# FINDING THE ENERGY TO HEAL

By the same author
*Healing the Divided Self: Clinical and Ericksonian
Hypnotherapy for Post-traumatic and Dissociative Conditions*
(with Claire Frederick)

A NORTON PROFESSIONAL BOOK

# FINDING THE ENERGY TO HEAL

*How EMDR, Hypnosis, TFT, Imagery,*
*and Body-Focused Therapy*
*Can Help Restore Mindbody Health*

Maggie Phillips, Ph.D.

W. W. NORTON & COMPANY • New York • London

For information about permission to reproduce selections from this book,
write to Permissions, W. W. Norton & Company, Inc., 500 Fifth Avenue,
New York, NY 10110

The text of this book is composed in Berkeley.
Composition by Bytheway Publishing Services, Inc.
Manufacturing by Haddon Craftsmen

Library of Congress Cataloging-in-Publication Data

Phillips, Maggie.
  Finding the energy to heal : how EMDR, hypnosis, TFT, imagery, and
body-focused therapy can help restore mindbody health / Maggie Phillips.
      p.    cm.
  "A Norton professional book"—P.
  Includes bibliographical references (p.) and index.
  ISBN 0-393-70326-6
  1. Mind and body therapies.   I. Title.
RC489.M53 P475 2000
16.89'1—dc21        00-056858

W. W. Norton & Company, Inc., 500 Fifth Avenue, New York, N.Y. 10110
www.wwnorton.com
W. W. Norton & Company Ltd., 10 Coptic Street, London WC1A 1PU

1  2  3  4  5  6 7 8  9  0

# Contents

## SECTION III. IMAGERY: OPENING
## WINDOWS OF THE MIND

## SECTION IV. SOMATIC ENERGY THERAPIES:
## COMING HOME TO THE BODY

# Acknowledgments

Anyone who has written a book knows that it is anything but a solo effort. Many talented people have made it possible for me to complete this project.

I am deeply grateful to my teachers from diverse traditions, particularly Elgan Baker, Joan Borysenko, David Cheek, Milton Erickson, Steve Gilligan, Bob and Mary Goulding, Peter Levine, Dick Olney, Ernie Rossi, Francine Shapiro, David Steindl-Rast, Lenore Terr, Jack and Helen Watkins, and Jeff Zeig. I am also indebted to the earlier pioneers in the fields of psychology, science, and the healing arts who set the stage for creation of the mindbody movement.

Numerous colleagues have helped me refine my clinical practices or otherwise contributed to the evolution of this book with their useful feedback and suggestions. Heartfelt thanks to: Andy Avins, Louise Bettner, Claire Frederick, Judith Fleiss, Seena Frost, Harriet Hollander, Ellen Hughes, Peter Levine, Shirley McNeal, Nancy Norris, Laurel Parnell, Noelle Poncelet, Sally Sadler, Virginia Scott, Francine Shapiro, Alan van Winkle, and Landry Wildwind. Thanks also to the friends and family who brainstormed during different writing stages and helped to critique the manuscript: Barbara Berkeley, Christina Floyd, Linda Gebroe, Mark and Cathy Hall, Francie Kendall, Win Bailey Loria, Anita Schriver, Cathy Henderson Stein, Wendy Storch, Liz Tarpley, and Sally Wherry.

There would be no basis for this book without the clients I have been privileged to serve. I admire the remarkable courage, strengths, and creativity they have brought to our healing endeavors, the deep trust they extended to me, and the opportunities they have provided for me to learn.

Special appreciation goes to Susan Munro, my wonderful editor at Norton, for her expansive vision and precise attention to the mechanics of good writing, and to Deborah Malmud at Norton, for her clear leadership and able organizational skill.

There would be no final version without the persistent and dedicated efforts of Susan Fleisher, my assistant, to refine the manuscript and the willingness of Jean Wing to complete the final proofing and printing. Special recognition is extended to Andrea Bryck for her artful design of the jacket and illustrations.

I also want to recognize those professionals who supported my emotional, physical, and spiritual well-being during the process of writing *Finding the Energy to Heal:* Diane Elise, Alan Leveton, Angie Specter, Alan van Winkle, and Barbara Wilt.

Finally, I express my deepest gratitude for the circle of love, laughter, and acceptance created by Andrea and Jennie, companions of the heart. I acknowledge my parents for their generous gifts of life and love, and my brother Jim and sister-in-law Nancy for their unwavering support. Thank you all for sustaining me through the many challenges of this journey, and for your ongoing encouragement to find my own energy to heal.

# Introduction

I HAD AN INTRIGUING DREAM during the time I was writing the first part of this book. In my dream, I was an apprentice in training to become what my teachers called a "healer of distinction." The methods they were teaching me were unlike anything I had ever encountered before.

My task was to sit quietly. A single person was ushered in to sit before me. I was to assume that each seeker who appeared was concerned about a distressing symptom that was creating illness. No talking occurred during the healing process. Instead, the curative approach involved nonverbal exchanges of energy between me and my client.

How this energetic exchange took place was complex and subtle. Sometimes, I was advised to "stare down" the negativity that I perceived in the guise of physical pain or self-doubt. At other times, I needed to intuit how to draw out inner conflict from the client's mind and body and to release it safely away from both of us. A third approach was to mobilize all of the positive healing resources from within myself and wield this positive force to overpower the lack of hope in the person across from me.

Gradually, I learned to assess the success of my efforts by looking into my clients' eyes until I could sense that they felt enough of a transformative shift inside of them to resolve the illness. My mentors stood by silently, beaming and nodding their agreement when my client and I had achieved what they considered a healing breakthrough.

Perhaps this dream scenario seems farfetched in terms of the real-life healing that can occur for people who have health problems. Yet its symbolism expresses an important message about where I believe the heart of healing really beats in clinical practice.

During more than twenty years of professional life, I've studied numerous therapies that appear to be useful tools in helping people resolve symptoms that compromise their health and well-being. Yet the healing moments that have occurred do not come from any specific modality. They appear to arise from a fluid, ever-changing coming together of all the available healing resources that are assembled when we sit together in contemplative focus on the departure from health. It is within this synchronistic, transformative process, which defies description, that the healing shift suggested by the dream takes place. It's a shift toward wholeness, a change that brings resolution.

This kind of radical healing is urgently needed. As a psychologist, I have worked with individuals who are confronted with disabling organic or stress-related health symptoms for the first time. Life, as they have known it, is at a standstill. They feel paralyzed and panicked, unsure about what moves to make to begin recovery. I have also seen many people who have long-term emotional and physical scars from health-related traumatic events that happened to them or to their families while they were growing up or after entering adult life. Many of them struggle with fears that prevent them from obtaining and responding to adequate health care.

Other clients in my practice who have experienced childhood trauma related to abuse, loss, and neglect seem to suffer from exceptionally mysterious health issues. Their lack of success with traditional medicine interventions seem to echo their lack of success with traditional psychological approaches. These survivors of past terrors appear locked in desperate holding patterns, as if circling their lives and waiting to land again.

The emerging fields of energy medicine and energy psychology offer new hope. Alternative healing methods, such as acupuncture, tai chi, reiki, qi gong, yoga, and meditation, are believed to work because they stimulate energies similar to what the Chinese call *qi* (pronounced chi) and the Asian Indians have called *prana*. Although there is no exact translation of qi, it is commonly thought of as life force energy. A more accurate understanding involves a rather puzzling paradox. Qi may be thought of as matter on the verge of becoming energy or, alternatively, as energy on the verge of becoming matter.[1]

This riddle suggests that qi represents dynamic harmony or balance in the mindbody system based on energy transformations. From the Chinese perspective, disease takes place when disharmony occurs in an organ, within an organ system, or inside the meridian network of the body, through which qi flows.

The Eastern concept of healing is therefore different from that of Western medicine. While Western doctors look for the underlying *cause* of health symptoms, Eastern healers look for *relationships and patterns* within an individual's complete psychological and physiological situation. Their task is to diagnose the nature of the *disharmony* that has blocked qi, thereby creating symptoms and disease. Eastern healing is concerned with correcting this imbalance or disharmony so that qi, the source of harmonious transformation in the body, can flow freely again.

It's a compelling possibility that methods from the field of psychology could be used to resolve clinical issues in a similar fashion. We know that disharmonies that occur in the body when qi is blocked have significant correlates in our psychological systems. According to authorities in Eastern medicine, qi can become blocked by anxiety, past traumatic events, depression, and various other inner factors.[2] If that is true, it would appear that psychological issues that affect our health negatively could also be treated by addressing the subtle, yet powerful, energy systems in the body.[3]

From this perspective, psychological tools can be used to reopen pathways that impact on the body's energy systems,[4] much as acupuncture and other tools of Eastern medicine are used to stimulate the meridians and other elements of the bioenergy system for healing. In other words, just as energy medicine works to activate meridians and other energy sites in the body to heal illness,[5] the technology of energy psychology may work through the psyche to help heal psychophysiological aspects of health imbalance.

Diverse approaches to energy psychology and medicine are emerging in the press. In *Why People Don't Heal and How They Can*, Carolyn Myss has discussed her healing method of applying psychic intuition to realign the seven chakra energy system. Donna Eden, author of *Energy Medicine*, has proposed ways of promoting health by balancing the meridians, which serve as our energy transportation system, as well as the chakras, which she conceptualizes as the major electromagnetic energy stations. Eden also emphasizes work with the aura, five seasonal elements, and vital electromagnetic energy points to reduce stress and boost healing.

Attempts to incorporate Chinese energy principles and the meridian system directly into the practice of psychotherapy have produced a varied and sometimes bewildering array of energy psychology approaches. The program for the second International Energy Psychology Conference held in May 2000, for example, lists more than 15 methods, including applied kinesiology, emotional freedom technique (EFT), matrix work, neuro-emotional technologies, thought field therapy (TFT), the Tapas acupressure technique, and therapeutic touch. Since few of these offerings are recognized to date by national or state professional standards agencies, how can practitioners and consumers make sense of this labyrinth of possibilities? One of my goals in writing *Finding the Energy to Heal* is to offer an integrative paradigm for effective, responsible use of energy psychology methods as part of psychotherapy.

My most important learning about the energy frontier has been inspired by clients who have come to me when they found themselves at a complete health impasse. The Western science model of cause and effect has already failed with them. Somehow, they have helped me to think more like a Chinese healer about the relationship of all the patterns in their life tapestries, rather than looking for a single underlying cause.

Participating in this kind of healing process, which my dream portrayed, has taught me new ways of using the wide array of technologies that psychology offers. I have found that more traditional models of psychological healing, such as self-object relations, ego psychology, cognitive behaviorism, and developmental psychology, along with theories of trauma, dissociation, and attachment, are invaluable in helping to identify the general patterns of disharmony that can activate illness.

Once my clients and I have sketched the broad outlines of where and how their pathways to healing may be blocked, then we can use the relatively more precise implements of hypnosis, EMDR, imagery, and body-focused therapies to reopen them again. The basic strategy illustrated throughout this book, then, is one of combining traditional psychological models for assessment with special tools to activate energy shifts that can rebalance the mindbody system.

Although I have chosen only a handful of methodologies to explore here, there are certainly many others that may be effectively used within the same or similar energy paradigms. Since further investigation is beyond the scope of this book, the reader is directed to many suggested references presented in the notes for each chapter.

What do hypnotic states, the impact of EMDR lateral eye movements, tapping on acupuncture meridian points with thought field therapy, and activating imagery and body responses have in common? First, each can be viewed as a unique method that can enhance psychological and physical well-being. Secondly, from the perspective of Eastern healing, these methods seem to open the flow of qi so that more complete mindbody transformation can take place, much as acupuncture needles, acupressure, and herbal remedies are believed to do.

Although hypnosis[6] and imagery[7] have a long history of successful applications with health-related conditions and symptoms, EMDR has been used almost exclusively to date with trauma and its sequelae. Relatively new on the therapy scene, in its earliest phases EMDR was viewed as an experimental technique that explored the effects of lateral eye movements on cognitive and emotional processes. As it has evolved over the last ten years following its discovery by Francine Shapiro,[8] EMDR has become a full-fledged therapy that incorporates many elements from the major psychotherapeutic traditions, including hypnosis and imagery. Its uses have similarly expanded to encompass a variety of psychological conditions, including complex PTSD, the dissociative disorders, postpartum depression, personality disorders, major depression, and symptoms related to low self-esteem.[9] There is a growing body of well-controlled empirical research to support the positive results reported in these areas.

One of the important contributions this book hopes to make is to extend EMDR even further—into the important area of health-related concerns. Although EMDR practitioners have reported and published cases where health symptoms were part of the clinical picture, there is very little previously published work that applies EMDR when health symptoms are a primary focus.[10]

Thought field therapy (TFT), developed by Roger Callahan,[11] psychologist and kinesiologist, is relatively new on the energy psychology scene. Based directly on the meridian system of energy used in acupuncture and acupressure, TFT is designed to diagnose and treat what is called the thought field related to a particular mindbody symptom. Clients are asked to tap gently with two fingers on designated energy points along various meridians on their bodies, in a prescribed sequential order. From the beginning, clients themselves are in charge of applying all treatment techniques. All TFT treatment, therefore, is self-treatment. Although TFT received high ratings of effectiveness in one comparative study,[12] its long-term effects have not yet been adequately studied.

Three kinds of common stressors associated with problematic health provide the framework for this book:

1. *General stress-related symptoms,* which plague a huge percentage of individuals and families. A substantial amount of our personal, organizational, and collective resources continue to be spent on this category of health problems. This category concerns the treatment of stresses that contribute to the formation of mindbody symptoms.
2. *Psychophysiological symptoms that result from posttraumatic stress,* triggered by illness, accident, and injury, as well as by the invasive medical interventions used to treat them. Catastrophic events that generate debilitating traumatic stress also include childhood abuse and neglect, exposure to violence, experiences with natural disaster, sexual assault, and war trauma. Although many therapies have been formulated to identify and treat reactions to trauma, many people are still seeking relief for related health symptoms.
3. *Stress connected with organic conditions* such as cancer, head injury, high blood pressure, cardiac disease, and autoimmune syndromes. Although these illnesses have a biological basis, there is always a stress component to consider. When a stressor interacts with genetic vulnerability or organic damage and can be resolved, better health almost always results.

For all three categories, *Finding the Energy to Heal* attempts to examine how pathways to healing have become blocked and how the tools examined here can impact essential mindbody energy systems so that more complete healing can take place.

The blueprint for treating these three kinds of stresses that often provoke or are related to health conditions is the *four-step SARI model*.[13] First presented in my earlier book, *Healing the Divided Self*, this framework was designed to treat posttraumatic and dissociative conditions. Because I have found the approach so helpful with all types of clinical problems, I have modified it for use with health problems. Its four steps are used to structure the healing experiences you will read about throughout this book. At times, they are made obvious. At other times, they are used more subtly as guiding principles. In some cases, each step requires multiple sessions. In others, the entire SARI model can be completed in two or three meetings.

1. In the first phase of work, *safety and stability*, it is essential to find a sense of internal and external safety in the therapy situation as well as in everyday life. The focus is on strengthening and empowering people to begin to take charge of health problems in new ways that lead to mastery and a sense of personal control over their symptoms. The guiding principle here is to gather and build on strengths already in place.

2. During the second "A" stage, clients are helped to *activate* psychological stresses related to health symptoms and the inner resources needed to resolve them. The tools offered in this book are used to help identify these underlying contributing factors, which are often unknown to the client at a conscious level. Each method used is also efficient in activating various internal strengths and capacities to help defuse the impact of past and current stresses.

3. During the third "R" stage, the health symptoms are usually *resolved*. If traumatic experiences are involved, they are reprocessed or repackaged so that they do not evoke the previous health imbalancing reactions.

   Often, corrective experiences are introduced or occur spontaneously as energy therapy promotes resolution. These may include the resolution of unfinished developmental business and creation of renurturing experiences that reopen pathways to healing. In some cases, stage two and three work is orchestrated simultaneously, though in more complex situations the two are usually undertaken separately.

4. In the final *integration* stage, successes that have taken place during therapy, positive progress toward health, and other healing gains must be *internalized* so that they can be maintained consistently. If inner conflict and personality fragmentation have been an issue in health impairment, there may be an added focus on personality integration, so that progress made can continue to generate positive health. Methods of energy psychology are used in the "I" stage to focus on future possibilities, transcending past experiences that have challenged and unbalanced health.

THE FIRST THREE SECTIONS OF *FINDING THE ENERGY TO HEAL* showcase EMDR, hypnosis and ego-state therapy, and imagery. The fourth section presents two somatic methods, TFT and body-focused therapy. At the beginning of each section, there is an introduction that may be useful if you do not know much about the method or if you want to learn more about the specifics of how it is used.

Each chapter presents specific techniques derived from the method being presented that my clients and I have found to be highly effective and efficient in resolving various types of health problems. Vivid examples illustrate how these tools can be used to resolve a variety of mindbody symptoms related to health imbalance. Each chapter also includes answers to questions that often arise, such as: How do the therapist and client decide which approach to use in a given situation? What kinds of healing benefits does each method seem to provide? How can you anticipate whether one therapy will be more effective than another?

The final section of the book explores three models for interweaving modalities. Combining technologies can offer some people a dynamic, highly effective, and cutting-edge psychological treatment for the resolution of more complex health problems. Although the potency of each method is distinct, synthesizing them can magnify some of their effects. These integrative models may be especially helpful in increasing the healing possibilities for clients who do not respond to any single approach.

*FINDING THE ENERGY TO HEAL* IS DESIGNED TO APPEAL to readers interested in cutting-edge mindbody technology. If you are a practitioner within the healing professions, I hope you will be moved and inspired by the promising benefits of energy psychology presented in these pages.

If you are seeking solutions to perplexing challenges to your own health, my wish is that the healing stories you read here will stimulate new understandings about how your pathways to healing may be blocked and suggest how they may be cleared and opened again. The results reported here range from the dramatic to the ordinary. It is likely that you will find some element of your own health crisis, as well as some clues to finding the key that may unlock its solution.

This is *not* a "how to" or a "self-help" book. I do not present complete protocols for any of the methods. It is not my intention that anyone attempt to use these techniques without proper training and supervision. Rather, I hope to present intriguing possibilities for how these methods can be used to assist in healing. Many useful references are included for the reader seeking a more step-by-step approach.

I have the greatest respect for each of the approaches presented here. I use them every day in my practice and I've seen firsthand the results they can produce. Yet the essential ingredient to their success is not their dazzling technology but the efficiency they lend to helping us discover the amazing strengths that we bring to our own healing. (To make your reading about them more efficient, please use the glossary as needed to review definitions of unfamiliar terms.)

Thich Nhat Hahn teaches:

> Many of us tend to focus on the question "What is wrong?" and we forget to ask the question, "What is right?" . . . We also have a tendency to get obsessed with the past. But you cannot go back to the past in order to repair the damage done there. The only moment available . . . is the present moment. If you can get into this moment deeply, then you can fix the things done in the past and also take good care of the future. . . . I would like to propose that we all reflect on the human capacity to connect with what is wonderful and healing in this present moment.[14]

He urges those of us who are therapists to "plant good seeds." What I appreciate most about these methods of energy psychology is that they empower us to plant good seeds in each healing moment.

# FINDING THE ENERGY TO HEAL

# Section I

# EMDR:

## MOVING TOWARD HEALTH

# Introducing EMDR

On a golden fall afternoon, as sunlight filtered through the trees and spilled into my office, Sam's eyes followed my fingers as they moved rapidly in front of his face. He had started this set by focusing on an image of a recent episode of chest pains. After about 40 side-to-side eye movements, I asked him, "What did you experience?"

He told me, "I thought about the earthquake we had a few years ago and how scary it was for me and my wife and kids. Then for some reason I thought about my father. I saw him standing in the doorway of my bedroom. He was looking at me with such an odd mixture of love and, I don't know, disdain. And I remember right after that, he had his first heart attack. He was gone so much of the time—I never knew what he was really thinking. He really didn't see me and who I am at all. It was so sad, how we all missed each other. I don't want to do that with my family. I want to learn how to take better care of myself than he did. That's why I'm here."

WHAT ON EARTH COULD BE INTRIGUING ABOUT A THERAPY approach that involves shifting your eyes rapidly back and forth from side to side while following someone's moving fingers? How can what seems like such a ridiculously simple method make the claim of resolving a challenging condition like PTSD (posttraumatic stress disorder) in only a few sessions? Had the therapy world gone mad again? These were some of the questions that plagued me when friends and colleagues first started telling me about this radical new approach to the treatment of trauma. In California, we're used to revolutionary new therapies. Here we go again, I thought.

I paid no serious attention to EMDR (eye movement desensitization and reprocessing) until one of my close therapist friends shared with me her own extraordinary EMDR healing experiences from childhood abuse. Because I had the deepest respect for her, I could no longer dismiss EMDR without finding out more about it.

Two months later, in the spring of 1989, I was sitting with a group of therapists in Palo Alto in what was then called an EMD training workshop. I listened as Francine Shapiro, originator of the model, explained the principles and steps involved. I watched videotaped examples, including one of my friend. Later, I practiced the EMDR method in a small group. Although some people in the room reported very powerful experiences, mine was uneventful.

Some months later, remaining skeptical, I invited Dr. Shapiro to present her workshop to the membership of the Northern California Society of Clinical Hypnosis Society, where I was president. If only a few clients were reached who otherwise would not be helped, learning about EMDR seemed worthwhile. I used EMDR on an experimental basis after that with a handful of people and found myself filled with more questions than answers. There were a few cases where fear-based symptoms were resolved. Some problems remained unchanged. Other clients remarked that it seemed to induce a state of inner focus that was similar to hypnosis, but they preferred hypnosis because it was more familiar and comfortable. Still others did not like the arrangement of holding their heads still and following my fingers from side to side. They found EMDR "too mechanical." Furthermore, my arm grew tired (a common complaint!) and I grew more reluctant to use EMDR.

I decided to place EMDR on a mental back shelf for a while. Nonetheless, I kept reading and hearing about the astonishing results that others were having with this method. I explained my lack of resonance with EMDR to myself in several ways. I was so successful with hypnosis that learning a new approach seemed like a waste of valuable time. This was especially true since I was getting ready to write a book on the uses of hypnosis in the treatment of trauma and dissociation. I also worried that there were too few safeguards in the model. I had heard reports that EMDR moved clients so quickly into and through traumatic memories that they were flooded with reactions, sometimes retraumatized. And, I had always resisted jumping on the bandwagon when a new "too good to be true" modality came along. There was, however, one major problem with all of these objections. I could not argue with or explain away the dramatic results that were being published.

Finally, in the middle of writing my first book, *Healing the Divided Self*,[1] I took myself to task. How could I put myself out as an expert in the field of trauma when I did not actually know how to use a therapy that so many clinicians who treated trauma were finding to be invaluable? I decided to take the Level I EMDR training over again. I was glad to see that more attention had been given to ways of helping clients achieve feelings of safety while exploring powerful moments that had been so dangerously unsafe for them. Additional flexibility in the protocols seemed to allow more healing possibilities for greater numbers of clients. I began using EMDR with more confidence. After completing the Level II EMDR training, where I learned about many exciting and creative new ways of using EMDR beyond the basics, somehow the method clicked for me. As my confidence grew, so did successful outcomes with my clients.

At this point in my professional journey, I use EMDR to treat many PTSD symptoms my clients present. It is becoming a primary approach I use to resolve health symptoms. And, sometimes, I interweave EMDR with hypnosis, ego-state therapy, and somatic approaches in ways that you will read about later on in this book.

## The Birth of EMDR

EMDR originated from a serendipitous discovery in 1987 by Francine Shapiro, then a graduate student in psychology in Palo Alto, California. She noticed that certain disturbing thoughts lost their negative charge immediately following a series of diagonal eye movements she made spontaneously while walking, lost in thought, through a park. Later, she experimented with lateral eye movements and found that they helped to resolve posttraumatic symptoms in a group of Vietnam veterans as well as in a group of women who had been sexually assaulted.

Shapiro began to test her model with other types of trauma. Her impressive results, which claimed to clear trauma-related thoughts, beliefs, fears, and somatic reactions, were replicated by other researchers, including the distinguished behavioral therapist, Joseph Wolpe.[2] As the body of empirical clinical results expanded, findings were used to construct specialized training protocols for various types of posttraumatic issues, including depression, phobias, grief, anxiety, and substance abuse.

EMDR continues to evolve. Ongoing testing of the EMDR approach in recent traumatic situations, such as the war in Kosovo, the Oklahoma City bombing, and the Littleton shootings, adds valuable data. As more therapists worldwide use EMDR with diverse clients and clinical problems, their feedback and findings are being used to strengthen, expand, and deepen this model.

Eye movements, of course, have been used since ancient times in various healing practices, such as yoga, Reichian therapy, and hypnosis. But EMDR is more than just a set of eye movements, which can appear deceptively simple. The complexities of EMDR include many dimensions, such as the accurate targeting of symptoms, precise phrasing and promotion of desirable beliefs about self, skillful introduction of interweaves, appropriate pacing of processing, and other competencies. These powerful in-

gredients can only come together in the hands of competent therapists
who have completed at least Levels I and II of the EMDR training
program.

Much of what EMDR offers to clients resonates with many other types
of effective psychotherapy. In addition, EMDR offers a different view of
how symptoms are created. Shapiro's theory emphasizes that the way we
store disturbing, unprocessed early experiences, and link them uncon-
sciously to subsequent events through complex information pathways,
contributes to many of our difficulties. The key to healing and resolution
of many symptoms we develop, from the EMDR perspective, is the *reprocessing* or reconfiguration of these original and linked experiences so that
they promote healthy responses.

## What Happens in EMDR?

The brief description of Sam at the beginning of this chapter gives you
only a glimpse of what happens during an EMDR session. When I work
with health issues, before introducing EMDR, I interview my clients about
the history of the health problem they want to resolve. I try to gain a
thorough understanding of each person's life in general and other therapy
experiences. I also make sure clients have received appropriate medical
attention. We then identify specific mindbody symptoms (e.g., insomnia,
muscular pain, dizziness, or tinnitus), prioritize our list in order of their
importance, and select one to target for change first.

If we choose EMDR as a method, I test the procedure with a *positive
target image*. This image represents a recent time free from the health
symptoms we will be working on. An example of this kind of positive
target is the *conflict-free image*, described in Chapter 1.

The goal here is to find an image that evokes only positive feelings that
can be sustained or even strengthened and expanded over several EMDR
sets, which usually consist of 20–50 lateral or side-to-side eye movements. These movements are created when clients follow my fingers, as
Sam did at the beginning of this chapter. My fingers and hands[3] make
lateral sweeps a comfortable distance in front of their faces, as they hold
their heads still (see Diagram 1 in Appendix A). We *install*, or put into
place, a conflict-free image or other positive target image using these sets.
Clients notice their inner experiences and tell me what happens during
and after the time that their eyes were moving.

Usually, several important inner resources surface spontaneously when
we associate to eye movements. Resources may be additional images,
memories, thoughts, symbols, or body sensations. We also experiment
with the speed, angle, and number of eye movements to make sure they

are a "good fit" during this phase. If we are not able to install a positive target image of a time when the health symptom was absent, I introduce other types of strengthening experiences. If the strengthening phase is successful, we then find and explore a *clinical target image* connected to the symptom. (I do not use the term *negative target image* because of its pejorative connotations).

With Susan, a 39-year-old lawyer who has low blood pressure, for example, the *clinical target* (i.e., what we want to change) is anxiety related to a recent episode of dizziness. I help her form an image of that episode. I ask her to describe the thoughts, feelings, mental pictures, and somatic reactions that seem to appear when she focuses on the image. We rate on a scale from zero to ten how distressing the image is now to her. This rating, called SUD (subjective units of disturbance scale), can be taken at different times to measure progress and to determine how much of the symptom still has not resolved.

Susan is also asked to notice what negative thoughts and beliefs about herself accompany the target image. She says, "When I feel that dizzy feeling, I am helpless. I'm afraid I'm going to die young just like my grandmother did." Next we formulate a positive statement of what Susan wants to believe about herself, called a positive cognition: "I am capable of learning many ways to manage this problem."

We then begin reprocessing the image connected to dizziness. To accomplish this, Susan moves her eyes to follow my fingers and then tells me what she notices. After the first set of eye movements, Susan says that her body feels as if it is leaning to the left. Next she begins to feel slightly more dizzy, and then remembers a fall that she sustained while she was skiing in the Sierra Mountains a few years before. I simply ask her to stay with each of those associations as a new target, and we start the next set of eye movements.

In this way, Susan moves organically through the internal links she might have to the dizziness that accompanies a drop in her blood pressure. Periodically, we test to see whether the symptom target has become less distressing for her (i.e., whether the SUD rating has dropped) and whether Susan is moving closer to the positive beliefs she wants to have.

At the beginning of sessions that will follow this one, we will check to see whether there have been any shifts in Susan's symptoms of dizziness or in any other symptoms. *Tracking changes that occur between sessions is extremely important.* With any healing modality involving the unconscious, which includes all of those featured in this book and many others besides, the changes may not be predictable ones. What is most important here is that the shifts continue in a positive direction through any channel that we use to process information. In accord with principles of energy medicine, healing can take place *only* if the flow of energy is kept moving. In Susan's case, the shifts that occur resolve her dizziness in only two meetings.

## How Does EMDR Achieve Change?

Although there is no simple answer to this complex question, Shapiro has developed the Accelerated Informational Processing theory[4] to explain the treatment results she and others have obtained with EMDR. To understand this theory, you must first understand the impact of traumas,[5] since EMDR was initially developed to resolve posttraumatic stress symptoms.

When a traumatic experience of any type takes place, it overwhelms temporarily, or even permanently, our usual ways of coping. The traumatic events, and our unique responses to them, are stored in what we can think of as memory networks.[6] These can become frozen in time due to the protective mechanism of dissociation as well as from the action of protective body/neurological responses.[7] When any element of the trauma is triggered, the entire traumatic reaction, or some part of it, may recur again and again.

This explains why people who have had a traumatic accident, loss, or illness, or who have witnessed or experienced some other type of trauma such as abuse or violence may have recurring sensory flashbacks, thoughts, beliefs, or dreams. Posttraumatic reactions remain connected to the traumatic events even though we are not consciously aware of them while the reactions are taking place. Since the traumatic reactions cannot be fully processed due to blocked or frozen mindbody pathways, the traumatic reaction can remain pretty much the same in intensity and quality. This can be the case even though many years may have passed and many intervening healing events may have taken place. EMDR therapy seems to help traumatized people reenter frozen memory and informational pathways, reprocess past memories as well as recent related events, and prepare for situations that may occur in the future. Because past, present, and future are connected in our information systems in many complex ways, positive changes spread or generalize throughout the system so that benefits are maximized in a short time period.

The eye movements used in EMDR are believed to impact two different types of networks, which facilitate multifaceted reprocessing. First, they seem to stimulate the memory network where the trauma is stored. The eye movements may also activate the informational networks that can restore a traumatized person's ability to process an event fully. When both networks operate simultaneously during the eye movement sets, it appears that the traumatic information is rapidly processed. Traumatic reactions such as fear, panic, despair, and grief are replaced by more positive ones that emerge from a new place of balance and completion.

Along with other therapists who use EMDR,[8] I believe that the eye movements operate similarly to the rapid eye movements (REM) that occur during our sleep cycles when we dream. One biological function of REM sleep appears to be clearing away the stimuli that have triggered anxiety and stress during a day of living so that we can awaken with a "clean slate" the next morning, ready to move on to new life experiences. The eye movements of EMDR seem to mimic this function by clearing the stressful debris from our psychological selves so that we can "awaken" to take in new information that will help us go on to new life experiences. Since the eye movements move from right to left and left to right, they may also help to stimulate both hemispheres of the brain to promote a "whole brain" approach to healing.

When the trauma appears to be an isolated incident, the traumatic symptom can be cleared within one or two sessions of using this efficient therapy. But when multiple traumatic events contribute to a health problem, such as physical, sexual, emotional abuse, parental neglect, or severe illness, accident, injury, or other health-related trauma that result in chronic impairment to health and well-being, the time to heal may be longer.

# 1

# EMDR and Stress Symptoms

MARTHA: INCAPACITATING INSOMNIA

Martha's voice told me more than Martha's words. In our first phone encounter, she sounded weary and hopeless, her tone filled with despair and anxiety. When I showed her into my office, she began her story hesitantly, her voice almost a whisper, her eyes not meeting mine. "You're my last hope," she said softly.

Five years ago, Martha began developing a series of health problems. She had just been promoted to a new job as director of a home health care agency. Although she enjoyed helping to meet the growing need for good homecare in an aging society, Martha's new position was immediately beset by difficulties. Her staff was downsized so that she was responsible for many more administrative duties. She was also required to travel to supervise a number of caseworkers in her region.

In addition, her own supervisor, who had recently joined the company, proved both incompetent and abusive. Her boss treated employees unfairly, giving preference to African-American coworkers and creating an atmosphere of reverse racism. She never acknowledged Martha's achievements, offering instead biting criticism that was devastating to her.

Martha struggled for the first six months of her new job with a range of symptoms, including numb hands, stomach pain, insomnia, and depression. Finally, she sought medical attention and was prescribed Prozac, an antidepressant. This intervention only seemed to worsen Martha's stress, since she experienced side effects from the medication that included nausea, irritability, and sleeplessness. She alternately tried Zoloft and amitriptyline. Neither provided relief from feelings of depression or help with her continuing insomnia.

Becoming more desperate, Martha consulted an acupuncturist and herbalist. Kava, valerian root, and Chinese herbs helped her to relax but still did not ease the insomnia. Over the next four years, Martha consulted a variety of medical doctors, specialists, and clinics. Thyroid and heart problems were ruled out. A low dosage of estrogen was prescribed by a gynecologist who theorized that her difficulties might be perimenopausal. Diagnosticians at two well-known sleep clinics pronounced Martha depressed and prescribed more antidepressants along with the use of a light box. None of these suggestions significantly reduced the insomnia or other symptoms.

Martha told me at our first session that she had had a brief trial with hypnosis years ago and found it intriguing. During her first hypnotic trance, she had seen a very dark room that was completely empty. At the time, she wasn't ready to explore this image. In fact, she had found the inner room terrifying and had not returned either to the therapist or to hypnosis.

Three months before seeing me, after struggling five years with her health problems, Martha had decided to quit her job. Her company had offered her the option of medical leave followed by early retirement. Though she felt some relief from stress, her persistent insomnia remained incapacitating. She decided this was the symptom that most impaired her health and targeted it as the one she wanted to resolve first. She also let me know she could afford only a few sessions.

DURING OUR SECOND MEETING, I PRESENTED ALL OF THE relevant therapy approaches to treat insomnia, along with their potential benefits and risks. As I explained the EMDR method, I told her that EMDR had the possibility of helping to rapidly resolve the stress and anxiety related to her sleep problems. If her sleep cycle restabilized, I thought she might then have the energy to approach some of her other difficulties. Although Martha wanted to try hypnosis because she found her previous experience to be so powerful, I pointed out that the mixed reactions she had described to hypnosis seemed to parallel her responses to all of the medical interventions she had tried thus far. I believed it would be better to begin with something new to her; if within a few sessions no significant movement had occurred, we could return to the idea of using hypnosis and imagery or other interventions.

Martha agreed to this plan somewhat reluctantly, but admitted, "I've got to trust you. I haven't trusted anything else so far. And that's probably why nothing has worked."

IN MARTHA'S FIRST EMDR SESSION WE BEGAN WITH *positive target image*. I asked her if she could find a time in her life when she recalled having *no* trouble sleeping, a time when sleep was easy and restful. Martha immediately recalled her freshman year in college when she could always sleep. She said, "I long for that ability now. It was a womb-like experience."

Her positive target image was walking in the door to her studio apartment. The thought that accompanied this image was, "Within 10 minutes, I'll be asleep." I asked her to focus on that image as well as the accompanying thoughts and feelings during the eye movements. (The symbol // indicates instructions to "stay with that" or "focus on that" followed by 20–50 side-to-side eye movements.)

M: I saw your hand as a magic wand and thought this might have potential for me. //

M: This time I got a picture of a blackboard. You were beginning to erase whatever was on the board.

MP: Can you tell what I was erasing?

M: I think you are erasing accumulated bad experiences of my being unable to let go and go to sleep. //

M: I saw the same image of the blackboard . . . I felt calming in my arms and stomach. Then I had an image of a pipe filled with too much gunk and you were cleaning the insides of that. Then you continued to erase those bad experiences off the board. //

M: I feel calm in my stomach; my arms are heavy.

Standard uses of EMDR suggest beginning with a *clinical target image*. These include images of the events from the past that created the problem, current situations that trigger distress, and the skills that are needed for change.[1] In Martha's case, a therapy target might be a time when Martha was not sleeping well and felt anxious about it, or a past event that is believed to have triggered the insomnia. However, I start my work a bit differently—by focusing first on the strengths already in place. I call these *positive target images*.[2]

A **positive target image** is *a sensory image that contains an experience of mastery related to the client's therapy goals*. Not necessarily a visual image, it can represent a special event or an interlude of time before the symptoms began or when they were in remission. The positive target is installed using several sets of eye movements in order to provide strengthening at the beginning of therapy and to uncover linking resources that can be helpful for healing.

Here I ask Martha to identify a time in the past when she has experienced an abundant supply of what she wants to have now—deep, restful sleep that comes easily to her. She quickly recalls her freshman year of college when sleep was a delicious, "womb-like" experience. We are able to install this image as a positive target during several sets of eye movements. Martha holds the positive feelings evoked by this image and expands their meaning. My fingers become a "magic wand" and then a hand erasing a blackboard of past negative experiences, which include insomnia.

I wanted to start with the possibility that even though her sleep might have been very poor during the last five years, there might have been some time before that when sleep was not in any way a problem for her. If she had not been able to find a positive target image closely related to her therapy goals, we might have started with another kind of positive image. As you read through this book, you'll learn more about the many types of images that can be used as positive targets.

As we continued to focus on the positive target image, Martha discovered some familiar negative thoughts:

M: I started having thoughts that I'm not doing this right. It's just going to be like everything else I've tried. I know I'm going to be disappointed.

MP: Do you have a sense of what you might want to do with those thoughts? That is, could you use the blackboard image in some way?

M: I could let you erase them. //

M: We erased the negative thoughts together; we kept erasing the board. //

M: This time I had the image of you as a priest giving me a blessing. It was lovely and sweet. You were giving me grace. The amazing thing is that I was receiving it; I could take it in. I've had a hole in my stomach for so long. I feel relaxed now. My arms and legs are like lead.

EMDR can be very helpful in changing negative ways of thinking. Here Martha's self-critical thoughts intruded as she found herself judging her process as not good enough. *When EMDR clients cycle again and again through the same negative thoughts, feelings, sensations, or images in such a way that progress is blocked, they are said to be* looping.[3] Fortunately, steps can be taken to remove these barriers so that healing can flow freely again.

One way to break through looping and other negative thought patterns is to use EMDR interweaves. *An interweave is a way of adding new information not available*. This may be because mindbody pathways have closed in response to trauma and other factors. Usually the interweave is suggested by the therapist at appropriate times when EMDR processing is not moving forward.[4]

The blackboard image Martha discovered early in this session is used as a special type of interweave called a *resource interweave*[5]. *A* **resource interweave** *can consist of an image, symbol, body sensation, thought, inner voice, or any other somatosensory experience that appears to be strengthening.* When it is installed during sets of lateral eye movements, the resource interweave should expand and the positive feelings that are evoked should deepen. This resource occurs spontaneously during an EMDR session or in between sessions. I have found that the most effective resource interweaves are those that appear spontaneously in the rich stream of feelings and sensory associations that occur during and immediately after sets of eye movements. My role is to identify these resources and to utilize them as interweaves when appropriate.

I used Martha's image of me erasing a blackboard as a *resource interweave* to remind her that she could make choices about letting critical thoughts interrupt her positive focus. Throughout the rest of our EMDR work, the blackboard image became a powerful resource to help interrupt self-judgmental cycles so that Martha could take in the positive shifts she was making in a more permanent way.

MP: Because our time is almost up, I'm going to ask you to return to our positive target image of you walking in the front door of your freshman apartment. Tell me what happens when you bring up that image now.

M: I'm moving this to the bedroom I sleep in now. I can only do it a little bit, but I think if I practice, it will get stronger.

We decided Martha would practice bringing up the image of entering her freshman apartment to reinforce our meeting and to prepare her mind for the experience of sleeping restfully. If any negative thoughts came up, she would use the image of erasing them from the blackboard.

Two weeks later, Martha reported that she had slept well every night but one. I suggested that we take one more trial with a positive target image so that she could continue to feel even more confident about this change.[6] We started with the task of forming a positive target image of the last two weeks:

M: When I look at the last two weeks there is a definite shift. I feel really blessed, and there are tears of hope. //

M: I feel more relaxed. My hands feel warm and I'm feeling full. These are nice feelings. //

M: I have a heavy feeling in my hands and arms . . . I'm also feeling very sad. I don't know why but it's OK. //

M: I felt my arms get even heavier. I'm not sure how I feel. I want to believe that this exercise will somehow clear me . . . //

M: It feels like everything from my chest is draining into my arms. The release through my fingers and chest is lighter. Feels good. //

M: I feel lighter. It literally feels like this gunk in my chest is just coming down and then out. It's comforting to know that. . . . Now I'm judging myself. I'm thinking this isn't good enough. I'm starting to get off the track and I know it, but I can't stop myself.

MP: Do you have a sense of what you might use to help with those judgments?

M: Right, you're reminding me that I can erase it from the blackboard. //

M: Your hand erased that thought. It was nice. . . . I'm laughing now because bodywork has been so frightening for me. It's lovely I can do it now. My body has been carrying a lot. I'm grateful for my body, for faith in my mind and body that I can let go of all this. //

M: It's very calming to feel all that gratitude. I'm surprised at my sense of faith. Your hands are like a benediction and a blessing. . . . Is that OK? //

M: My hands are very heavy now. I had an image of you cleaning my lungs, my chest cavity. . . . //

M: I feel calm and goodness and heavy. I'm lighter in my chest. I feel pretty damn good.

Martha's story also gives us a chance to examine the role EMDR can play in helping people find and use the resources of relationship. In most kinds of therapy, relationship issues that occur between client and therapist are referred to as transference and countertransference.[7] In the first EMDR session, Martha perceived me as the instrument of change. It was I who waved a magic wand, then erased the blackboard and removed her past negative experiences, which included insomnia. I was transformed into a healer, cleaning "gunk" from her body. Later, I became a priest, using my hands to offer her blessings, benedictions, and spiritual cleansing.

Unlike other therapies, EMDR does not involve giving suggestions, manipulating, or interpreting reactions toward the therapist. These transferential responses are fully accepted and allowed to move with the eye movements, just like other inner data. Most reactions toward the therapist that surface during EMDR are then naturally assimilated by clients in healthy, organic ways.

Martha seemed a bit uncomfortable with her images that involved me. She asked in the second session, "Is this OK?" Rather than responding, I simply invited her to stay with her images of me and to incorporate them into the rest of the inner connections she was making. One of the strengths of EMDR is its clear focus on the client's experience. When feelings, whether positive or negative, come up about the therapist, they become another link in a complex chain of associations that lead clients to a new sense of self and others.

Martha's initial sense of me as healer and priest shifted naturally to one of her providing the nurturing. At the end of our second EMDR session, I asked Martha to go back to the target image of the last two weeks, her sense of the definite shift that occurred, feeling blessed, feeling tears and hope:

MP: What happens when you bring up that image now?
M: I see a little encapsulated egg. . . . It's white and surrounded by light. I feel full of new beginnings, like a rebirth. . . . The egg is very fragile. It needs care. It needs me to coddle it. (*sobbing*) It's like this egg has been given to me so many times and I've brushed it aside. //

As we talked for a few minutes about the egg, Martha told me that she thought it represented a neglected part of her that she had previously brushed aside because she did not know how to help it. Now she felt ready to nurture the egg self and felt confident that, with practice, she would be a good mother.

My sense is that because Martha was allowed to have and use freely her transpersonal images of me as a good parent and a comforting spiritual presence, she was able to incorporate those roles fairly quickly into her own identity. We will explore later how other kinds of transpersonal reactions, including negative ones, can be used as positive pathways for change through EMDR.

Two weeks after her second EMDR session, Martha reported that her sleep was absolutely fine. After three months, her debilitating insomnia still had not returned. The other health symptoms, including depression, stomach pain, and numbness, had vanished. She is appreciative. Her parting words to me were, "I could be a poster child for EMDR."

How did two EMDR sessions resolve a five-year bout of insomnia? I attribute the rapid change to several factors. First, EMDR's multifaceted system enabled Martha to *reprocess*, or transform, information related to her insomnia at cognitive, physical, emotional, and even spiritual levels very quickly. Second, the use of positive target images strengthened Martha's self-confidence and sense of mastery by demonstrating to her that she already had the necessary resources to resolve her symptom.[8] Third, from an energy psychology perspective, Martha's response to the positive targets images clarified rapidly the psychological issue that was blocking healing. *Her own self-criticism* was the culprit! Once we found a resource (i.e., the image of erasing the blackboard) that was more powerful energetically than her judgments, the block was cleared and Martha's healing pathways were open again.

## RICHARD: NEGATIVE PATTERNS
## OF OVEREATING AND EXERCISE

Windy days at the airport only intensified Richard's already high levels of stress. His job as air traffic controller required completely steady levels of concentration of every moment during his eight-hour shift. He had anxiety dreams and waking worries about any lapse that might cause a plane full of people to crash to their deaths. At 41, he was overweight, having gained 50 pounds since beginning training for this second career three years ago.

Richard and his doctor were both worried about damage to his health, because he came from a family with a history of high blood pressure and cardiac problems. He had already been placed on medication to lower his blood pressure and cholesterol. It was ineffective, however, since his stress remained high, his diet poor, and his exercise nonexistent.

During our first meeting, Richard described his work days as marathon tests of visual, cognitive, and emotional acuity, broken only by brief breaks when he paced restlessly up and down airport corridors enticed by junk food and soft drinks into sugar and caffeine highs. Although he countered these binges with strict adherence to a vegetarian diet during off-duty hours, his weight had steadily climbed.

Active in sports as a teenager, Richard was now a self-described couch potato, preferring quiet visits with friends, reading, and watching television to fill leisure time. When he did venture out into the world of nature to walk his dog or hike, Richard always rediscovered the pleasures of physical activity. He determinedly renewed his commitment to any one of numerous work-out regimens, which would ultimately fail when he found himself too tired from the rigors of his job or too disinterested to pursue it in subsequent weeks.

Exhausted by these dysfunctional cycles, he called me for an appointment. Richard explained that he had found EMDR helpful two years earlier when he had first confronted physical and sexual abuse by his father. The abuse had surfaced during his participation in a therapy group for adult children of alcoholics. "I don't want to go back into all that pain again with EMDR, but I know that you use hypnosis and that hypnosis can help some people lose weight. Do you think hypnosis might work for me?" he asked.

After reviewing more of his history, we considered our possibilities. I explained to Richard that there were now many more ways of using EMDR in addition to focusing on trauma. I told him we would start with his health strengths, expand them further, and then use sets of eye movements to try to interrupt his negative patterns of eating and exercise. I also advised Richard to let me know if at any time he felt we were getting too close to the traumatic abuse of the past because there were many other ways we could proceed at that point. We could begin with hypnosis, I pointed out, but because he had found EMDR so useful before, we might want to build on that success as a starting point instead. Richard opted to begin with EMDR.

To achieve thorough resolution of symptoms believed related to past traumas, Shapiro recommends beginning with the earliest traumatic event first when using EMDR. Yet, because I respect Richard's right to work differently in this case, I choose to embark on a more experimental course.

Finding and installing a general positive target image proved relatively easy. We then shifted our focus to the symptoms of eating and exercising in more consistently healthy ways. Richard identified a specific positive image of eating his favorite vegetarian food in a relaxed, enjoyable way. While installing it (i.e., putting it into place using eye movements), we discovered an important clue to Richard's difficulties with eating and exercise:

R: I hear an inner voice saying, "I don't want to eat this way all the time. It's boring."

MP: Let's find out about this inner voice. Stay with that voice and invite it to share more. //

R: The voice says that I work too hard all the time and that eating is the only reward he has. . . . It's funny. I got an image of myself when I was about five years old. I was kind of chubby then. //

R: This time the voice seemed more frightened . . . I don't know why . . . I feel the fear in my body right in my gut. . . . (long pause). It's like he eats to calm himself down or something. //

R: Nothing much happened that time. It seems like that voice went away.

MP: Are you willing to find out more about that voice and why he might be frightened?

R: I'm not sure whether I am or not. I'm afraid it has something to do with the incest.

MP: I understand and respect the fact that you don't want to go back into the pain of the abuse experiences. How about if we proceed by trying to find out more about the feelings and needs of this part of you we seem to have found without getting into the details of what may have happened to him?[9]

R: Yes, that's OK. Let's try.

MP: Is it OK with you if I talk to that voice inside now and then we'll let him respond during the eye movements?

R: Sure. OK.

MP: (*To the voice:*) I wonder if you're still here even though you did not communicate with us during that last set of eye movements. I want to reassure you that we only want to get to know you, not to hurt or upset you in any way. I have a feeling that you are a very important part of Richard and that you are trying to help him. I'd like to know more about that. //

R: Well, that was interesting. I completely relaxed inside. It was like that part of me really heard you and feels safe. //

For Richard, healing pathways began to open when we started to work with this inner voice. The spontaneous appearance of inner self parts can happen frequently during EMDR, especially with people who have been exposed to "inner child work" or other therapy methods that involve working with different aspects of the inner self. The approach I use is based on ego-state therapy,[10] which was developed by Jack and Helen Watkins. This model will be presented in Chapter 5.

*An ego state is an aspect or part of the self that contains personality energy. It has its own history, beliefs, needs, sensory experiences, and purpose. It functions like a subpersonality. An ego state can appear in any sensory form—as a voice, an image, a somatic sensation, an emotional feeling, or even a symbol or color.* When an ego state is dominant, or "takes charge," we say it is directing the personality.

Ego states that have been hurt in the past often fear hurt in the present. When I reassure Richard's five-year-old ego state that I do not want to hurt him, there is an immediate feeling of calm inside. During the next few sets, we discover that there are good reasons for this part's need for reassurance:

R: He told me this time that he used to feel very unsafe, especially at night. That's when bad things happened, when Dad would come in the room and do things that were scary and he couldn't make them stop. So he'd sneak out later and find something to eat in the kitchen, like a reward for getting through it. //

R: Now I see that he's still doing that. I work hard and there are lots of scary things that happen or could happen, things that have to do with things intruding into my space, like the airplanes going where they shouldn't. And that's why he eats during breaks, because he got through it, because he doesn't know what else to do (*sobbing*). //

R: I asked him whether he would trust me to keep him safe now in a way I couldn't when I was growing up. But he doesn't think I can. How can I prevent planes from crashing? I'm really stuck here.

We learned that this child state seemed connected to incest experiences with his father. Eating was his reward for "getting through it." In Richard's adult life, the potential danger of his job triggered danger for this little boy part of himself, who again coped by eating. Although the link between past and present became clear, Richard's processing was stuck because he could not find a realistic way to provide safety for this child ego state.

When there is a child ego state that seems to be contributing to health issues, I first check to see whether the client can provide his or her own resources for renurturing. In this case, Richard let me know that he felt unable to figure out how to respond to the needs of this part of himself. So I helped him search for role models to give him new ideas. We can use these ideas to construct what I think of as *renurturing or reparenting interweaves.*[11]

Renurturing interweaves *can be drawn from the media, from past memories of nurturing adults, or from current experiences that demonstrate abilities to nurture others.* They are invaluable ways of repairing past parenting that was inadequate, abusive, or damaging.

My preference is to let these interweaves emerge, whenever possible, directly from the client. I believe this enhances self-confidence and prevents undue dependence on me. When it is obvious that access to these resources is blocked, I provide simple links to information needed to activate the interweave. In this situation, I function as a witness who sees someone floundering in deep water and quickly throws out a lifeline.

I asked Richard whether he knew of any models of parents who provided appropriate kinds of safety and protection. After some hesitation, he finally selected a TV sitcom where the parents seemed to provide good role models for their children.

R: I saw these TV parents talking to the five-year-old part of me. They explained that they could not protect him all of the time, but that they would do all that they could to keep him safe. They want him to tell them if anyone does things to him he doesn't like because they will put a stop to it. Then they hugged him. //

R:   This time I was giving this part of me the same messages. I was telling him I wasn't perfect but I could be like the TV parents and stay connected to what he needed. I told him that if I'd been around when Dad was coming into his room, I would have stopped him. Now I will try to stop anything that hurts or scares him. //

R:   That felt good. Like everything inside me fell into place.

MP:  Since we're near the end of our session, let's bring up the image we started with, of you eating your favorite vegetarian food. Tell me what you experience now when you find that image.

R:   This time I'm eating and feeling really good, like I'm really taking care of myself and that small part of me too. I think I'll try to remember this every time I eat.

Following a second session where we reinforced and expanded the changes that were taking place, Richard went on a business trip to complete a training course for his job. When he returned, he told me that his eating had been much more consistent, even though he ate out much more than usual. He had been easily able to seek out and to choose healthy foods. He commented, "Even though we didn't work on this, I was able to notice when I was getting full and stop eating. I've never been able to do that before. It's like there was no struggle inside and all of me wanted to help."[12] Satisfied with the results of our work, he was now ready to begin a different approach to exercise.

We decided to start with a positive target image of playing soccer in junior high school. When we reinstalled it with eye movements, he connected with positive feelings in his body. After the third eye movement set, other important associations began to appear:

R:   I'm feeling strong, like my body can do anything. This is how I want to feel. //

R:   This time I was thinking about how when I went to high school, I stopped being interested in sports. Somehow I got the feeling from my father that I couldn't be smart and good at sports at the same time. The last thing I wanted was for him to ridicule me for being stupid. He did that to my mother. I couldn't have handled his doing that to me. //

R:   I can see how I pulled myself away from sports. I couldn't be good at sports and get the best grades. //

R: That makes me sad. I missed out on a lot. It's like there's a split inside me that's been there for a long time. I don't know how to fix it. //

R: I'm feeling really stuck. Just thinking about how hopeless everything was back then. I don't think this is helping. I feel like I'm digging myself in a hole that I can't get out of right now.

Richard confronted an old unconscious belief that prevented him from sticking with exercise. Because his father belittled his mother for her intellectual inadequacies, Richard could not take the chance of appearing inadequate academically. As if to ensure this, he stopped playing sports and concentrated on schoolwork, thereby protecting himself, he believed, from the humiliation his mother suffered.

Our transcript indicates that the necessary information seemed available at this point for Richard to change this old decision. But Richard had trouble putting the information together. This misfiring is common when trauma is part of what is contributing to childhood decisions. It seems to be part of the freezing effect that occurs in the mind's memory and thought networks as well as in the body's nervous system. I decide to initiate a *cognitive interweave* here in the form of a question that helps him identify the dysfunctional belief that is blocking his progress.

**Cognitive interweaves** *are part of the standard EMDR protocol or procedure developed by Francine Shapiro. They are used to interweave positive statements with previously stored information that is negative or dysfunctional so that new information can be processed.* Questions and comments can be used to help stimulate new positive information that will connect with the therapy target network.[13]

MP: Do you still believe now what you believed then—that you can't be smart and good at sports at the same time?

R: Of course not. Oh, I see. That's how I'm still stuck. No, I know it's possible to be smart and a good athlete, to do well at my job and enjoy physical activities too. //

R: That feels great. I want to run out of here now and go for a hike. //

R: I was thinking that this is always what happens. I get very enthusiastic about exercise and then I just get bored and quit. I can't stand going through that cycle again. It's like it's not safe to have those good feelings because they always disappear and then I feel worse about myself than before.

It appears from Richard's reaction that the cognitive interweave takes hold briefly but then he encounters another barrier. And, although he is clear about the negative cycle that happens when he starts to feel good about exercise, he remains unclear about its source.

In thinking about how to find the source of this repeating pattern while respecting Richard's wishes not to go back into past trauma, my intuition was sparked by the word "bored." I wanted to explore whether the child ego state we found earlier was somehow connected to the problem of exercise. From experience I know that key ego states can be linked to characteristic emotional or mood states, such as boredom, that reappear with different symptoms. I decided it was worth a try.

MP:  You mentioned that part of the negative pattern you get into is to feel excited and then bored. I'm wondering whether the boredom might be connected to the inner voice we found last time when we explored your eating. When the voice appeared, it said it was bored when you ate in healthy ways. What do you think?

R:  You're right. That's true. Maybe that part of me is involved in the exercise thing too. Can we find out?

MP:  Let's ask if that part of you, the five-year-old part, would be willing to communicate during the next set of eye movements, to tell us if he has some feelings about exercise that we need to know about. //

R:  Oh he has things to say, all right. He's telling me that when I exercise, I don't pay attention to him. If he's tired, I ignore him. I just keep on going until I burn myself out. Eventually, he digs in his heels and refuses to let me do any exercise at all. //

R:  I'm going to have to involve him somehow but I don't know how.

MP:  Let's see if he'll tell us how during the next set. //

R:  I got a picture of my little friend Michael. He's the son of one of my women friends who's a single parent. I'm sort of a big brother to Michael. I take him on walks and to movies. I've been thinking about taking him to the ice skating rink. That would be fun. //

R:  I went blank. There's something important here about Michael but I lost it.

The need for reparenting recurred when Richard recognized that he might be ignoring the needs of this child part of himself when he exercised. This time a resource spontaneously appeared during eye movements in the form of an image of his young friend Michael. I proposed an external situation parallel to the inner one to remind Richard of the nurturing ways that he already knew. Then Richard could easily make the leap between his loving responses to an external little boy as a model for new responses to the internal one.

MP: If you took Michael ice-skating and he got tired and wanted to stop, what would you do?

R: Well, we'd stop. I'd let him know that was OK. We could stop and rest, or we could stop completely because what matters to me is that he has fun. Not that we skate a certain amount of time to prove we can. //

R: I see now that I need to do that with the little boy part of me. What needs to matter the most is that he enjoys himself. I can see how I've ignored that. . . . it makes me sad *[long pause while Richard is tearful]*. When I go out for a walk with my dog, I can check in with this part of me to see if he's OK, if he's enjoying himself. . . . It's a little scary because I'm afraid he will want to stop right away and I won't get any exercise. //

R: He's reassuring me that if I take care of him, he'll be fine. He likes to feel his body being strong too. //

When I saw Richard two weeks after this session, he was beaming. "I've been doing some kind of exercise every day since I was here, even on work days. No struggle. No problems. It's been very easy and that's because I haven't pushed it. Checking in with the little boy inside me really is the key."

Six months later, Richard continues to maintain improved exercise and healthier eating habits. After getting involved briefly in an intimate relationship that did not work out, Richard now wants to focus on any issues that appear to block his ability to select partners that offer him healthy support. We anticipate that they will be connected to his early experiences of abuse.

BARBARA: COLITIS, DERMATITIS, AND ECZEMA
RELATED TO PAST SEXUAL ABUSE

Barbara's boss had sexually harassed her. He had begun with sexual innuendoes in their conversations, then graduated to inappropriate touching and seductive propositions. When Barbara refused his advances, he threatened her job. Fortunately, with a counselor's support, she was able to negotiate termination from her job with full disability benefits.

Six months later, however, the health problems that resulted from the cumulative stresses of this situation still persisted. She had episodes of dermatitis and eczema. She suffered from nightmares and panic reactions when he called her house occasionally to see how she was. The worst symptom for Barbara, however, was colitis. Colitis flare-ups kept her close to home and dependent on her mother and grandmother, who lived next door. Because she was not improving, her physician referred her to a psychiatrist, who prescribed an antidepressant and then referred her to me for help with her stress symptoms.

When she entered my office, Barbara bounced with energy. She spoke rapidly, her voice filled with nervous tension. "I need to balance myself out somehow," she said. "I know that part of this nervous energy is fear. My father physically and sexually abused me growing up. I know what happened with my boss is triggering me, but I don't know how to stop all this stress. And then when my skin breaks out or I have a colitis episode, I get down on myself. I should be able to relax—I'm not at my job anymore. He can't hurt me now, but it's like my body doesn't believe that."

After seeking more information, I suggested that we begin with EMDR since her finances were limited and EMDR can work rapidly. Finding a positive target image of a time when she did not have health symptoms, either in the past or the present, proved difficult. Unlike Martha and Richard, Barbara was not able to find a positive target when she was symptom free related to her health goals. So here I used a different kind of image, the *conflict-free image.*

**Conflict-free images** *represent moments or longer periods in time when there is full engagement in an activity, when all of the person is in agreement so that there is no inner conflict. There is a sense of wholeness. There is no anxiety, stress, pain, discomfort, or any other symptom during this time.* Only positive feelings are evoked when the experience is recalled. Only positive inner responses occur when the experience is represented as an image. The image is not necessarily visual; it can be somatosensory. When the conflict-free experience is accessed through an inner focus, there needs to be a clear positive connection between mind and body that can be felt and expressed.

Since there are many positives in life that stimulate mixed feelings when they are recalled later on, some sorting is needed to find one that is wholly positive for EMDR purposes. My use of conflict-free imagery is based on the belief of Heinz Hartmann, founder of ego psychology,[14] that *every* individual has a conflict-free area of self or ego functioning. No matter how debilitated a person's health may be, no matter how much emotional suffering he or she may have sustained, this conflict-free "zone" can be found and used for healing.

In my clinical work, I have found that *every* client can find conflict-free images. The avenues to detecting conflict-free images, however, may be very challenging to navigate. Individuals who are trapped in long-time negative reactions tend to have the most difficult time finding these important resources. Barbara claimed, "It just feels like there's never been any time when I didn't feel like this." I helped her locate a conflict-free image by asking, "Is there any time in your everyday life when you are comfortable enough that you aren't focused on your symptoms? Maybe it's when you're doing something that takes your full attention so you just don't notice your problems."

Barbara looked doubtful, then smiled. "Well, I would have to say that the only thing that makes me happy is my cat, Simon." I asked her if she could form an image of Simon and she answered, "That's easy. He sits right here on my shoulder."

As we installed this as a positive target for strengthening, Barbara reported feeling very relaxed and comfortable during the first several sets of eye movements; however, during later eye movement sets she began to seem agitated and upset:

B:  I'm starting to worry that this good feeling won't last. This is what happens to me all the time. I feel good for a few moments and then I start worrying and bring myself down. It's a vicious circle and I hate myself for it. //

B:  I'm still doing it and I can't stop myself. I feel so hopeless. As long as I'm like this, it won't matter what starts to help me. I'll just undo it again.

Since we were at the end of the session and could not seem to move to a place of resolution, I asked Barbara to bring up the image of Simon and to notice some of the things that she appreciated about him so that we could end in a positive way.

The negative looping pattern from Barbara's worries of losing good feelings repeated itself again and again at the beginning of our second EMDR session.[15] I realized that we needed to use the image of Simon in a different way. My hunch was that part of Barbara's difficulty was that she could not hold her positive connection with Simon or with herself when the image, or the feelings connected with it, changed in any way. This pattern prevented her from building a stable connection to any kind of positive experience. When clients seem unable to hold a stable positive connection to themselves or others, I use a special kind of resource interweave called the *developmental learning interweave*.

**Developmental learning interweaves** *can be used to help clients who have unfinished developmental business that can interfere with EMDR processing.* This can include problems with boundaries, difficulty regulating strong feelings, or inconsistent attachments to self and others.[16]

I directed Barbara back to her image of Simon. When she told me she had the picture of him on her shoulder, could feel his warmth, hear his purr, and feel comfortable feelings of contentment, I continued:

MP: Barbara, I want to point out something now. What seems to happen is that as your inner reactions to the image of Simon begin to change a little, you become anxious. Are you afraid you're going to lose the good feelings and won't be able to find them again?

B: Yes that's it exactly. That's what always happens to my good feelings.

MP: Isn't it true that even though your reactions shifted, each time you bring up the image of Simon again, you find some good feelings? In fact, the good feelings get even stronger sometimes, don't they?

B: Yes. Now that I think about it. That's true. I guess I can find that image of Simon and the good feelings it brings whenever I want. //

B: I started to worry that I would lose them [*the good feelings*] again but I reminded myself that the picture comes back each time just like you said. It's not lost after all. //

B: I'm feeling more relaxed inside. I'm not as worried. //

B: More of the same. This is nice. //

B: It's the same. Nothing different. //

MP: What do you think of that, Barbara? That you are having the same good feelings?

B: Well, it's nice, but what if they started to change like before?

MP: What if they did? Could you find them again?

B: Well, I can find the image of Simon again and if I find that, then the good feelings will come too. //

B: I tried it. I let the image go, then brought it back. It works. //

B: I told myself that I don't have to be afraid of losing good feelings. They're going to change a little because everything does—oops, now I'm starting to feel anxious again.

MP: Barbara, let's talk about things changing. We know the weather changes, doesn't it? And is that a good thing or a bad thing?

B: Neither. I mean, sometimes it's good. We need to have rain, and we get it and then the sun comes back out. It changes but the things we need always come back around again. //

B: I guess it can be that way with feelings too. The fact that they change is neither good nor bad. It just is, like the weather. //

B: I have a little more control over my feelings than the weather. I can find the image of Simon and the good feelings come back with it. //

B: That time I saw some colors and the feelings in my body got more deep, that's how I'd put it. And I didn't get worried because I

know now that I can find Simon anytime I want. Besides, the
colors were interesting. Maybe I'll have more kinds of good feelings if I can just learn to trust more.

Barbara's inability to sustain positive feelings for any length of time
seems to point to a lack of permanence and constancy in her connections
with herself. A classic example of this is the distress that occurs when a
baby loses sight of the ball he or she is playing with as it rolls under a
sofa. The infant may cry in distress because it appears that the ball is
gone forever. Each time the ball is retrieved, the baby is joyous. When it
rolls away again, the tears return. Between nine and twelve months, children gain a sense of object permanence. With this new skill, the child
searches for the ball when it rolls away. The hide and seek element becomes part of the game. Similarly, children learn that their parents come
and go, but still exist when out of sight.

However, when a child grows up in a daily environment of turmoil,
violence, and inconsistency, the sense of permanent attachments to self
and others can be fragile or severely damaged. Barbara's father was living
with the family and abusing her when she was under the age of five.
Around that time, her mother found out about the abuse and made the
father leave. Clearly, the damage done from those early years persisted,
so that she could not sustain attempts to heal from the harassment of her
boss and from the earlier abuse by her father. The turning point came
when Barbara learned to hold a more permanent attachment to herself
and her feelings, using the unshakable bond with her cat, Simon. She
could then begin to learn about self constancy, realizing that her feelings
could change their form and still remain useful, positive experiences.
These joyous discoveries allowed Barbara's pathways for healing to begin
to open.

Developmental repair can be one of the most valuable uses of EMDR
and other healing work. It is an important avenue of exploration when
clients like Barbara are unable to form and keep a steady connection to
any positive experience of healing.

During the next weeks, Barbara practiced finding the image of Simon
whenever she was starting to worry about her health symptoms or any
stress in her everyday life. She learned that even when the image changed
she could still stay connected to various kinds of positive inner reactions.
After first reprocessing clinical target images related to her father's abuse,
we worked directly on the dermatitis and the colitis a time or two using
EMDR. Gradually Barbara's health symptoms dissipated almost on their
own. The changes seemed to come about as a cumulative outcome of our
focus on developmental learning, which allowed her to move toward

more permanent resolution of childhood abuse and to hold positive, healthful feelings.

By the beginning of her twelfth meeting with me, Barbara had news to report. She had gradually stopped taking the medication for her skin and colitis symptoms because she no longer felt the need for them. She decided to make a geographical move out of the area because she needed to be on her own. She had found a waitress job through a friend of hers who owned a restaurant. Her plan was to support herself while she went back to school to study business.

Ten months later, Barbara called me for an appointment to explore reactions triggered by her new boss at the restaurant, as well as her inability to separate successfully from her mother and other family members so that she could live on her own. She stopped after two sessions, citing finances and her own resistance as obstacles. "I know that I need to do more work," she said. "It's just that I'm so angry that I still have to pay for things in the past that weren't my fault." Barbara reminded me that not all clients are ready to go the distance. Old resentments, in her case, proved to be a formidable barrier to further change.

# 2

# Beyond Trauma: Enhancing Mindbody Health

When Kate opened her eyes, she found herself looking into the troubled face of Matt, her assistant. "Don't try to move," he told her. "You've had a bad fall. I'm going for help and I'll be right back. You're going to be OK, Kate, just lie still."

When she woke up again, she found herself in a hospital bed. Her mother was talking in hushed tones with someone in the corner of the room. Hearing her soft moan, the doctor quickly turned around. He told her that she had hit her head during a fall down a flight of steps at the museum where she worked as a curator. Kate managed, "This is so weird. I don't remember anything that happened. . . . Wait, I do remember waking up and Matt telling me he was going for help. That must be how I got here."

For the next 48 hours, Kate lay completely still. Any movement of her head was excruciatingly painful. In the days that followed, her vision was blurred. She had terrible headaches. She was exhausted. Moving around enough to take care of basic needs took all the stamina she had. Reading and concentrating for any length of time seemed out of the question.

The neurologist who followed up with her was reassuring. "Your CAT scan is normal. That's a good sign, though it's too early to tell what the permanent effects may be. My diagnosis is post-concussive syndrome. We'll watch you for a while and run some more tests. It might also be a good idea to have some neuropsychological testing done to document how this has affected you so we can measure your progress through the coming months."

Kate called me because she was having trouble adjusting when she went back to work. Even on a reduced schedule two months after her accident, she was struggling. She had difficulty sorting out simple tasks. She often could not find the words she needed to finish sentences. She felt withdrawn and did not know how to respond to the questions and concerned comments of her friends and coworkers about the changes they were noticing. Her self-confidence was shattered.

Many people think of EMDR as a method for treating past and present types of psychological trauma, such as that resulting from childhood abuse or disasters like the Oklahoma City bombing. Less well known are the effective uses of EMDR with acute and chronic medical trauma, even though a specific EMDR protocol for illness and somatic problems is provided.[1] Research has shown us that it is common for individuals who have accidents, illnesses, and injuries that impair their health to experience symptoms of posttraumatic stress. People who undergo surgeries and other invasive medical procedures also frequently report posttraumatic stress difficulties.[2] In light of this evidence, it is important to include EMDR among the tools that can address symptoms resulting from medical trauma.

During our first meeting, we talked about Kate's injury in detail. Although she had had good medical care, no one had talked to her about the acute symptoms of posttraumatic stress that she was experiencing. I explained that a psychological diagnosis of PTSD (posttraumatic stress disorder) often accompanies serious trauma to the body. We discussed the fact that she seemed to have several kinds of intrusive symptoms: negative thoughts that she could not control, startle reactions, nightmares, and high irritability and frustration. Like many people after a traumatic event, she was also experiencing symptoms characterized by avoidance and dissociation. These included lethargy, depression, feeling withdrawn, isolating herself socially, emotional numbing, and avoidance of triggering situations at work. I explained that these were normal traumatic stress responses and would probably resolve over time, especially if we worked to help her manage her emotional reactions to them.

As we discussed the symptoms related to the accident that were most troubling, Kate selected two targets, or goals, for change. One was her tendency to withdraw from others, and the other was her anxiety when asked to concentrate on more than one task at a time.

Kate told me she had used imagery successfully in previous therapy. The main question for me about including imagery in our plans was whether she could concentrate consistently enough to make this approach work well at this point. I gave her some information about EMDR. "It's fairly easy to hold a focus with EMDR," I said. "However, there is a very slight chance that you might experience headache,[3] so we will need to watch out for that with you." Kate seemed curious about trying a new method and so we began with EMDR.

During Kate's first EMDR session, as we searched for a positive target image to begin our work on her tendency to withdraw from others, Kate revealed her needs for safety. "I've been feeling so unsafe since the accident. I sometimes jerk awake in the middle of the night and feel like I'm falling, almost spinning out of control. And when I go anywhere that's crowded, I feel like I'm going to pass out. I think that's one reason I'm staying home more right now."

When trauma plays a role in an individual's difficulties, whether they are related to health issues or to other problems, it is important to evaluate the need for basic safety. Because any kind of trauma, including abuse, disaster, war, accident, or illness, can dramatically disrupt a sense of basic trust that we live in a safe world, it is essential to find ways of restoring feelings of inner safety and security as quickly as possible.

To help Kate begin to find a sense of inner safety that had been disrupted by her injury, I asked her if she could recall a time before the accident when she felt secure and had a sense of safety that was missing for her now. We used this to construct a conflict-free image, which we installed using several sets of eye movements (remember that // = the instructions "Stay with that" followed by a set of eye movements):

> K: I remember a beach I used to go to when my family vacationed in Hawaii. I feel relaxed and at peace there. There's nothing to bother me. The sea is this beautiful deep blue color. I can feel the sun, the wind. I can smell the flowers. I feel good all over. I'm floating in the water and I am exactly where I want to be. //
>
> K: I feel like I can rest right now. I haven't been able to really let down since the accident. There have been so many scary things, so many things I can't do now to feel bad about. This feels safe. //
>
> K: I could almost go to sleep right now, I'm feeling so comfortable . . . hmm, I just want to stay here forever.

As you can see, Kate was able to find and install an image connected to safety quite easily. We proceeded cautiously at first because of the slight chance of headache, using short sets of 5–10 eye movements, which can be a good way to use EMDR if any caution is indicated. It turned out, though, that Kate was quite comfortable with EMDR and experienced no discomfort at all.

In standard EMDR work, identifying the *safe place image*, like Kate's beach scene in Hawaii, is an important part of preparing for therapy with each client. Although most clients can benefit from deeper feelings of inner safety, establishing a safe place image as a solid resource before beginning EMDR is *essential* when past or present trauma is a known part of the picture.

*A safe place image evokes specific feelings of safety and security.* It can be a real setting or an imagined one. The safe place image serves as a container for calm, safe internal feelings. Like other positive targets, it is important that this image stimulate wholly positive feelings before, during, and after installation with eye movements.[4]

When someone demonstrates special needs for safety, it may be important to elaborate safe place imagery. Because Kate is still reacting to the trauma of her recent injury, I decide to see if we can expand her safe place image beyond its initial form to strengthen her sense of security. One simple way of accomplishing this is to bring up the original image to find out whether there has been any change since first installing it during the eye movement sets.

MP:  Let's bring up the image of Hawaii again, Kate. What happens when you bring it up right now?

K:  It seems to have shifted a little bit. At first, I was looking at the beach scene. I was outside it. This time, it's like I'm really in it more or it's inside me. //

K:  That time the good feelings seemed to go deeper. It's nice to know that feeling safe is more inside me. //

K:  I feel like feeling safe belongs more to me. It's not outside of me or somewhere far away.

This was an important discovery for Kate to make—that the source of safe feelings is now *inside*. Sometimes when a safety image is revisited, the scene itself changes. That kind of shift can lead to the realization that there are multiple resources for safety, or that safety can remain constant even when places change, ideas that are further reassuring. Other people benefit from drawing, sculpting, or journaling about their safe place, recreating it in many ways as a calming resource between sessions.[5] I have also found that posttraumatic clients like Barbara in chapter 1, who have developmental needs for permanence and constancy in relation to themselves and others, can benefit from reconnecting with their safe place at the beginning and end of every session. (See Appendix B.)

Kate moved on through the other three stages of the SARI model. She used EMDR successfully in her two goal areas. After first reprocessing the traumatic events related to her accident, Kate learned to relax more about fluctuations in her concentration. She also gained more confidence about her social interactions with people. Six months after the injury, her acute PTSD symptoms had subsided. We shifted our emphasis to intimacy and trust issues as well as to the persisting posttraumatic symptoms that seemed to expose deeper layers of vulnerability. It's as if the work we did to resolve some of the difficulties after her head trauma helped to set the stage for deeper levels of work. I have found that this is often the case when people with health problems aren't aware of childhood trauma. If they do know about these events in their histories, they may not be aware of possible links between current health trauma and other types of trauma in the past. This was true of Helen, whose story you'll read next.

## HELEN: TRANSCENDING THE TRAUMA OF ABORTION

"Having kids has always been very important to me. I think that's why the abortion hit me so hard," Helen gasped between sobs. I strained to understand her as she tried to express her reactions to a difficult abortion that occurred almost a year before. She explained that, although she and her boyfriend were clearly not ready to have and raise a child, she had felt particularly close to the unborn baby. She had dreams in which she was happily washing the clothes of a little girl. She found herself talking to her unborn child many times a day. And she knew the abortion would be emotionally difficult.

What she didn't know was that the abortion procedure itself would be a nightmare. Apparently, everything that could go wrong did. She had gone with her boyfriend to the hospital where her HMO plan was based. A health worker who explained the procedures told Helen that if she'd had more benefits she could have chosen a less painful procedure. Because her insurance covered only one type of abortion, however, she would receive the low-cost approach.

Helen recalled that the room where she was taken looked unclean. She had wondered if it were sterile. The nurses who prepped her were rushed and gave only minimal answers to her questions as they flew by.

The rumpled doctor who performed the abortion was preoccupied and brusque. She could see that he was inserting what looked like a metal hook inside her cervix. It reminded her of stories she had heard about coat hanger abortions. The pain was excruciating when she felt the hook go in. The medication she was given a half-hour before the procedure did not provide relief. When she saw blood oozing out, she began vomiting and was given a shot, which only seemed to trigger more vomiting and anxiety.

When Helen was released later that day, she had terrible cramping and pain, which was not managed by the medication she was given for after-care. When she started vomiting, bleeding, and running a fever a few hours after arriving at home, her boyfriend called the hospital and took her back in. She ended up seeing three different doctors, who prescribed strong antibiotics for a staph infection.

Since the time of the abortion, almost a year before she called me, Helen had suffered numerous posttraumatic reactions. She had been un-able to go to the gynecologist because she couldn't tolerate a pelvic exam. She awakened every morning between 3 and 4 A.M. feeling nauseous and experienced intermittent episodes of vomiting. She had trouble eating some days because the smell of food was aversive. Her ability to partici-pate in sex had been very limited, since she didn't like her boyfriend to touch her pelvic area. The only thing that helped was marijuana, which dulled the nausea and relaxed her, allowing her to eat on her "bad" days.

"It's as if I still have morning sickness. We had a goodbye ritual for the baby on what would have been her birthday. I've tried to grieve and put it behind me, but I can't seem to get past this. My life is on hold. I can't concentrate so I can't finish school. I can't work so my boyfriend is supporting me. This is the lowest point in my life. Can you help?"

During our opening interview, I asked Helen whether the difficulty she was having in healing from the abortion reminded her of any other time in her life. After a long pause, Helen said thoughtfully, "I've never fallen apart quite like this . . . and I've been through a lot in my life. I guess I'm shocked that I've been having such a hard time. I can't control it, I can't stop it, I can't resolve it. The only other time I felt like that was when I lost my virginity when I was 15. Actually, I was raped. . . . "

Helen went on to tell me about a time when she and her best friend from high school had gone out with two college students they had met at a party. Lying to their parents, they had gone to the men's apartment. The four of them had done a lot of heavy drinking and then the couples separated as the evening became more sexual.

Helen recalled that suddenly her date pinned her arms and pulled out a condom. "I told him to stop, but he kept on going. All I remember next was that he was hurting me, I was screaming, and my friend and her date ran into the room. They pulled him off of me and the other guy hit my date. My friend was shocked and scared. She took my arm, helped me get my things, and then we left. Now that I think about it, back then, I couldn't control what was happening to me either. It was the same kind of helpless feeling I had during the abortion."

As we explored the possible connections between the abortion and the date rape, I commented, "It must have felt during the abortion like you were raped all over again." That statement seemed to resonate deeply. Helen responded, "Absolutely. You're really helping me to understand why I'm reacting the way I am. Now it's all starting to make sense."

Before using EMDR or any other therapy method, it is important to try to find out whether there are links from the current traumatic event to past trauma. Often this information can be found by asking a simple question about whether the current symptoms are reminiscent of any other time in the client's life. Sometimes I use some of the structured interview questions available in various instruments designed to obtain a trauma history.[6]

In Helen's case, making this connection at the end of our first meeting had dramatic results. At our second meeting, Helen reported that she had slept better, had experienced less nausea, and had not vomited. She also told me about several intense dreams about her grandparents, now dead, who had been very nurturing during her early childhood. She had also made links between the abortion and other traumatic events from the past, including sexualized contact with a male babysitter.

In previous therapy some years before to help her deal with her parents' divorce, Helen had appreciated the benefits of imagery and dreamwork. But there had been no financial pressures then, since her parents had paid her therapist. Now, as a university student, Helen did not have the money for therapy with me. A concerned friend was donating funds for just a few sessions. Because our time together was so limited, and it is usually possible for me to tell whether EMDR is workable after a relatively short time, I suggested that we begin with EMDR. We would then have time to shift to another method if EMDR wasn't bringing the results we wanted.

Because trauma, both past and present, was a definite focus for our work, I asked Helen to find a safe place image. She immediately recalled a recent experience working as a nanny to two small Asian children with whom she had fallen in love. When I expressed my concern that this image might trigger feelings related to the trauma of the abortion, Helen agreed and searched for another one. This time, she selected the art studio where she worked with clay almost every day:

H: When I'm working with clay, time stands still. I feel so peaceful inside, so secure in myself. It's like I know who I am. I don't worry about anything. And I love the feel and smell of the clay. //

H: I felt stronger, like my heart is lifting up. I saw the color red like a red heart. Then I saw bloody fingers . . . the ends were cut up.

Like many people who have been traumatized, Helen had a difficult time installing a safe place image. She shifted almost immediately from an inner feeling of safety to terrifying associations. Sometimes when there are rapid shifts away from safe place imagery, it helps to seek resources that evoke feelings such as comfort or relaxation. This is especially true when someone has been in an anxious state for a long period of time and may not remember what it is like to feel a sense of safety. Because Helen has told me that her past therapy was positive, I decided to utilize her experiences with her previous therapist as a *safety interweave.*

A **safety interweave** *is the addition of new information that can be installed in EMDR to strengthen a stable sense of safety within the client and in relationship to other people.* Like other resource interweaves, it can take the form of a question to stimulate new learning, an image or other sensory experience, or a past memory of safety.

I asked Helen at this point to draw on a past therapy situation where she felt secure:

MP: Helen, I'd like to pause here for a moment and ask you to think back to your previous therapy where you had so many valuable experiences. Did you feel safe then?

H: Oh yes. I really learned a lot. I remember feeling safe from the very beginning and the feeling lasted all the time I was going there and even afterward.

MP: Can you form an image of that time or is it more of a feeling?

H: It's both really. I see my therapist's office, her chair, and the couch where I sat. I feel very comfortable, almost like I'm in a cocoon. //

H: That time for some reason I saw an underwater scene like a treasure chest or open box with jewelry in it. //

H: I am floating in the water. There are bubbles coming up and I'm laughing. . . . I feel like I'm on vacation, on a big adventure.

This time, Helen was able to hold the feelings of comfort and safety over several sets of eye movements. She ended the session feeling relaxed and good.

AT THE BEGINNING OF OUR NEXT SESSION, SHE TOLD me that she continued to feel better and that she'd thought about the image of swimming underwater several times during the week. Each time she imagined the scene, it had helped her to feel better. She was sleeping well with less nausea and had even enjoyed her boyfriend touching her more freely.

We decided to use the image of swimming underwater as a positive target to strengthen her stability.

> H: I liked swimming underwater as a kid. I could escape. I didn't hear my parents fighting. . . . When I swam on the swim team, I used to put a scuba tank on and float on the bottom of the pool. //
> H: I feel free, in my own world. It's a complete time-out.

Because Helen was able to link the image of swimming underwater with consistently positive feelings of safety during her second session with EMDR, we moved on to SARI's "A" phase—activating information related to the trauma along with healing inner resources.

In this stage of work, pacing becomes a very important issue. This means that we must balance Helen's safety and stability with the important mission of focusing on different aspects of the traumatic experience so that they can be reprocessed through EMDR. Finding inner resources is crucial to achieving this balance.

The standard EMDR method for beginning to activate aspects of a traumatic event is to form a *clinical target image* of a recent time when traumatic anxiety from a past experience was triggered. It is best to begin with the earliest known traumatic experience. In Helen's case, we decided to begin with the sexualized contact with her babysitter when she was seven. We reprocessed the targeted events during a series of eye movement sets.

In her third EMDR session, Helen selected the therapy target of the scene where her date was beginning to rape her. The SUD (subjective units of disturbance scale) level was a 7 and the positive belief she wanted to hold about herself and this event was: "That's all in the past. I can keep myself safe now." We reprocessed this successfully and the SUD for the date rape image dropped to 0 and her confidence in her positive self-belief increased.

Since we had time left in the session, Helen next selected a more recent image of her boyfriend touching inside her vagina, which she believed was linked directly to the abortion:

> H: I imagine Michael touching me, my whole body is tied in knots, like the inside of me is coming out. I'm losing all of my power, I feel helpless, invaded. My hands are sweating. //
> H: In boarding school, I remember helping a friend who got raped. I could empathize so much it felt like it was happening to me all over again. . . . Then I felt this suction cup feeling inside me. It was horrible. //

H: It felt like I was dead on top of a pool, like a detached, heavy, floating feeling.

At this point, we have to make a choice. It is possible that negative looping is taking place because we need to choose a target image that is more clearly related to the abortion. As I mention this to Helen, she becomes more anxious. "No," she tells me, "I'm not ready to go there yet. This is all I can handle." With this feedback, I decide the best plan is to shift more toward safety and stability for the time being. We steer toward a more positive image of Michael that might counterbalance the traumatic material that is surfacing:

MP: Helen, let's step back for a moment. What do you think is happening here?

H: It seems like I'm getting deeper into a negative hole of some kind, the kind I can't easily get out of.

MP: It seems that way to me, too. Let's go back to the image of Michael touching you for a moment. Can you find an image of Michael touching you in some other way, emotionally or physically, that really feels safe to you?

H: Yes, sure. Michael touches me all the time. He's wonderful, affectionate, loving, and he says the sweetest things. Like I remember him telling me that the baby knew we weren't ready to have her but she came to help us get ready. That was so reassuring to me. //

H: I'm remembering some psychic connections. One with my best friend Bonnie. We would have the same dream at the same time. . . . Then with Michael, the first week we met, we had this great connection. We talked for hours about how we both wanted to have children and really do it the right way. //

H: I thought about another psychic link between us. Michael and I both want to give back to society in some way. Maybe by adopting kids or doing some volunteer project to help kids. //

MP: Let's check how we're doing with the target image we started with of Michael touching your vagina. When you bring up that image right now, what happens?

H: It's not as uncomfortable. . . . Somehow I think of him touching me right now as a way of preparing together to make a place to receive a child someday when we're really ready.

By checking back with the original target, which was an anxiety-producing trigger, we saw that Helen had been able to use the interweave to *counterbalance* some of the negative traumatic effects that were starting to flood into her awareness.

A counterbalancing resource interweave *is used to counterbalance the overwhelmingly negative effects of a traumatic reaction.* For many posttraumatic clients, when negative looping persists for more than three or four sets of eye movements, it can be helpful to identify a sensory image that is "counter" or opposite to the one that seems to be triggering the looping. If looping is allowed to persist, the person can become flooded or overwhelmed with distressing feelings, which can reactivate trauma.

Checking to make sure that the counterbalancing interweave has been appropriately installed is important. When using any interweave, it is important to introduce it in such a way that does not interrupt reprocessing. If there is negative looping after the interweave is introduced, this may be a sign that reprocessing of the traumatic event is incomplete. At that point, it is best to reassess the target image to see whether adjustments need to be made.

AT THE BEGINNING OF HER NEXT SESSION, HELEN told me she'd had several dreams that had seemed quite positive. One of them was a dream that her grandmother, who died ten years before, was taking care of the unborn daughter she lost. This and other dreams brought a sense that healing was taking place. Other signs were that she was sleeping all the way through the night, able to eat all of her meals without sensitivity, and feeling freer during sex.

Because she seemed to be holding the gains we had made in the previous session, we decided to select a clinical target image related to the abortion that triggered a higher level of distress than the one for the previous session. This time, Helen selected the image of inserting a tampon, a task she had not been able to do since the abortion. After reinstalling her safety images of swimming underwater and sitting in her previous therapist's office for added stability, we shifted our focus to explore this new target.

> H:  I feel like the tampon is like the abortion hook being stuck inside me. It's like the inside of me is coming out. . . . I'm lying with my feet in the stirrups and I don't want to be here. I knew he was going to put something inside me that I didn't want, and it was going to hurt.

Helen had quickly shifted from the image of inserting a tampon to the traumatic abortion during the first set of eye movements. We now enter the third phase of work and begin actively to *resolve* the current abortion trauma. If Helen begins to destabilize, I know that we can return to stages one and two again.[7]

Two important factors that can help facilitate the resolution of past traumatic events are related to time. First is the realization that many instinctual responses that are made during the time of the trauma itself are useful and adaptive. The second is the understanding that important learning has taken place as a result of the trauma, which would lead to different reactions now. As one client told me, "That was how I reacted back then; I would react differently now based on what I have learned."

Identifying these and other kinds of temporal resources is essential when the decision is made to reenter the traumatic event. Temporal resources can help the person participate more fully in the present moment, free of the contamination of past dangers. Because Helen begins to loop negatively when she focuses on her distress about the abortion, I decide to introduce a *temporal resource interweave.*

MP: Helen, your instinctive feelings—that you didn't want to be in that room, that something was going to be put inside you that you didn't want there—were those feelings accurate?

H: Yes, I was right about that. //

H: I'm having the feeling that I can trust my instincts. //

H: I keep thinking I was right—the whole room was dark and weird, like I shouldn't be there. //

H: I didn't want this doctor to touch me at all. When he walked in the door, I didn't see him wash his hands. He didn't put gloves on until after he touched me. Since the abortion I've been really careful about cleanliness. Maybe I've been a little paranoid. . . .

MP: Can you trust those instincts you had about cleanliness at the time of the abortion?

H: Yes. It turned out that I got a terrible infection. I'd never put myself in that kind of situation again. //

H: If I walked into a room that didn't seem clean, or if a medical person tried to touch me and I wasn't sure about sterility, I would ask first, "Did you wash your hands?" I would make absolutely sure. //

H: Yeah. I know after that I can act differently now to keep me safer.

We worked our way through other elements of the abortion during the remainder of this session and the next. Especially poignant was the moment when Helen sensed that the spirit of her unborn baby left her body. Deciding that she could allow herself to trust these intuitions as well, Helen concluded, "I'm somehow relieved because I knew that she and I both were going to better places." She then began to orient toward the future and link the pain she felt during the abortion to future childbirth: "I'm thinking about labor pain and how it's going to feel good to bring a child here that I'm really ready for."

When we returned to her clinical target image of inserting a tampon at the end of the fifth session, a major shift had taken place:

> H:  I can let go of some of the discomfort [*of inserting the tampon*] with my breath . . . and I can think about it without thinking about the abortion. Now I have a choice about how to feel. Before I didn't.

After our seventh EMDR session, following the reprocessing of several more aspects of the abortion that linked to newly identified traumatic experiences from childhood, Helen reported that she had been able to use tampons with no difficulty. She had also cleared another major hurdle, which signaled movement toward the integration phase of the SARI model. Deciding she was ready to make an appointment with a private gynecologist, she used her learning about exercising choices in the here and now to tell the doctor she wanted an interview session first. "That way," she said, "I can let my intuition help me. If I don't feel safe in any way, I won't come back. If I do, I can schedule another time for a pelvic examination."

As we discussed her readiness for ending therapy, she told me that she and Michael had decided to get engaged. Their delighted families were helping them buy a house. Although this was bringing up issues about having children, Helen seemed content to wait. "I've learned that it's the most important thing in the world for both of us to work toward creating a space where we can welcome children. Until then, we can grow in lots of other ways."

After eleven meetings, nine of which were EMDR sessions, Helen was happy with the changes. All of her symptoms had resolved. She was sleeping and eating well. She enjoyed a full range of sexual experiences with Michael. And she felt good about the care she was getting from her new gynecologist. No longer uncomfortable around friends or relatives who were pregnant or new mothers, Helen was looking forward to finding a job and completing her degree before she and Michael decided to have children.

## Benefits OF EMDR

Although all of the approaches presented in this book can lend effective help to the resolution of medical trauma symptoms and the stresses related to organic health problems, EMDR offers several important benefits. First, it can help people install needed resources of strength and safety at heightened times of vulnerability. Second, EMDR can help achieve rapid shifts toward more positive attitudes that support a rapid return to health. Third, its strong orientation towards action can offer hope to many individuals whose victimization by healthcare systems has often contributed to their inability to heal. EMDR also appears to stimulate energetic shifts during the eye movements that aid in resolving distressing reactions to past events while simultaneously awakening new possibilities. Though EMDR is hardly a panacea, as one of my clients said, "EMDR takes solutions that are already inside me and helps me begin to use them in my healing before I even realize what has happened."

# Section II

# Hypnosis:

## THE POWER OF HEALING TRANCES

# Introducing Hypnosis

Stephanie, a pediatric nurse in a busy intensive care unit, sank down in my office chair with a heavy thud. "I really need to relax today. Can we do some hypnosis to help me with my stress at work?"

I suggested that Stephanie close her eyes when she felt ready to close out all the pressures presented by the outside world and let herself sink more deeply into the chair. I commented on the body changes I noticed and suggested ones she might explore. I mentioned the softening of her face, the flutter of her eyelids, a loosening of her shoulders, and a deepening of her breathing. We then followed a structured induction that we had used before. I counted slowly from 20 to 1, letting my voice soften and recommending that she allow each number to lead her into deeper feelings of comfort. At her signal that she was feeling relaxed, I suggested that she could find a special container for all of the tensions in her body, negative thoughts, distressing memories, and stressful emotional reactions.

After reorienting to a waking state, Stephanie told me that she had imagined finding a special file box where she had filed some of the stressful events of her work day. "I feel really calm inside. Now maybe I can leave my job at the hospital where it belongs."

## Clinical Hypnosis: The Royal Road
## to the Unconscious

Modern views of hypnosis grew out of Anton Mesmer's experiments with animal magnetism beginning in the late eighteenth century. Like many of his time, Mesmer believed that disease resulted from an imbalance of fluid within the body and that cure was accomplished by redirecting the flow. Mesmer's methods involved passing his hands over or placing them directly on his patients' bodies. The controversial results he obtained included body convulsions and twitches, amnesia for what happened during magnetizing sessions, reports of increased clairvoyance, and perceptions that such changes occurred beyond the patient's conscious control. Although investigations of Mesmerism by his government in France discredited his claims, Mesmer was clearly a pioneer in energy psychology. Using the energy of his moving hands, he believed he could shift the liquid energy inside his patients' bodies to cure ailments of mind and body.

One of the attacks on Mesmer was that he obtained dramatic results only when patients were encouraged to have miraculous expectations. This objection is reflected in the ongoing debate about whether hypnosis is a truly distinct state of consciousness or whether its results stem instead from a positive set of client and therapist expectations. The theory that hypnosis, like Mesmerism, works primarily because of positive expectation is closely aligned with placebo theory in the field of medicine. From a placebo perspective, medication has been proven effective at least partly because patients expect that it will work, rather than purely as a result of its chemical properties.

Current allegations by the False Memory Syndrome Foundation against hypnosis also follow this line of reasoning. Therapists who use hypnosis are accused once more of skewing clients' expectancies, this time toward the idea that they have repressed memories of childhood abuse.[1] Although this specific issue is beyond the focus of this book, it illustrates the swirls of controversy that have surrounded hypnosis at every turn of its cultural and scientific development.

Despite controversies that have been waged throughout its history, hypnosis has remained a celebrated method within the field of psychology. Freud called it the "royal road to the unconscious." Clinicians since the beginning of time have been fascinated by its parameters and continue to demonstrate its effectiveness in healing mindbody difficulties.

## How Does Clinical Hypnosis Help to Create Changes?

Hypnotic suggestion may be direct or indirect. *Direct suggestion* involves the use of straightforward communications to promote desirable changes. They are offered during a state of relaxation, which has been formally induced by directions from the therapist. When used with health problems, direct suggestions refer to decreased pain levels, increased feelings of comfort, lower blood pressure, stronger feelings of well-being, and better self-regulation of various physiological processes. Chapter 3 describes some of the methods involved in using direct suggestions to stimulate healing responses.

The mindbody connection was firmly established in the hypnosis world by the contributions of Hippolyte Bernheim. His term, *ideodynamic healing*,[2] was introduced to describe the impact of ideas, or suggestions, on the dynamic processes of the body. Many others in the field of hypnosis have built on Bernheim's ideas. A review of 30 years of research on hypnotic suggestion concluded that hypnotic suggestions can direct specific physiological events in the autonomic nervous system.[3] In fact, there are numerous published cases, as well as carefully controlled scientific studies, that demonstrate successful hypnotic effects, such as the self-regulation of bleeding among hemophiliac patients, the management of hypertension and cardiac problems, the healing of burns, the relief of headaches, the control of anxiety, pain, and nausea in cancer patients, and the enhancement of the immune response.[4]

These and other health-related changes are reported to take place independently of the type of suggestion used. That is, significant changes are reported whether the hypnotic language used is the direct suggestion of clinical hypnosis or the indirect communications of Ericksonian hypnosis, which you will read about in Ted's story.

## TED: A NEW KIND OF "PACE MAKER"

Ted,[5] a 51-year-old man, was so anxious that he literally could not sit down in my office. As he paced back and forth in a highly agitated state, I learned that he had been to a number of doctors and therapists and that no one had been able to help him. He announced in staccato phrases that he had been diagnosed with heart disease a few weeks before after a series of angina attacks related to work stress. Rising to the challenge, I walked along next to him and suggested that he keep pacing while he talked. After a few minutes of pacing together, I asked him to keep going but to make some variation in the direction or pattern of his strides just to see if a movement in a different direction would make any difference.

To Ted's amazement and my own, when he turned left instead of his usual right at the end of the room, he found that he felt a little more relaxed: "I can't tell you why," he said, "but somehow I'm not quite as upset as I was a few minutes ago." We continued to experiment, having him walk in different configurations until he sat down in the chair and reported that the anxiety state had all but disappeared. I asked him what had gone through his mind during his pacing. "At first," he said, "I was thinking how ridiculous I must look. But then when I made that left turn and I started feeling different, I realized that maybe that's all that I needed to do—just move differently in my life. I got this memory of running back and forth with a kite, like I used to do as a kid. When the wind suddenly changed, I had to move in a different direction too or the kite would start to come down. If the kite wasn't flying up as high, I wouldn't be having as much fun anymore."

Ted learned to remind himself of the kite whenever he began to feel anxious or worried. Over the next few weeks, he decided to develop a new role for himself at work that led to greater satisfaction and less stress. His doctor told him just before his last meeting with me that if his health continued to improve, he could look forward to a long and happy life.

## Ericksonian Hypnosis

Ted, and other clients like him, have taught me many important lessons about how healing takes place. Much of what I learned from working with Ted is based on exploring principles from the work of Milton Erickson, whom many have called the father of modern hypnosis.[6] A physician trained in conventional hypnosis that incorporated direct suggestion, Erickson found that many patients rejected or resisted the use of more authoritarian language. Beginning in the 1930s, he became interested in experimenting with other kinds of verbal suggestion and discovered that using indirect language permitted him freer access to the unconscious domain of possibility than more direct suggestions would allow. He also believed strongly in the uniqueness of each individual and the necessity of tailoring hypnotic interventions to fit each client's needs and style. This practice was in stark contrast to the standard practice of giving the same suggestions to each hypnotic subject.

Ericksonian principles explain why altering the direction of Ted's pacing opened the door to other, far more important changes. Erickson believed that interrupting a client's habitual ways of thinking, behaving, feeling, or experiencing would lead to change not only in the target area of concern but in other areas as well.[7] Family therapists who worked with Erickson extended this idea to develop parallel theories of systems change.[8] From a systems perspective, if any one component in a system changes, the rest of the system will also change out of adaptive necessity. This concept implies that the smallest possible unit of change that can be encouraged, like a pebble dropped in a pool of water, will ripple out to other areas far beyond its immediate influence.

TED'S EXPERIENCE ALSO ILLUSTRATES ERICKSON'S BELIEF IN the importance of internal resources. When Ted tuned into his inner experience during that first small change of pacing across my floor in a different direction, he found an important resource from childhood: the memory of flying a kite.

The kite eventually became a living metaphor that he used to expand the range of possibilities in his work life.

One of Erickson's more empowering teachings is that all of us possess the resources needed to make any changes that are important to our health and well-being.[9] The therapist's job is simply to help clients learn to tune into their inner worlds in order to identify the significant aspects of past history stored inside, elements of here and now awareness, and possibilities for the future that can all be used to make needed changes in targeted areas.

Why didn't I choose to focus my first conversation with Ted on the emotional and physical liabilities that threatened his health and were so upsetting to him? Why did I concentrate instead on finding and utilizing the creative resourcefulness that ultimately emerged to allow Ted to make changes he had not believed possible? I was determined, within the first few minutes, to identify some aspect of Ted's behavior, attitudes, values system, sensory experience, or communication style that could be used in a positive way to begin the change process. This was particularly important because he was in such despair.

I selected this strategy because of my appreciation of Erickson's *cooperative and utilization* approaches. Traditional hypnosis requires the client to cooperate fully with the hypnotist's suggestions. For many years, this literally meant the singular goal of having the client go into a "deep sleep." If hypnotic subjects did not comply with this kind of suggestion, they were considered to be resistant or willful.

In contrast, Erickson believed that it was the *therapist's* task to cooperate with the client. This means that the therapist must understand and communicate about clients' attitudes, behaviors, and symptoms in such a way that they feel fully understood and will then choose to cooperate fully with the therapist's suggestions. One advantage to this kind of approach is that no initial change is required of the client, which can be reassuring to individuals who fear change and loss of control. It is actually the therapist who must make the initial change, by accepting and figuring out how to utilize, or make positive use of, whatever the client presents.

With Ted, I thought it was very important at first not to require him to change *anything* about how he was feeling or what he was doing. Instead, I opted to accept his pattern of pacing around my office as being useful. My intention was to send a message that I found Ted as a person, as well as his pacing behavior, completely acceptable to me. I also wanted to let him know that I would be his partner in whatever took place in our meetings. So I joined him in pacing the floor.

As it turned out, Ted's pacing provided an entrée into his inner world. From the perspective of energy psychology, we also discovered that when

Ted allowed his kite resource to guide energetic shifts in his behavior, his anxiety decreased, access to his creative imagination increased, and he was able to convert his inner momentum to outward change in a powerful way.

CHAPTER 4 PRESENTS MORE IDEAS ABOUT USING INDIRECT Ericksonian methods to open pathways for healing. Used energetically, they can stimulate a flow of ideas that might be inconceivable or unacceptable if offered in a more direct way.

## Hypnotic Ego-State Therapy

There are some occasions when health problems and other kinds of clinical symptoms do not respond to the usual direct and indirect hypnotic methods described here. Sometimes this is because hypnosis is not a good "fit." At other times, a client's inner fragmentation or self-division can make it impossible for hypnotic suggestions, or any other therapeutic intervention, to be fully accepted and used.

In *Healing the Divided Self,* Claire Frederick and I wrote about how conflicts that exist among different parts of the self could cause emotional and physical symptoms to form. If the inner state of conflict is strong enough, pathways to healing may be blocked by energies in the personality called *ego states* that are at odds with one another. When this is the case, it is important to find and work with positive parts of the self that can bring the self together in a cooperative effort to seek physical, emotional, and spiritual wholeness.

Since the early days of psychology, experts have believed that our personalities are divided into parts or ego states. Freud wrote about the id, ego, and superego. Carl Jung studied complexes, or hidden aspects of self. William James concluded that the mind operated under the control of several subpersonalities. Pierre Janet described aspects of personality that had separate patterns of feeling and cognition and could only be activated by hypnosis.

In modern psychology, the idea of personality division is commonly accepted. We have developed many approaches to study and work with subpersonality parts or ego states. Some of these include gestalt therapy, transactional analysis, psychosynthesis, imagery, voice dialogue, neurolinguistic programming (NLP), and ego-state therapy.

The ego-state model of therapy, developed by Jack and Helen Watkins,[10] is presented in chapter 5. The Watkins's unique way of working with self-division features various uses of clinical hypnosis to find and activate dynamic personality energies that operate at a less conscious level. Indirect hypnotic approaches can be added as well.[11] When ego states are found to contribute to the formation of health symptoms, they can be redirected instead to contribute to improved health.

## Resolving Health Symptoms with Hypnosis

The three chapters that follow present many ways that direct clinical hypnosis, indirect Ericksonian hypnosis, and hypnotic ego-state therapy can be used to resolve a variety of health issues. Why, when, and how to use these different approaches is discussed in light of each health situation and the outcomes that took place. Decision points shared along the way may be helpful in understanding more about how various uses of hypnosis can assist in opening vital inner pathways so that creative healing energy can flow more freely.

# 3

# Clinical Hypnosis:
# The Inner Healer

Mason slouched in his chair and looked down at the floor. He said defensively, "For the last two years, I've been using cocaine almost every day and I get drunk almost every night. It's not a big deal for me. It doesn't change my personality or keep me from working or anything, but my wife left me because of it and now I have to figure out how to be a good father to my little girl. I can take the end of my marriage, even though it's really painful, but I can't imagine losing Jessie. My wife will file for sole custody in a minute if I don't quit using. . . . Don't bother telling me to go to a 12-step program. I've got to do this my way or it won't work. But I need help. I know you use hypnosis and it seems to me I need a really powerful tool like that to lick this thing. Will you work with me?"

It's these kinds of challenges some days that make me want to run for the nearest exit. How was I going to help an addict who wouldn't consider AA or NA? Despite his defiance, however, there was something special about a man who loved his daughter so powerfully.

I've always been drawn to paradoxical clinical puzzles. So I thought for a few moments about how to respond. First meetings present important opportunities to form a partnership. I had a feeling that if I missed this chance, I wouldn't have any future ones.

"You're laying things on the line, so I will too. I don't know if I can help you, Mason. In some ways you're tying my hands. You don't want to stop abusing drugs and alcohol for yourself—because you don't feel *you have* a problem. Doing this for other people's reasons is not a good way to approach addiction. You won't consider 12-step programs when they're probably the best tool we have for treating addiction. And you want to go your own way, which isn't a great sign that you're really open to my ideas. But, on the positive side, you really love your daughter; I can see that. I'm impressed very much by your commitment to being a responsible father. That kind of strength may be just what we need to solve this problem. So, if we can come up with a plan that both of us *fully* agree to, I'll try my best to help you."

Sometimes situations like the one I found myself in with Mason require me to think about making exceptions to my usual ways of working. When a client's health picture involves addictions, I almost always require participation in 12-step programs, because the research clearly shows that psychotherapy combined with 12-step work is significantly more effective than either one alone.[1]

I also rarely use formal hypnosis until a client has actively confronted the issue of addiction through AA or NA and has had at least a few months of recovery. This is because some people become dependent on the good feelings formal hypnosis can bring and may try to use hypnosis to avoid the hard work of dealing directly with their addiction. It is also possible during hypnotic sessions to connect inadvertently and prematurely with heavy clinical material, such as childhood trauma, which people in early recovery are often not ready to process. Should this occur, the risk of triggering relapse into using substances is quite strong. There are also other considerations for using clinical hypnosis that need to be weighed carefully before beginning to work with any addiction using formal hypnotic states.[2]

If I bend my rules, as I did with Mason, I make it safe to do so by forming a secure agreement for how we will proceed. I usually insist on a trial period, so that we can assess our progress carefully as we go along.

As we outlined our plans for using hypnosis, we began looking at the needs Mason wanted to address with me. His main worry was that he wouldn't have the strength to stop his drug habit and that he would let Jessie down, as well as himself. I pointed out that his drug use was also jeopardizing his health, a subject that he had avoided. Mason appeared dangerously thin and admitted that he existed mostly on junk food when he ate at all. He realized that he was setting an unhealthy example for Jessie, a nine-year-old who was beginning to express a strong interest in snack foods.

"I also smoke cigarettes," he said, "I have ever since I was in grade school. Jessie's been after me recently to stop. I guess I might as well quit everything while I'm at it." I explained to Mason that we would need to pace the changes carefully so that we would not trigger a relapse back to drugs. We would build on small successes that would start with discovering his inner strengths.

ONE OF THE BEST HYPNOTIC TECHNIQUES I HAVE FOUND for strengthening clients was developed by my colleague, Shirley McNeal.[3] Called "Inner Strength," this method involves using a script that leads with a brief hypnotic induction followed by guidelines for discovering a special energy in the personality that is connected with the survival instinct. I described the approach to Mason and we agreed that we would begin with Inner Strength after first exploring his responses to different kinds of hypnotic suggestion.[4]

I started by giving Mason some simple hypnotic suggestions for relaxation. "Mason, I'd like you to get as comfortable as you can there in the chair. That's right. Let your body show you what it needs to do to feel more relaxed. Notice how you can find a position that brings just the right feeling of comfort and balance. Become aware of your own way of breathing . . . in and out . . . in and out . . . and of your own unique rhythms . . . and notice just when you're ready to close out the world around you by letting your eyes close very comfortably, but only when you're ready to let go of a little more tension."

We continued on in this way as I proposed various ways that he could deepen the feelings of comfort that were beginning to develop, for example, finding some limp sensations in his body and a drowsy, drifting feeling in his mind. Mason confirmed these two experiences with a nod of his head when requested, and after several more suggestions I asked him to signal by lifting a finger when he felt as relaxed as he wanted to feel.

At his signal, I began to lead him through a variation of the Inner Strength script:

MP: Mason, I'd like to invite you to take a very special journey . . . a journey to the center of your very being. This is a place inside you where you will be able to connect with an energy that's been with you since before you were born. This is an energy that is part of the life force of the universe. It is afraid of nothing and no one. It has helped you through many difficult times of hardship, times when you thought you might not survive. This is an energy that we'll call your inner strength. . . . I'm going to count now from 5 to 1. Each number can guide you deeper inside yourself, down

toward the center. 5 . . . getting more and more relaxed . . . 4 . . .
feeling a gentle pull like gravity pulling you into yourself . . . 3 . . .
noticing how easy it is now just to be with all of yourself . . . 2 . . .
discover how all of you can come together on this special mission
. . . feeling at 1 . . . with yourself now and the world around you.
I'd like you now to meet your Inner Strength. Be open to whatever
you find. It may be a sensation in your body, or an image in your
mind . . . or a voice or sound that you hear . . . or an emotional
feeling . . . or a memory . . . or a symbol or color. Just allow yourself to connect with whatever is in your awareness right now. . . .
If you'd like to, you can tell me what you're discovering or just
stay quietly with your own experience. . . .

M:   . . . I'm feeling some very powerful feelings in my chest. I feel full
of energy like I could climb a mountain or something. It's a feeling
that I could do anything I want to do. It feels great.

After giving Mason suggestions about finding Inner Strength whenever
he needed the energy he had found, I reoriented him to his surroundings.
We discussed his experience and some ways he could practice finding
inner strength when he was confronted with urges to use cocaine or
alcohol.

When Mason came in the following week, he told me he had found
Inner Strength very helpful on several occasions, but that it was more
difficult to use on his own than with me. I explained that self-hypnosis
was different from guided hypnosis, because when he attempted to use
hypnosis for himself, he had to be the operator while he was trying to
have the experience.[5] Recommending that for the time being it might be
helpful for him to be free of this dual role, I told Mason we would make
an audiotape that he could use to help him stay more focused on his
inner experience.

We went through the Inner Strength script a second time as we made
the tape. This time, Mason reported that the sensations in his chest were
even stronger. He seemed to have no additional responses to the script. I
added the following posthypnotic suggestions after Mason told me how
good he was feeling:

MP:  Listening to this tape can expand and deepen the "natural high"
you have found in the inner strength exercise. Each time you listen, you will be reinforcing these good feelings even more. There
will be many moments of decision, many situations when you will
find yourself at a crossroads. Will you focus on what inner strength
can bring into your life or will you focus instead on the predictable

highs that drugs have brought? Only your creative inner mind can help you find the resources inside yourself to give the answers that will lead you toward the changes that are so important, and so challenging, for you to make. . . . We really don't know how quickly or how slowly you will make the shift inside yourself . . . toward health . . . toward being the kind of good father to Jessie you've always wanted to be . . . toward feeling the pride in yourself you have long wanted to feel. . . . And over time, as you keep listening, this voice on the tape will more and more become like your voice, the voice of your own inner mind. . . .

AT HIS THIRD HYPNOSIS SESSION, I WAS PLEASANTLY surprised to learn that Mason had been motivated enough to play the inner strength audiotape two or three times a day. He was finding it easier to cope with ongoing urges to use drugs and alcohol to medicate daily stress and had created his own form of self-hypnosis to interrupt them.

"Every time I'm tempted," he said, "I think of losing Jessie, I take a deep breath, and I find those feelings of strength in my chest. Sometimes I have to do it 20–30 times a day, but it's working. I haven't used drugs or alcohol at all since I've been coming here. And you know, this inner strength thing has been helping me with the rage I feel toward Jill for leaving me. Sometimes I'm so angry for the way she's acting, like she's so perfect, and I'm scum. I know I can't give into my anger so I use the same 1-2-3 approach. I think of Jessie, breathe deeply, and feel the strength in my chest. It's like magic!"

During the part of our meeting where we used hypnosis, we continued with the basic Inner Strength script. Then we modified the process to add a step. After Mason followed the induction and found again the familiar sensory energy in his chest, I suggested that he take a few moments to communicate with Inner Strength, calling on this energy inside for special strength in the evenings when he was alone. When I asked Mason what was happening in response to these suggestions, he told me that he saw a white light and heard an inner voice saying, "I'm here for you now instead of drugs and alcohol." This message was followed by a deep sense of calm and peacefulness.

Following an opportunity for further responses, Mason signaled that his experience felt complete. When he reoriented toward an outward focus on his surroundings, we discussed the meaning of this inner message. "Before Jessie was born," he said, "Jill and I were like soulmates. We traveled, we wanted the same things, we were really close without even trying. Then, when Jessie came along, I don't exactly know what happened. . . . Jill spent more time with Jessie, and we spent less time as a couple. We just drifted. Looking back, I guess I felt a void that I didn't know how to talk about or fill. I started hanging out with guys that used cocaine . . . and that's all it took. For a while, Jill and I used cocaine and drank together. Then she got disgusted and stopped, but I partied on with my friends. I can see it all now, but I couldn't see what was really happening to us then."

In the next few weeks, we began to address the relational aspects of his addictive behavior.[6] We agreed that the message he had received from Inner Strength seemed to refer to the fact that, at least for the past several years, alcohol and cocaine had been his primary relationship. Mason noted, "That really makes sense. You know, I started smoking cigarettes when I was about nine years old and it was because I didn't know how to make friends. I had friends all right, but I didn't feel really connected to them. I didn't know how to feel close because in my family nobody showed any affection. We all were pretty separate from each other. It was like a bunch of strangers under the same roof. So cigarettes made me feel cool, like I was the kind of kid that other people would want to know."

In light of this piece of history, I recommended that Mason reconsider his decision about 12-step programs, since meetings were filled with people who had the same problem he did: They had made alcohol and drugs their strongest relationship and did not really know how to experience intimacy any other way. I further recommended that he continue to work with Inner Strength to find out how he could form a satisfying type of relationship with this inner source of energy.

Mason met those two challenges. He reported that he had confided in another mechanic at the garage about his decision to stop drugs. His friend's wife turned out to be a recovering alcoholic and had invited him to go to some meetings, which Mason had decided to do.

Mason began practicing meditation, structuring the times he meditated to be in the late evenings when he usually felt restless. He followed the steps he had learned in a meditation workshop and then added his version of the Inner Strength technique. "That way," he explained, "I clear my mind and get quiet and centered first. Then I find Inner Strength by counting down from 5 to 1 like we do here. I don't really need to use the tape anymore now although I listen every now and then when I feel urges to get stoned."

After a few months of sobriety, we explored other hypnotic techniques to address changing needs that emerged in Mason's recovery. None of them, however, worked as well as Inner Strength, which we kept as the centerpiece of our therapy plan. Over time, we expanded the uses of this tool to help him rise to the challenges of negotiating custody issues with his former wife, taking risks with new friends he was making who did not use drugs or alcohol, instigating healthier self-care habits, which included better nutrition and exercise, and finally, assuming a new identity as a nonsmoker.

At our last of 15 meetings spanning six months, Mason was happy about the changes he had made. He felt confident about his role as a single dad. He had moved his workplace to a garage that had a smoke-free environment. He had gained weight and was eating well. And he worked out regularly at the gym and also enjoyed bicycling and roller blading with Jessie on the weekends.

How did all of these changes come about? When I asked him, Mason explained that he felt he had been able to trust me because I kept the agreement we had made and inspired him to do the same. "I think I needed to relate to a woman who believed I could do it. Jill had lost all respect for me. Yet even though I was an addict and a boozer, you respected me." "What role did Inner Strength play?" I inquired. Mason paused and then said, "It's hard to describe. I mean at first your belief in me was my Inner Strength. It was all I had. But because I had that kind of strength, then the tape and the hypnosis we did helped me to find my own type of strength inside. It felt real and I could always find it, even during the times when I felt like I was bottoming out. I guess the truth is, when I found inner strength, for the first time in a long time, I found something better than a burned-out marriage or whiskey and cocaine."

THE INNER STRENGTH TECHNIQUE IS ONE OF THE MOST consistently effective hypnotic tools I've found to work with various kinds of addictions. My theory is that it gives people who have become dependent on drugs, alcohol, cigarettes, food, gambling, sex, or some other substance outside themselves a tangible way of developing positive dependence on themselves and their own inner resources. One of the important predictors for successful completion of recovery from addiction is *self-efficacy*, or the degree of confidence that the addict has what it takes to stay clean and sober.[7] It may be that the Inner Strength technique strengthens this confidence.

Many other types of health and clinical problems respond well to the Inner Strength method. My clients have used it to help manage anxiety and depression related to medical diagnoses, lower their blood pressure, reduce and eliminate stress symptoms, and even conquer needle and dental phobias. Although there are certainly many other techniques that can help people tap into sources of strength within them, this method lends itself well to self-practice and is easily modified to fit a variety of individual needs.

## MIRIAM: HYPNOSIS AND SEIZURE DISORDER

Miriam was on a collision course with terror. She worried every time she went out in her car that she would black out. She had nightmares of losing control while driving and of killing others or killing herself in head-on collisions.

Miriam had just been diagnosed with complex partial epilepsy. Although the warning signs had been present since her pregnancy with her now college-age son, her symptoms had escalated during the last two years as she entered menopause.

One of her major dilemmas involved the use of medication. With large doses, she was seizure free. The down side was that she felt tired, lethargic, and barely functional. In her medicated state, she was also acutely aware of her handicap. She sought my help to find out if hypnosis could help her manage the seizures so that she could lower her medication and live a more normal life.

When someone is referred to me specifically for formal hypnosis work, as Miriam was by her acupuncturist, we always discuss the nature of hypnosis, what the possible benefits might be, any questions or concerns there might be about hypnosis, and any reservations either of us might have in using hypnosis.[8] I also discuss alternatives to formal hypnosis so that the client can make an informed choice with the understanding that, if hypnosis for any reason is not helpful, there are many alternative approaches that might be useful. Since Miriam was well informed, and neither of us had doubts about using this method, we decided on hypnosis.

Because she was so anxious, we began with methods to help Miriam connect with an inner sense of safety and comfort. The safe place technique, which is in every hypnotherapist's tool kit, was her first hypnotic experience. After a basic induction designed to help her find comfortable feelings in her body as well as a deep inner focus, I suggested that Miriam drift back in time to find a time and place where she felt as relaxed and comfortable as she wanted to feel right now in her life.

After a pause, Miriam told me that she was thinking about the beach near her house where she often walked. No matter how burdened with stress or worry she felt when she went there, she was able to let the beauty of her surroundings restore her. As we explored together, she told me she could easily feel that sense of safety and well-being as she pictured herself walking along the beach. She described the scene in vivid terms— the bright sunlight, the salt spray, the spongy sand she loved to sink her feet into as she walked along, the cries of the seagulls, the sound of the surf lapping the shoreline.

When she realerted back to the room, we discussed how she might pull up the image in her mind whenever she recognized any of the signals connected with her seizures. I suggested that she notice what happened whenever she remembered to do this, rather than expecting any specific outcome.

At the beginning of our next meeting, Miriam told me that going in her mind to the safety of the beach really helped her to feel less anxious during the week. She felt hopeful about learning more about how her imagination could help with her seizures. As we discussed our course of action, I suggested that she might want to add a step to the explorations she had just told me about so that she could learn more about how her seizures began, whether she experienced different types of seizure activity, and, if so, what pattern each kind followed. I explained that this kind of approach might help her to have a sense of mastery over her symptoms instead of feeling out of control about them.[9]

Miriam was intrigued by my questions, since she was largely unaware of her seizures until after they occurred. In order to explore patterns related to her symptoms, I introduced a technique called *ideomotor signaling.*

**Ideomotor signaling** *is an approach that is often used in hypnosis to activate the mindbody connection.* Although based on the work of Milton Erickson, it is a direct, more structured technique that involves linking "yes" and "no" answers with unconscious (motoric) movements of identified fingers.[10]

After describing the technique, I led Miriam in a brief induction (though none is required), using the same basic approach from the first session, so that she could strengthen the links she was forming between relaxed sensations in her body, the imagery of her safe place at the beach, and the emotional feelings of security and belonging. Once she signaled her readiness with a nod of her head, I guided her to establish finger signals for "yes," "no," and "I'm not ready to tell you." Miriam's right index finger was linked to "yes"; her right thumb was her "no" finger, and her left index finger was her privacy signal.

MP:  OK, fine. Now, I'm going to ask a series of questions. I'd like you simply to relax and allow the answers to come through the responses in your three finger signals. That is, even though your conscious mind might be thinking an answer to my question, the answers we are most interested in right now are the ones that resonate through your fingers. Since I am asking these questions of your unconscious mind, there is no way your conscious mind can know the answers in advance. As I ask each question, when you can tell which finger has responded, you can help or make it move so I can have the answer too. OK?

As Miriam and I continued exploring, we first focused on finding the sensations in her body that preceded different types of seizures. Miriam's responses indicated a symptom pattern beginning with an overpowering sleepy feeling, followed by a brief lapse of time, after which Miriam was aware of being detached from her body. This basic information obtained through the finger signals seemed to be confirmed by a spontaneous memory Miriam accessed of a seizure that occurred while she was watching TV. Though it was important to continue gathering information, we could begin to use what we had to help her begin to regulate her symptoms using inner resources.

Our next step was to use ideomotor signals to find the resources that would allow Miriam to begin regulating her seizure activity. When we asked her unconscious to indicate a resource which would help her stay more present in her body during seizures, we discovered that Miriam could imagine walking on the beach, digging her feet into the wet sand and feeling the pull of her undertow as her legs felt very heavy. We then practiced the use of this technique by asking her inner mind to take her back in recent time to one of the seizures that began with a very sleepy feeling. Miriam accessed a common experience of sitting in her family room reading a magazine while listening to the news on TV. As she imagined simultaneously her beach scene of digging her feet into the wet sand, she reported feeling very heavy in her body, putting her magazine down, and going into the kitchen for a snack. When I asked her how she was feeling, Miriam replied, "Fine. Normal. Like I've got some more energy for the rest of the evening."

We spent a minute or two reviewing the steps involved so that Miriam could practice this strategy at home. I let her know that her future feedback would give important clues about where to focus next.

"I HAD A VERY GOOD WEEK," MIRIAM TOLD ME AS SHE came in the office for our third hypnosis session. "I was surprised to find how easy it was to imagine digging into the sand whenever I felt that sleepy feeling coming on. My body felt more normal and the seizures began to fade out rather than continuing to build. I don't think I had any seizures of that kind. But I had some other ones so maybe we could find something to help me with those today."

We decided to focus on the type of seizure that was most disturbing to her—those that occurred while she was driving. Again using ideomotor signaling, we explored the sequence of this type of seizure and found that it seemed to begin with a visual aura, shifted to a spacey, unfocused feeling, and ended when she pulled off the road and rested. The inner resource that Miriam found to help her modify this kind of seizure was the image of a red warning light accompanied by the words "Not Safe."

She had not even begun to practice this approach during the next week when she had a seizure after stopping at a stop sign at the end of a freeway exit ramp. Unfortunately, during the seizure, her foot slipped off the brake and she rolled into the car in front of her. Miriam was devastated because it meant the suspension of her driver's license for a year and dependence on family and neighbors for transportation. Yet she remained hopeful: "I hate this because I'm going to have to confront my disability more directly. I guess I have a lot of shame. In a way, though, it's good that it happened because it makes the epilepsy more real for me."

We discussed several ways she needed to come to terms with her condition. For example, Miriam was already aware that she needed to pay more attention to her diet. Although she had talked with her acupuncturist and medical doctor about her need for more protein and less wheat and sugar, she was not consistent about her eating habits. We added the nutrition issue into our plan for self-regulation.

Over the next few weeks, Miriam began to monitor her seizure activity whenever she was a passenger in a car. She found that by imagining a red warning light and hearing the words "Not Safe" in her head whenever she was aware of the initial stages of an aura, she could become more aware of times when she felt at risk for having a seizure. She learned to ask the driver to pull over to the side of the road while she did some deep breathing or relaxation techniques or ate the snack that she now always carried with her. Occasionally, when she followed this plan, she would decide that she needed to rest in order to prevent a seizure and would change her schedule so that she could go home. Using these strategies, Miriam was able to interrupt almost every seizure that occurred while she was in a moving vehicle or that began with a visual aura.

We also used ideomotor signaling to identify a third type of seizure, which began with intense tight pressure in her temples. This turned out to be the most challenging type of seizure because the onset was more sudden. Over time, we learned that this category was usually related to fatigue, emotional stress, or hunger. With practice, Miriam learned to recognize and prevent or interrupt most of these seizures as well.

After about six months of hypnotherapy sessions, Miriam was able to begin reducing her medication. We took this process very slowly because of her fears about relapse. At about the nine-month mark, Miriam had reached the right dosage, one that allowed her to manage the seizure activity and yet have enough energy to increase her activity level. After

15 months of therapy, she had reclaimed her driver's license and had had no further problems while driving, though she always took a passenger along as a precaution.

When she decided that she had completed her work with me, we discussed together the changes she had made. "Now," she said, "I can read my own signals that I'm entering a critical period. I know the signs of anxiety and stress that can bring on seizures and I can trust myself to respond to them. I usually have just the beginnings of seizures now, which are like little clouds passing by. I've learned how to check in with myself so that I can add whatever is needed."

### JUNE: MANAGEMENT OF CHRONIC PAIN

June's voice trembled as she spoke of her excruciating pelvic pain. Constant burning and throbbing in the right side of her vagina. Occasional hot spears of pain in her rectum. Knives of pain down her right leg, through her lower abdomen and under her groin. "I've been in pain for so long, I don't know if anyone or anything can help me."

Her problems had started four or five years ago with a diagnosis of endometriosis (inflammation of the lining of the uterus). Surgery removed 14 pounds of endometrium, leaving behind a great deal of scar tissue. Two years later she had had a full hysterectomy. After that, the pain intensified.

Ever since, June had used all her resources to pursue help. Currently, she was working with a well-known urologist who directed a center for pelvic pain. She received weekly treatments of acupuncture, physical therapy, and biofeedback. Yet even though objective measures showed that her pain had lessened, June was feeling, if anything, more panicked about her condition.

"I organize my life around this. I obsess about it all week long. I hate to sit because it's so painful. The whole thing makes me crazy trying to figure out and avoid situations that might trigger me. Living this way is insane."

June could identify very brief pain-free periods of time. When she was with friends, playing with her 11-year-old daughter, or walking her dog, her focus changed and she could leave her pain behind. When she reentered a state of pain, however, she beat herself up emotionally because she was not able to remain in whatever comfort zone she had found. "I know it doesn't help," she confided, "but I just can't stand the fact that I have so little control over the quality of my life."

ONE OF THE MOST DEBILITATING HEALTH ISSUES IS chronic pain. Pain can be associated with a number of serious conditions like rheumatoid arthritis, lupus, chronic fatigue, and multiple sclerosis. Pain is also a byproduct of accidents and injuries and is an unavoidable aftermath of surgeries and many medical procedures.

Hypnosis has had a long and successful history as a positive tool for managing acute as well as long-term pain.[11] When people are in the throes of discomfort for long periods of time, they often cannot even recall a time before pain took over their lives. One of the main benefits of hypnosis is to introduce those who live in extreme states of painful suffering to comfortable states of relaxation, inner exploration, and wholeness.

When June and I discussed the options we might use, she very much wanted to explore hypnosis first. "I've used EMDR and it helped me to resolve the shame I've been feeling about my condition, but it hasn't helped with the physical pain. I think hypnosis can help with that; at least I want to find out by giving it a try."

I reminded June of the benefits of *progressive relaxation* to promote health by releasing tension. A simple skill that has become more mainstream as our society has become more health conscious, this technique is easily taught. But, like any competency, it requires regular practice to receive full benefit.

I call this tool the "head and shoulders, knees and toes" approach to hypnosis, because specific direct suggestions are given to induce relaxation in the muscle groups of the body progressively, usually starting with the head and moving gradually down the body to the legs and feet. Many clients with physical discomfort issues respond very well to progressive relaxation as a tool to help them enter a new world where their bodies can finally experience complete rest.

Making an audiotape, which I did for June, allows for reinforcement of the positive benefits of relaxation many times a day. As June began to trust that she could find a state of complete comfort whenever she wished, she found that the relaxation tape began to replace her preoccupation with pain as a daily focal point.

RELAXATION, SAFETY AND SECURITY, AND HEIGHTENED positive awareness, which Mason, Miriam, and June discovered through the use of hypnosis, are only a few of the many special states of awareness that hypnotic suggestion can facilitate. Another one that is often helpful to people with virtually any type of health problem is the state of *mindfulness*.

**Mindfulness,** *associated with a type of Buddhist meditation developed by various practitioners, teaches an opening of the awareness to embrace the fullness of any moment in time.* Although mindfulness meditation can require extensive practice to learn and master, there are several modifications that can be used effectively in a brief format.[12]

One of my favorite modifications was created by my friend and colleague, Noelle Poncelet. I have used it successfully with many health-related problems, and find it especially useful for anxiety and depression related to medical conditions, for acute and chronic pain, and to intervene with addictions. Although it does not require the use of hypnosis, I have found that hypnotic suggestions seem to deepen the experience for many people.

Since June mentioned that she was struggling to start a daily meditation practice, the mindfulness approach seemed like an important next step. I told her that I would like to guide her through a meditation exercise that might help her to feel more centered while also helping her with the other goals we had been working on. I asked her to sit in a comfortable position and close her eyes, if that would help her to focus more on her inner experience. Then we went through the following steps:

MP: June, I'd like you to take a few easy, slow, comfortable breaths. . . . That's right, easy and effortless. . . . Then take a moment to notice all that is happening inside and around you . . . what you can hear . . . what you can feel in your body or emotions . . . what thoughts are traveling through your mind . . . any pictures or symbols that might appear. . . . When you're ready, let me know all that you are aware of at this moment in time.

J: I'm aware of that familiar burning feeling as if a nerve is being pinched. I'm uncomfortable and I'm thinking that that's the way I've been feeling for so long. There's been no change. I feel such despair that I don't want to go on living this way . . .

MP: All right. I'd like you to gather up all that has filled this moment of awareness—the familiar burning feeling as if a nerve is being pinched, the discomfort, the thoughts of despair that there's been no change, that you don't want to go on living this way. Gather them all up now and take a deep breath in and hold it. . . . That's right, hold it along with all of those other sensations, thoughts, and feelings . . . and when you're ready, let it all go. . . . Let it all go. And then with the next breath in, step into a new moment as if for the very first time. . . . Be open to what this *new* moment brings. Begin to explore what you are becoming aware of now in this new moment. And when you're ready, let me know what is in your awareness now.

J: I don't feel quite as much panic. My chest is a little more relaxed. I still have the burning feeling but it's mainly in my left leg. I was thinking about how I'd like to be able to move my body and wondering if I'll ever be able to. . . . That's all.

MP: OK. Now I'd like you to accept all of that with great compassion and kindness toward yourself . . . that you don't feel quite as much panic, that your chest is a little more relaxed, that you still have the burning feeling mostly in your left leg, that you're thinking about how you'd like to move your body and wondering if you will. . . . Just accept that kindly and gently and when you're ready, gather it all up as you take in a deep breath and hold it . . . hold it. And when you're ready, *let it all go*. . . . With the next breath in, step into the next new moment as if for the very first time. . . . Explore this new moment and all that it brings you. When you're ready, let me know what you find in your awareness now.

J:  My hip feels relaxed and my knee feels relaxed. I'm finding that I can move some of the good feelings from my right to my left. My left foot feels normal and my right foot feels fatigued and I have a little of that burning there.

After three or more cycles through the exercise, June reported feeling much more comfortable and had some positive thoughts about her future. She learned, as many people do, that having what Buddhists call "beginner's mind" allowed her to use her cycles of breathing to let go of much of the pain while being open to new experience. We made a tape so that she could practice at home, using this method as a way of clearing away negative thoughts, detaching from physical pain, and opening pathways to possibilities for more comfort and mobility.

AFTER THREE 75-MINUTE SESSIONS, JUNE CALLED TO SAY that she wanted to stop her work with me for now. "I've learned some good tools for managing my pain and I feel more confident that I can use them. My pain levels have dropped almost 50%. I'm determined to get them even lower. In fact, I've decided to pursue the idea of surgery to remove some of the scar tissue. I think I need to be more aggressive in my care. I've been afraid of the pain involved in another surgery, but now I think I can handle whatever discomfort comes. I know I can let go of the pain over and over, with each breath if I have to."

I checked with June after her surgery and learned that it was quite successful. She was feeling significantly less pain on a daily basis, was far more active, and was enjoying her life a great deal more.

In June's case, once she discovered that it really was possible to enter a pain-free state, and that tools she could use easily helped her find a state of mental and physical comfort, her confidence grew and helped her push for a more complete recovery.

## Using Hypnosis to Uncover and Resolve Past Trauma Related to Health Symptoms

Some clients who use formal hypnosis do not experience the positive outcomes that Mason, Miriam, and June were able to achieve. Although there are many complex factors to consider, sometimes a lack of movement toward health can occur because of past trauma that may be contributing to health problems.

I believe it is important to take a careful health history with *every* client, regardless of the beginning complaint. This includes screening for traumatic events such as serious or chronic illness, accidents or illnesses, experiences with surgery, the need to cope with health problems of family members, any episodes of violence or threats of violence, and various types of abuse experiences. If the client and I suspect that unresolved trauma from the past is somehow contributing to current health problems, we may decide to use hypnosis to help resolve unbalancing effects of the underlying traumatic event still stored inside.

Hypnotic techniques can provide effective means of identifying unconscious past distress that may be driving current symptoms, bringing them to conscious awareness, and disengaging them. Like EMDR, formal hypnosis can remove barriers that may be blocking healing pathways so that full health can be restored.

# 4

# Ericksonian Hypnosis:
# Activating Unconscious Pathways

In addition to helping to provide an inner diagnosis that can pinpoint important needs for correction, metaphors can also be used to plant seeds for growth and healing that can be received at an unconscious level. This avenue was especially useful in Sarah's situation, where presenting the same message at a conscious level might not have been effective.

### SARAH: METAPHORS AS CATALYSTS FOR CHANGE

Sarah came to see me because she had been diagnosed with a condition known as alopecia arieta, which refers to premature hair loss generally believed to be stress-related. In her early forties, Sarah was the active mother of three school-age children. She was frightened about how much of her hair had fallen out over the last several months and desperate to find a solution.

Sarah had already made the rounds of several dermatologists, who had told her that there was no known cure for this condition, and she had found the cremes and medications they prescribed ineffective. My primary impression of Sarah was that she was obsessed by her hair loss. She told me that she literally counted the hairs that appeared in her hairbrush or on the surface of the sink and tub several times a day. Each accounting led to stronger feelings of anxiety and helplessness. Although I wanted to search for possible links between her surgery and her symptoms, I felt that I first needed to connect more with Sarah, to let her know I understood, and to offer her hope. My hunch was that because she was so distraught, direct attempts at reassurance would not be useful.

As I sat quietly after listening to the story of Sarah's mysterious symptoms, I felt at a loss about what to offer her and how to respond. Unexpectedly, an anecdote from my own experience popped into my awareness. Since my Ericksonian training has taught me the value of accepting the spontaneous gifts of my own unconscious, as well as those of my clients, I decided to tell her the following story (italicized words were given vocal emphasis):

> Sarah, I'm not sure why but I'm reminded right now of something that happened to me last summer. It was an awful experience, but I'm happy to report that *this story has a happy ending.* I'm a very inexperienced gardener, but I recently bought a house with a lawn, so last summer *I decided the best way to learn* about caring for the garden *was by taking action.*
>
> The first task I set for myself was to fertilize the lawn. I went to a nearby nursery and talked at some length with people there about my options. *I did a lot of research.* I finally decided I could handle renting a machine that dispenses the fertilizer as it is pushed along. So I was given instruction in using the equipment, purchased a sack of fertilizer, and headed home to try out my green thumb. I loaded the spreader and began walking along, *feeling very good about spending time taking care of myself* and my home in this way.
>
> But after a few minutes, I noticed with alarm that most of the fertilizer had been distributed. I did not know much about gardening, but I knew something was wrong. I went inside and *called for help. That was a good decision* because the nursery people were quite helpful. They asked me to bring in the machine, which they adjusted, and gave me a new bag of fertilizer. They also told me *how I could repair what had gone wrong.* I started off again with a little less enthusiasm and more caution. Unfortunately, the same thing happened again. I was horrified. Even though *I tried to even things out,* spreading the fertilizer as best I could, *I had a terrible feeling inside that there would be permanent damage.*
>
> Sure enough, in the next few days, big brown patches appeared in the lawn. *The grass disappeared, as if the blades had been burned away. I was devastated. Each time I came out of the house, I imagined that my neighbors were laughing at me, or at least judging me, for this eyesore. Their lawns looked so immaculate by comparison that I felt*

*humiliated. I asked many people for advice and each one had different ideas. None of them seemed particularly helpful* until one neighbor said to me, "The same thing happened to me once. *It was horrible. I suffered terribly but then I realized that this sort of thing happens in nature all the time. There are fires and grassland and trees are destroyed. But the wonderful thing about nature is that it restores itself. What is lost will grow back. Just be patient. You'll see."*

*So I tried to hold those hopeful thoughts* for the rest of the summer as I watered faithfully every day. *Each day I checked those spots carefully, looking for new growth.* Yet as the weeks went by, *the surface still looked barren and awful, a shadow of its former self. I began to despair again. Just as I was about to do something drastic* like ripping the whole thing out and starting all over again, *I noticed some little green shoots one morning. I was filled with relief and joy. As I continued to nurture this new growth, I thought to myself, "The problem was that I was focusing more on what I had lost, rather than on the new growth that was trying to happen."* And, you know, *that experience taught me a lot.* My lawn is lush and green again, *though it took longer than I would have liked. I learned to trust that nature will meet me at least halfway and that its power to regenerate itself is stronger than my despair.*

Sarah sat in thoughtful silence for a few moments after I finished the story. We went on to talk at length about her interests in gardening, which she had not yet shared with me. She told me that she had been so busy in recent weeks that she had not been out in her large yard, where she usually enjoyed working.

We discussed how it was possible for her to *start small, focusing on the most rewarding part* of gardening, *which was watching new growth appear.* She decided to plant some seedlings in little pots at her kitchen window where she could easily watch them grow every day. Other seeds were planted in the indirect suggestions I gave her highlighted above.

When Sarah came back after our first meeting where I had shared the story of over-fertilizing my lawn, she remarked, "I felt more full of energy this week. It was unusual because I've been so depressed about things for so long." Her comments let me know that we were on the right track. From an energy psychology perspective, we had stimulated Sarah at unconscious levels so that she experienced greater energy inside herself and therefore had more energy for her life.

MANY ERICKSONIAN APPROACHES TO HYPNOSIS, INCLUDING metaphor, achieve this kind of indirect impact on mindbody energy systems through the use of special kinds of indirect suggestions,[1] which are designed to bypass the resistance of the conscious mind. The highlighted messages in the story I told Sarah were *embedded*, or concealed, within the storyline of my lawn ordeal. Marked with a subtle shift of voice to draw her attention, they were intended to imply several levels of meaning. Certainly, they proposed truth about the event in my life, but they were also true in a universal sense and undoubtedly true for Sarah in her own unique circumstances.

OVER THE NEXT FEW WEEKS, WE DISCUSSED THE PROGRESS of her little plants. When she raised the issue of going back to school to finish her degree, I gently inquired about how she was feeling about the problem that had prompted her to call me. "Oh that," she said quietly. "I don't think about the alopecia any more. The other day I noticed patches of my hair were growing back in. I'm ready to spend my time and energy on more important things now."

It seemed that the seeds my story planted bore fruit very quickly in her life. Could these changes have happened if I had suggested EMDR or some other approach? Perhaps. Yet my little story so closely matched her situation in an indirect way that it seemed to allow her to enter into a nonthreatening, shared experience with me. We then expanded the story into a living metaphor, which allowed Sarah to contribute equally to its meaning. Unaccountably, the story's metaphorical seeds worked their magic along with the literal seeds she planted in her windowsill pots. This powerful way of stimulating new growth and learning at an unconscious level, an unmistakable hallmark of Ericksonian hypnosis, was also central to my work with Alexandra.

## ALEXANDRA: ERICKSONIAN HYPNOSIS FOR
## PAIN OF RHEUMATOID ARTHRITIS

Alexandra almost crawled up the stairs to my office to keep her first appointment. Partially disabled with rheumatoid arthritis, she was in almost constant pain. Part of her distress was her worry about deteriorating like her grandmother, who had worn leg braces in later life when crippled by the same disease. During the earlier stages of her disease, Alexandra had become addicted to cocaine and to pain medication. She was also aware that food allergies, especially to wheat and sugar, worsened her condition, yet she struggled unsuccessfully with a special diet. Free of all drugs for the last ten years, she attended Narcotics Anonymous regularly and worked at her job as an insurance agent half-time.

As we explored together what most deeply "pained" her about her life, she revealed, "Pain is my recognition from others. If I get better, I won't be special anymore. No one will notice me. I'm just a fifty-year-old over-weight grandmother who does well at her job but that's about it."

Alexandra agreed that she needed to find other ways that she could feel special. She increased time spent with close friends and joined a support group. As she felt more confident about ways she stood out in the minds of others, she learned to identify three patterns of body discomfort: (1) times when she was relatively free from all discomfort, (2) periods when she felt a sense of pressure in her joints, (3) and episodes of intense pain mostly in her left knee. I helped her to be curious about which of these three patterns would emerge when she began to move her body, rather than tensing her body in anticipation of always feeling pain. She also began literally to move more in her life, enrolling in a water aerobics class and walking every day.

As her pain levels began to drop and mobility increased, Alexandra became preoccupied with family relationships. I observed that her physical pain was located in areas of joining between bones, tissues, and muscles. I wondered aloud if her relational "joinings" with others needed further healing in order to promote additional healing of her arthritis symptoms. We began to explore her relationships with her three daughters and five grandchildren, arriving at the conclusion that she felt great guilt about the years she had been drug-addicted, especially when her grandchildren as babies were left in her care. She shared these feelings with her daughters and was relieved to receive their love, support, and forgiveness. Her mood lightened and she felt less depressed.

Alexandra had already made several important changes that involved a shift in her attention and focus. First, she made an initial shift to expand the meaning of her pain from arthritic pain to the emotional pain involved in her addictions and in the dysfunctional ways she had joined with others. As she began to benefit from her openness to these new alternatives in her outer life, she also learned the benefits of refining her inner focus. She learned to discriminate types of discomfort and what they signaled. She learned to recognize and enjoy the many times during the day when she was free of pain. And, she learned to shift the ways she anticipated physical movement by using more positive self-suggestions.

ONE OF OUR THERAPY EXPERIMENTS WAS PARTICULARLY convincing for Alexandra. On a damp winter day, she was experiencing high levels of pain in her left knee as she sat in my office. I challenged her to give herself different types of positive suggestions before she stood up, a movement that usually increased the discomfort in her knee and hip joints. She discovered that when she told herself, "This is really going to hurt," her pain level shot up to an 8 or 9 on a 10-point SUD (subjective units of disturbance) scale. When she thought, "I wonder what this will be like," her discomfort dropped down to a 1 on the scale.

Alexandra practiced exploring the different types of suggestions she routinely gave herself, particularly just before she was about to make a movement that was challenging. Instead of lying awake in despair at the end of the day, she also learned to use that time to evaluate the kinds of self suggestions she had used, refining them further based on the results she had obtained.

Words came to make a big difference in Alexandra's everyday life. As she summed it up, "I've learned to talk differently to myself and everyone around me too. I notice when I approach my roommate in certain ways, I like what happens. If I lead with negativity, I feel bad and so does she. And I'm really starting to notice what kind of language works with my hyperactive grandson. There are certain kinds of messages he really responds to. That's what I'm learning with others and myself—to choose the messages that get the results I want."

## GWEN: BULIMIA AS AN ALLY[2]

Most people with health symptoms understandably view them as liabilities; however, symptoms can also function as assets to achieving growth and wholeness. I often ask my clients the question, "What can this symptom help you learn about yourself that you can discover in no other way?" Inevitably, the answers lead to interesting possibilities for our work together. This proved true in my healing journey with Gwen.

At her first visit, Gwen looked like a wooden mannequin. Her words tumbled over each other in a rush, as if she were afraid she couldn't get them all out. She spoke of recurring nightmares, of physical, sexual, and emotional abuses growing up, of attempted toilet training at the age of eight weeks (which she had read about in her mother's diary), of feeling that her body had never been hers, of her father's, grandmother's, and uncle's suicide deaths, of her own suicide attempts as a teenager. After ten minutes, both of us were overwhelmed by the enormity of her suffering.

Gwen was referred to me for help with her bulimia, which had begun in her early teens. She had worked on this problem in a previous therapy, where bulimic episodes stopped completely for a few months before starting up again. She felt her previous therapist focused only on the bulimia because she was frightened of Gwen's history and didn't want to delve into it. She had then started work with another therapist who had been willing to focus on Gwen's past. Unfortunately, the deeper they delved, the more depressed Gwen became and the more active her bulimic symptoms. Her psychiatrist, who was monitoring her on antidepressants, told her that work with me was a "last ditch effort" to avoid hospitalization, as the health effects of her bulimic episodes, if left unchecked, would soon become life-threatening.

After exploring the history of Gwen's symptoms as well as of her physical, emotional, and psychological health, we discussed our options thoroughly. I explained to Gwen that there were therapy techniques, such as formal hypnosis and EMDR, that had the potential to work relatively quickly. The risk, however, was that they might work so quickly that they would destabilize her further, and since she was already feeling suicidal and hopeless about the imminent possibility of hospitalization, I was not sure I wanted to take that risk with her.

Another alternative would be to *utilize* her bulimic episodes from an Ericksonian perspective to find out what they could teach her about herself in her present life. Gwen agreed with me that this was probably the best initial path. "I want to find and lay to rest the demons of my past as quickly as possible, so I'm a little disappointed that we need to go more slowly. But I'm interested that you believe the bulimia could be useful. I've never imagined that. I've always felt so ashamed and other people treat it like I have the plague. If you think studying my bulimia can help me, I'm ready to start."

We began very slowly to build an alliance. Every session was an opportunity for her to tell me more of the story she was hungry to share with someone who would not shrink away or be repulsed. Gwen also wanted help with current stresses, which included strained relations with her two teenage daughters. The oldest was drinking heavily and the youngest was preparing to leave for college. Gwen was also struggling in her clothing design business, which she had built over the last 15 years. Her current dilemma was how she could expand beyond the current payroll of 20 employees without more capital, which she did not have. Yet she believed that if she did not expand, she might not be able to stay competitive within the industry and the business would have to fold. Each night she came home so exhausted that she went to bed early and had little contact with her daughters or Gus, her live-in boyfriend.

During this time, I reassured Gwen that our goal was not to change her symptoms in any way, provided that they did not worsen beyond the four episodes per day baseline where we had started. Although Gwen was dubious, after a few times of testing me she became more trusting, as she found that I kept my word and stayed within our contract. At moments when she would mention the bulimia as something she had to get rid of, I reminded her that we still had more learning to do and that we were not yet at the time in therapy when we would begin to change the symptom.

Valuable information surfaced during our discussions about ways the bulimia was helpful to her. We learned about the soothing qualities of her bulimic cycles. "When I'm eating and I know I'm going to purge later, nothing bad can happen to me. It's like I'm in a cocoon. I feel happy, invincible, safe. Then later, when I'm purging, it's like a cleansing, it's energizing, a way to get rid of what is bad inside my body. I was brought up to believe that I had something bad inside me. I was told it was the devil. My mother wrote in her diary that she knew this about me because I was born a day early. My father often told me I should read the Bible every day to get rid of the devil inside."

We also learned that when Gwen tried to stop herself from bingeing and purging, feelings of despair increased. "This week, I had only one bulimic episode," she reported, "It was on Sunday when I was by myself. I felt really lost, like I had no place to belong in the universe. I felt like I had to die if I didn't do it, like I'd be sucked into a void that's so empty, I would be completely alone. It's like I'm a freak of nature."

I wondered aloud if these feelings might belong more accurately to another time and place in her history, since things were going relatively well in her adult life. Gwen said thoughtfully, "Maybe you're right. This is probably just how I felt as a little girl, only I didn't have the words to explain, and I didn't have anyone I could tell like I can tell you now."

Through our Ericksonian framework of utilizing the bulimia to learn more about her inner dynamics and her past history, Gwen's episodes had decreased on their own. She was less depressed and decided to reduce her antidepressants. For a few weeks, she was almost fully stabilized. Events in her life, however, began to gather like storm clouds to threaten her newfound well-being. Gus, her boyfriend of two years, began to express dissatisfactions with their relationship, perhaps a development related to Gwen's newfound strengths. Her business also seemed more fragile, as two possible sources of funding failed to pan out.

These changes in external circumstances triggered several psychological responses. First, her bulimic episodes began to increase again, up to two or three per day, so that she felt out of control and desperate. Nightmares also began to plague her. They brought jagged images of being forced to endure humiliating enemas as a small child, of being molested by an old man as she sat on the toilet, or of being chased by a rapist with a knife.

As we mused about the possible meanings of these reactions, Gwen became concerned about whether I would hospitalize her if the bulimia became worse. I told her that as long as the number of daily episodes did not climb above our baseline, I felt it would be safe to continue to explore what they could teach us about ways she continued to be vulnerable in her current life. I suggested that her bulimic behavior might even serve as an important guidepost, pointing us to necessary strengthening and repair work that we still needed to do.

In the weeks that followed, we focused on several important themes identified by Gwen's scrutiny of her bulimic episodes. One was the feeling of pressure that built up inside, which she felt powerless to release except through binge-purge cycles. Another theme was the sense of past and current violation that surfaced in her nightmares and in waking interactions with her boyfriend. A third was the physical trauma she had experienced throughout her childhood and adult life, most recently in an automobile accident the year before that had inflicted soft tissue damage and compression of nerves in her neck.

We addressed each issue with a careful eye toward any further destabilization of her health. Using imagery, Gwen learned how to regulate feelings of stress and pressure. We also worked with her dream imagery to expand the scenarios so that she experienced a sense of completion and mastery. But perhaps the most fruitful investigation was our study of the role physical and medical trauma played in her life. Her health history, which I had initiated in our first few sessions, became more detailed and comprehensive as Gwen felt more comfortable sharing events with me she had never told anyone before. She described having recurring bladder infections before the age of six, which she was told resulted from sitting on cold stones. Although her sister had remembered occasions of being sexually abused by her grandfather, Gwen was uncertain but had always held it as a possibility because when she became a sexually active adolescent her bladder and kidney infections had recurred and intensified.

Gwen told me accounts of her appendectomy at age 7, tonsillectomies at age 9 and again at age 18 to remove scar tissue, a thymectomy at age 22, and multiple dental surgeries resulting from medication overdoses during suicide attempts and from years of bulimic episodes. Gwen had also had an abortion in the fourth month of pregnancy without anesthesia. She had been diagnosed with an extended bladder due to the bulimia and with a mild form of myasthenia gravis that affected her muscle control in certain situations. When her children were young and after their father had left her, Gwen had been involved in a relationship where she was physically battered. In the past three years, she had also undergone several surgeries on her thumb, which had been injured in a fall while she was out jogging, as well as a lumpectomy.

Although this kind of history would be emotionally staggering to most people, Gwen seemed nonchalant about what she was telling me. When I checked in directly about how she was feeling, she told me, "I love having surgery. I feel safe in the hospital because nothing else can happen to me while I'm there. I feel special because I can get care for myself. I won't be expected to take care of anyone else. I actually like seeing scars on my body because they're proof that I survived, that I endured horrific things, and that I can be proud of making it through."

This kind of detachment, even elation, related to medical events can be a sign of unresolved posttraumatic stress related to medical and physical trauma.[3] Even though we had explored other types of trauma in her childhood, it was not until we reached this core that we were able to move toward resolution.

RATHER THAN OFFERING SOME OF THE OBVIOUS LINKS I could make between her health history and the early physical abuse where her body was invaded (though I was sorely tempted), I asked what all of this could teach us about her that we did not already know. For a long time, Gwen was silent. "I thought for sure you were going to tell me what I already know about myself . . . that this is the profile of a damaged person, that I shouldn't feel the way I do. You're constantly surprising me in good ways that let me know that I really can trust you to let me figure this out."

She went on to say, "I think what all of this means is that my body is not real to me. It's only a thing that has things done to it, which is why I don't feel much unless the feelings get really intense—like a surgery or an injury or even purging. The pain lets me know I'm alive and becomes a weird sign of my strength, like I'm invincible."

Since Gwen herself had pointed to the issue of having a detached and dysfunctional relationship with her body, we began to work intensively with techniques to help her form a positive connection with her physical self. During the next six weeks, we both noted that Gwen's bulimia had subsided.

With the latest bulimic cycle seemingly safe behind us, I questioned whether Gwen's most recent physical trauma, the car accident, and the recent calls she'd been getting from her lawyer about meeting to settle the case, had brought up body issues at a time when she felt very insecure that she would survive either financially or in her relationship with Gus. I reasoned that perhaps this difficult juxtaposition had triggered the latest activation of bulimia. If so, maybe on an even deeper level, the bulimia was an expression of her longstanding fears of survival.

To my amazement, Gwen latched onto the survival issue. "I think I'm finally ready to deal with this fear. I've needed to for a long time but I haven't felt safe enough." For several more sessions we plumbed the depths of her fears that she would "bottom out," that she could never heal, and that the only way out might be to die. Instead of reenacting her fears in suicidal behavior, however, she seemed willing and able to look at how these feelings were attached to times in the past, times as a young child when in reality she did not know whether she had the resources to survive. She was able to grieve these times without feeling shame, but rather as her right to feel whatever she needed to feel and emerge feeling empowered. Both of us were surprised when, despite this positive therapy experience, the bulimia escalated once more.

As the number of daily episodes quickly began to approach baseline again, Gwen challenged me. "So, are you going to send me to the hospital this time?" I thought for a few minutes, realizing that this situation posed a huge test of the hard-won trust in our relationship. On the one hand, I did not want to minimize risks to her health or deny the possibility that perhaps Gwen needed more help than our outpatient setting could provide. On the other hand, I would be betraying her if I took the decision-making into my own hands.

Finally I spoke. "Gwen, you and I have reached a very difficult point in our journey together. Perhaps it will be the most difficult one we will ever face. I think the best approach is to look carefully *together* at *all* of our options. This will include the full range of treatment possibilities for you if the bulimia intensifies further. But it will also include the option of not changing anything at all that we're doing. And it will also include the option of your choice to have bulimic episodes when and how you really need to have them, as perhaps your best option in a particular set of circumstances."

At my last statement, Gwen's head jerked up to meet my gaze. "Do you mean I can choose to binge and purge and you think that's OK?" I answered carefully, drawing on my understandings of the Ericksonian principle of choice. "We've learned a lot from your bulimia, during times when you've had a lot of episodes as well as during periods when you haven't had any episodes at all. This may be a time in your life when choosing to have a bulimic episode could be your very best choice for learning about yourself, out of all the other possibilities that you have. I don't really know—you have to be the one to decide whether that's true or not. I won't step in unless your life and health are truly at risk."

We agreed to assess the bulimia carefully during the coming days, increasing my availability by phone and making it the primary focus of our sessions until Gwen felt she was past a place of danger. As she left the session, she said, "I really want to make it through this time without giving into the bulimia. But I think you're right. It has to be my choice— you can't decide for me or I'll never learn how to resolve this."

At the beginning of our next appointment, Gwen looked weary. "Well, I did choose to have a bulimic episode this week. I tried all the techniques

I've learned but nothing worked. And you know, I had a curious reaction. I didn't feel any of the old feelings I used to have. I didn't feel elated. I didn't feel safe. I didn't feel the shame afterwards. I decided that if I were going to let myself purge, I would do it on the basis that I would pay close attention to whatever I could learn. And what I learned is that the bulimia doesn't fill the same needs for me anymore. I feel my body now so I felt all the disgusting sensations that are part of this—feeling uncomfortable and too full when I eat more than I really want, feeling disbelief when I retreat into the bathroom to purge because I have so many better ways to fill my time now. And I could taste and smell the whole time when I was purging and it was completely disgusting. I may choose to have another episode again in the future but I'm very clear that I don't want to go through this again unless I decide I absolutely have no other choices."

Gwen emerged with greater self-awareness from that one episode of bulimia. For the next four months, she weathered threats to her business and to her relationship. She worked hard in therapy to examine any bulimic urges that arose. We were able to connect them now to old survival issues and to find creative ways of working with current situations that brought a greater sense of confidence in her adult resources.

When another crisis period arose, Gwen allowed herself to go to the edge of a bulimic episode before deciding she did not want to complete it. Instead, she followed an alternative course of action that we had worked out, based on our learnings about the link between survival fears and bulimic behavior. We had reinforced the notion of her right to choose bulimia for the rest of her life and she felt more realistic confidence that she would make healthy choices, even at times of crisis.

Gwen has ended her therapy with me after more than two years of work. She is committed to continuing couples therapy with her boyfriend, to whom she became engaged. Her relationships with her children are thriving, and both of them are doing well. Her business is beginning to transcend the difficulties of the last year. She is starting a special exercise program to expand body awareness and to strengthen physical areas that have been damaged in various ways by past events. She is also starting to make friends, realizing that she now feels strong enough in what she has to offer others.

Recently she told me, "I feel steady about myself and the person I'm growing into. I now appreciate and crave a sense of balance in my life. I'm no longer on a roller coaster ride, being determined to prove myself invincible and then being devastated when the good feelings disappear. If I need to stay in therapy to solidify what I'm learning, I will. But I'm much more confident that I can find within myself what I need to live each day well. That's quite a change from looking inside myself for so long and seeing nothing but a dark bottomless pit of hopelessness and pain."

## Benefits of Ericksonian Principles

The work with Sarah, Alexandra, and Gwen included in this chapter featured no uses of formal hypnosis. Formal hypnosis was used with Sarah only after metaphors had planted the seeds of change. Ericksonian *utilization* was the primary intervention used to initiate a change process that led to the resolution of significant health symptoms. Several Ericksonian principles formed a framework that gently encouraged change for these women. For Sarah, metaphor provided an opportunity to reframe her diagnosis and initiate change that led to a healthier energetic focus. Utilizing symptoms as valuable avenues for self-learning allowed Gwen to approach the traumatic foundations of her bulimia gradually, gaining strength and reopening pathways to a full flow of life energy. As for Alexandra, Ericksonian hypnosis taught her how the power of language and suggestion can reduce emotional, as well as physical, pain, while helping her to develop an expansive inner focus.

# 5

# Ego-State Therapy:
# The Healing Presence of
# the Inner Family of Self

JEANNIE: EGO-STATE THERAPY AND
EMDR WITH MIGRAINES

Jeannie woke up at 3:00 A.M. with her head pounding and her stomach queasy. Remembering that she had a deadline later that day, she reached for the only thing that was sure to help. After swallowing one of the precious white tablets, she slept fitfully until the alarm rang at 7:00 A.M. She was tense most of the day. The usual refrain raced through her mind again and again. "Who do you think you are? You can't write like this. You can't write at all. Just give it up. Much more of this stress and you'll be unable to write or do anything else. See, another headache is coming on. Save yourself. Stop bothering."

Gripping the arms of her computer chair firmly, she tried to get a grip on her runaway mind. "Settle down. You can do this. You've done a million features for the magazine. They're always OK. This one doesn't have to be perfect either. Just breathe deeply. If the headache doesn't go away, you can take more medication. After all, that's what it's for."

When Jeannie called for an appointment, her voice broke. "I'm sick of it all . . . the headaches, the pills, the stress, this constant battle inside my head about writing. I've had a good experience with biofeedback. That helped for a while, but now the headaches are back with vengeance. Acupuncture and herbs didn't really do anything for me. I've even been to a headache clinic, where I learned meditation and deep breathing. That helps for a few minutes, but it's no long-term solution. I don't know if I want to go on living if this is the way my life is going to be."

Jeannie's distress was palpable as we sat down to assess her situation. She outlined a fairly complex health history. Migraine headaches had started about six years before, coinciding with the onset of menopause. MRIs and CAT scans were clear. She rotated the use of several medications, including Cafergot, Fiorinol, and Imitrex, on an almost daily basis. She had been diagnosed with Graves' disease about ten years ago; shortly after that problem went into remission, the headaches began. She had also been diagnosed with PTU, a condition involving a hyperenlarged thyroid gland, which had resolved with the help of medication, acupuncture, and herbs. Both of her parents had died within the last two years and her only sibling the year before that. Supportive therapy had helped her through those losses but the headaches lingered on. Although her doctors believed the migraines were linked to hormonal changes, everyone agreed that Jeannie was not a good candidate for hormone replacement therapy because there was a strong history of breast cancer on both sides of her family.

When she was seven, Jeannie sustained a severe head trauma when a truck suddenly backed out of a driveway and hit the bicycle she was riding. She was unconscious for more than 72 hours and convalesced at home for several months. She recalled being very worried during that time that her parents were going to be killed and fabricated illnesses so that her mother would come home from work. When she returned to school, Jeannie was far behind her classmates and struggled with learning new skills. Prior to the accident, she had been a happy, self-assured student, but afterward her self-confidence seemed shattered, never to be fully restored during her school life.

Jeannie's goals were to manage her headaches without medication and to interrupt the negative internal dialogue related to writing deadlines so that she could enjoy her work and lower her stress. In discussing several options for treatment, Jeannie wanted to try hypnosis first. She had read several articles on various uses of hypnosis in clinical settings, including a study where hypnosis was applied successfully to different kinds of headaches. Her reading gave us a chance to discuss different types of hypnotic approaches, including direct and indirect hypnosis as well as ego-state therapy techniques.

Because her procrastination and writing stresses seemed clearly related to some type of ongoing inner conflict, I theorized that the headaches could be connected to that conflict, depending on what we learned about its nature. I believed that ego-state therapy might be useful, and perhaps necessary, to identify and resolve the inner battle that seemed to underlie her symptoms.[1]

It also seemed likely that her current difficulties were fueled by self-doubts stemming from the aftermath of her head injury. If that were true, ego-state therapy could also help us explore and repair some of the psychological damage from that past traumatic event, with our ultimate objective to reintegrate parts of her personality and their diverse reactions to that challenging time in her life. As with the use of any hypnotic technique, however, we would begin with an introduction to hypnosis that would help Jeannie experience a sense of relaxation and safety.

Jeannie responded well to general hypnotic suggestions for mental and physical relaxation. She was able to surmount her acute sensitivity to traffic noises outside my office and learned quickly to clear headaches that she brought into the session. This was accomplished using ideomotor finger signals to help her to activate unconscious healing processes to release tension and reduce discomfort following a brief hypnotic induction. Once the signals were established, I asked Jeannie's unconscious to lower her headache pain by increments of one unit on a 10-point SUD scale after establishing her initial pain level at an 8. We used this process, called *calibration*, to move all the way down the scale to 0, where Jeannie was completely free of headache pain.

*Calibration*[2] *is based on the work of Milton Erickson. Like ideomotor signaling, with which it is often joined, it is a relatively straightforward technique that can help reduce physical discomfort in a gradual way that can be accepted by the whole personality.* Calibration is especially useful when larger incremental changes might be too threatening, too dramatic to maintain, or bring up questions of performance (e.g., "Can I do this correctly?") for individuals with chronic pain problems.

There are many other methods of pain reduction and management that can be used with and without hypnosis to promote comfort and a sense of mastery.[3] I prefer to start with the least complex, least intrusive approaches. If they are successful, this allows the client to build on a base of confidence. If they are not, we can move on to methods that address more unconscious psychological issues that may underlie the experience of pain.

Although she was pleased by her progress during our meetings, Jeannie was concerned that she could not reproduce this effect on her own. She had listened to audiotapes of our sessions and had tried to use the finger signals to no avail. "After all," she said, "I don't want to come here forever. I need to learn how to do this on my own. But each time I try, it's like some voice pops up inside and shuts everything down."

Jeannie was letting me know that we needed to deal with the problem of conflicting parts within her personality, because the conflicts were interfering with the necessary task of generalizing headache management beyond our sessions and into her everyday life. Here is an excerpt of how I explained the theory and practice of ego-state therapy to her:

The model of ego-state therapy was developed by Jack and Helen Watkins, who added hypnosis to the ego-state model of personality proposed earlier by a colleague of Freud's named Paul Federn. Federn was the first professional to use the word "ego state" to describe various aspects of the personality. He believed that each ego state has its own history, thoughts, feelings, sensations, and behaviors, and that each ego state contains personality energy that interacts with the energies of other ego states, somewhat like the members of a family.

Although families have a lot of shared history, each member has his/her own perspectives and feelings about family events and, of course, has separate individual experiences as well. As in an external family, sometimes the needs of different members come into conflict with each other. When this happens in an internal family, if there is no way to resolve the conflict, symptoms can occur like your headaches and the problems you have with deadlines for your writing. We have clues that these might be connected to ego-state conflicts because of the inner dialogue that you are aware of when you sit down to write or feel a headache coming on.

In order to be a successful person in our culture, we generate parts of our personalities that can take the lead when we need them to. That's true of every individual. In fact, ego states are formed under three different conditions of personality development. First, they help us to adapt to different situations. We learn as children to behave differently in church, or at school recess, from how we are at home with our families, and ego states make this possible. Second, ego states may be *introjects* of parents or other significant adults with whom we interact as we are growing up. That means we take in their energies when we use them as models of how to act and how to be. And third, ego states may help us deal with overwhelming traumatic events. They can be created to contain the trauma and protect us from having to think or feel about it, or they can help us cope better.

Sometimes, conflicts happen because, just as in external family systems, ego states become closed off from each other and isolated from the family as a whole. In other instances, some ego states have requirements that don't fit with the needs of others. And, in the case of trauma that has not been sufficiently resolved, ego states can be separated from each other more or less permanently by barriers of *dissociation*,[4] which is one of the brain's automatic responses to an event that overwhelms our usual abilities to cope.

Once Jeannie understood the basic process of ego-state therapy, she was ready to begin identifying and working with her ego states. The best place to begin for the purposes of strengthening and further stabilization is with helper ego states. These have been called internal self helpers or allies.[5] They are usually able to form a trusting relationship fairly quickly with the therapist and can often take on the role of co-therapist.

I usually start this process by asking clients what qualities in themselves they believe are needed for healing. Jeannie told me she felt she needed to connect with a part of herself who knew how to feel more confident. With this mission clearly in mind, our next step was to find and activate an ego state related to confidence. Any number of direct and indirect hypnotic and nonhypnotic techniques can be used to find ego states.[6] Because Jeannie was already comfortable with ideomotor signals, we decided to stay with that approach. The steps we took were:

1. Using a basic hypnotic induction to achieve relaxation.
2. Setting up the ideomotor signals.
3. Asking the unconscious if there were a part of Jeannie that knew how to feel very confident.
4. When her "yes" finger moved, asking that part of her to come forward inside in a way that she could recognize. Jeannie immediately felt a rush of energy and excitement in her chest.
5. Asking whether that part would communicate with us through the finger signals.
6. When there was a "yes" response, asking several general questions about the ego state's age and willingness to cooperate.
7. With this positive "yes set" foundation, asking whether the ego state would tell us in words what she knew about confidence. We found out that this part of Jeannie enjoyed playing touch football with her brother and other neighborhood friends. She felt carefree, strong, and completely confident.
8. We asked for and received agreement for full cooperation with our future work. Specifically, this part agreed to be present when Jeannie was writing and to lend her confidence as deadlines approached.

Jeannie was discouraged to find that the ego state connected to confidence, a 12-year-old tomboy part, did not solve her headache problem. "It was like her voice was overwhelmed. I could sense that a more positive attitude was trying to take root, but it just got blown away by the negativity that I'm always aware of when I sit down to write."

When health and psychological symptoms are related to relatively uncomplicated inner conflicts, sometimes focusing the presence of positive ego state energy will lead to full resolution of the problem. For Jeannie, however, this kind of immediate solution did not materialize. If anything, her migraines intensified after the positive ego state appeared. When this kind of boomerang effect takes place, it is usually an indication that the inner conflict is complex and requires more intensive interventions. The next step is to begin working with the ego states that are directly involved in the strife that drives the symptom.

For further strengthening, we explored Jeannie's safe place image of a gently curved river that she floated down into a deep state of relaxation. We also invoked "Inner Strength" (see chapter 3, pp. 56–60). These efforts seemed to shore up Jeannie's resolve and she was able to replicate the state of relaxation and strength by listening to audiotapes before each writing session. Her headaches seemed to improve slightly but returned in full force just prior to biweekly deadlines.

During the meetings that followed, we worked diligently to find the ego states that were entangled in the inner war that impacted the headaches. One set of ego states seemed to be associated with the time of Jeannie's head trauma. In a poignant exchange that took place after a brief hypnotic induction, a seven-year-old ego state shared the dark fears that surfaced during her early recovery:

MP: You must have been very scared after the accident.

J: (*As seven-year-old state*) Yes. I'm scared that my parents are going to die in a car accident, that they won't come back when they leave me. So I make up things to get them to stay with me. I know I'm bad but I can't help it.[7]

MP: Are you able to move around much on your own? In addition to being scared, it must be very hard to stay at home for so long.

J: The doctor told me I have to stay still. I lie on the couch all day and Daddy takes me upstairs at night to bed. I can't go outside so I just lie here.

MP: And then the scary thoughts come?

J: Yes, and they won't go away.

MP: Did anyone tell you that you are much better now? That you can go outside and play?

J: Oh, no. I'd better not. I don't want to get in any more trouble.

MP: Jeannie, I'm a different kind of doctor. And you're here to find out that many things have changed since you've been injured. You need to be brought up to date. You're well enough to go outside now. If you want to test it out while I'm right here, go ahead. Take it slowly at first until you get used to the idea, but I think you're going to find out that you're fine. Do you want to try?

J: OK . . . (*long pause*) I'm back now.

MP: How was it to be outside?

J: It was great. You're right. I must be better!

This is a good example of how traumatized ego states can be frozen in time, blocked from new information by inner walls of dissociation that separate them from the mainstream of conscious experience. Reconnecting these split-off personality parts and providing them with corrective learning is an important part of ego-state work.

Over time, we found more child ego states that seemed directly connected to Jeannie's head trauma. We began to see how their unresolved issues were linked to stresses in Jeannie's adult life as a writer. As deadlines approached, these self-parts would feel as if they were being "hit out of the blue" by an overwhelming force. As they reenacted the collision with the truck, they described falling into a dark abyss where they believed they were going to die.

We probed the possible comparisons between the coma state Jeannie was in for several days and the state of death. We provided new information about how the medical treatment of head trauma in children is different today, especially in terms of convalescence. We asked the ego states to reenvision what it would be like to go through recovery now. And we engineered several escape routes out of the abyss image that menaced many of the younger ego states as deadlines loomed. These included a human chain that connected the frightened personality parts to older, physically stronger ego states who could pull them to safety.

These interventions resulted in a more mature, unified attitude toward deadlines. Jeannie also initiated a writing schedule of two uninterrupted hours every morning, as well as other intervals during the day, which provided a more secure structure for the inner parts who were vulnerable to unpredictability. Her anxiety decreased and headaches improved. We worked out a plan where she would calibrate beginning headache sensations on a 10-point scale. If scores were four or less, she would take an aspirin and 1/2 Excedrin and use some of the imagery she had developed, including "Inner Strength" and the flowing river. Jeannie reported that about 70% of the time, this was sufficient to clear her symptoms.

As Jeannie became stronger, she decided to leave the magazine she'd been working for and actualize a longstanding dream of establishing her own business. Predictably, during this stressful transition, her headaches escalated again. I framed this as an opportunity to learn about any unfinished inner business that might still be triggering these symptoms so that we could achieve full resolution.

We worked with another seven-year-old ego state who had struggled to learn cursive writing when she returned to school following her head injury. We learned that her classmates were three months ahead of her, her teacher provided no extra support, and she was plagued with post-concussive symptoms that made it difficult for her to concentrate. Jeannie's recollection of this time was that the devastation and loss of confidence she suffered were so great that she had never fully recovered her self-esteem.

To design a corrective strategy, we speculated that many resources would be available today to school children in this situation. Jeannie envisioned a mature ego state who could serve as a special tutor, sitting beside "little Jeannie" in the classroom during writing lessons to help her make progress. With the help of this inner tutor, she was able to build more confidence about writing. Still, deadlines continued to trigger headaches, a stalemate that was frustrating for both of us.

I next introduced her to EMDR, explaining that I thought this approach might help us complete our work more rapidly, as finances were now becoming an issue in her therapy. Jeannie was agreeable to this change, and I explained that we could use the technique with individual ego states, if needed, as well as with the whole personality.

I had actually considered introducing EMDR much earlier in my work with Jeannie. When we began the ego-state work, which proved to be helpful in determining the extent of posttraumatic fragmentation and helping her to begin to unify her personality functioning, the need for constancy for the younger self-parts became obvious. Jeannie was hypersensitive to my absences and to any changes in our therapy routines. We addressed this need for stability by keeping our hypnotic induction the same each session, by reinforcing positive imagery repeatedly, and by beginning and ending our meetings in the same way each time. When we first discussed using EMDR, we both agreed that this might upset the balance created by hard-won inner trust and opted to stay with ego-state therapy.

At this later juncture, however, we had explored the head trauma and related childhood experiences that appeared to underlie the headache symptoms. Developmental interventions had helped to establish a much greater level of inner constancy and trust with a significantly lower level of fragmentation. Both Jeannie and I felt she was ready for a change and were hopeful that EMDR would help us move from actively exploring past links into fuller resolution and integration.

Our first step with EMDR was to install a conflict-free image of the river that we had found during hypnotic work, along with Inner Strength. This provided a sense of continuity for the younger aspects of self and provided an easy transition for the introduction of a new tool. During the second session, as we began with a target image of the onset of a headache as she was pushing her writing toward a deadline, Jeannie found herself feeling very small, grieving the loss of the brother who had been her childhood protector, and recalling some scenes related to her father's harsh discipline and criticism at the dinner table. Spontaneously, she brought in "True Self" and "Spirit," along with other ego states we had worked with previously.

Jeannie felt moved by the flow of feelings and awareness that occurred during EMDR. Her writing seemed to move more easily, but she still complained of many "false starts," times when she would sit down to write and felt paralyzed inside. We continued on during a third session, encountering scenes of physical abuse by Dad and various struggles in recovering from the head injury. Jeannie spontaneously added many of the resource images and suggestions we had used in our ego-state work and felt good after each session. She continued to struggle, however, with her writing and headaches.

Because we were not obtaining a clear resolution of the headache symptoms using standard EMDR protocols and adding resource inter-weaves, I decided to check with her about her current use of medications. I was surprised to learn that even though the headaches had not worsened, she had intensified the frequency of pain medications.[8]

Ideomotor signals indicated that Jeannie's recent return to drug dependency was related to two trauma-related ego states who called themselves "Fear" and "Panic." Although Fear had begun to feel more positive about writing and managing the headaches, she claimed that her remaining difficulty was to stand up to old negative messages of doubt and blame that originated from Jeannie's father. Panic added, "The headaches are so scary when they come out of the blue. The medication always works so I went back to that."

I explained to Jeannie, and to these individual ego states, that in order for us to obtain a true test of her own inner resources, she would need to taper off her medications, resuming our past plan of using over-the-counter medications for primary management. Because this change was so threatening, we agreed in consultation with her prescribing doctor to have two transition weeks where Jeannie was allowed two doses of Fiorinol during a seven-day period. She could decide at what point to use them when her pain rose above 4 on her subjective discomfort (SUD) scale.

When we next used hypnosis, various ego states reported that the first week of the medication plan had been challenging but that they felt good about being able to stay within the medication limits we had set. I suggested that we use EMDR to detect and resolve any remaining anxieties for Jeannie or any of her ego states about continuing to rely on inner resources for headache management.

During the first few sets of eye movements, Panic appeared and admitted that it was hard to trust the other parts inside as firmly as she could trust the effects of Fiorinol. We then did some individual EMDR work directly with Panic while Jeannie was in a hypnotic state.

"P": I'm feeling that it's just too hard without the medication. I can't find anything else that helps . . . I want to trust you that we can figure things out but I'm really scared. //

"P": That time I felt really bad. Everything looked really black. It reminded me of the abyss. . . . I can't stand to go there and that's how it feels every time there's a headache coming on. //

"P": (*Shaking and sobbing*) Why do I have to go through this? You're supposed to help me!

MP: I guess this is how you feel a lot of the time, that there's nobody to help you. Let's see if we can find another part inside who understands what you need and is willing to help right now. OK? (*nods yes*) During the next set of eye movements, let's see who comes to help you.[9] // Who came, Panic?

"P": It's Anger. I think she is angry with me.

MP: Let's ask her what she's angry about during this next set. // What did you get?

"P": Anger's mad that I'm having such a hard time. She thinks maybe we ought to try a yoga class to help me relax. Jeannie's friend is going to one every day and it's helping her. I guess I could try it. Anger says it isn't easy for her either but we all have to be willing to try new things. //

"P": I was in the yoga class. I felt a little weird twisting into different shapes but I'm calmer inside. //

Jeannie and I discussed the idea of a daily yoga class. She decided to try going with her friend while lowering her medication limits to one dose of Fiorinol during the coming week. When I saw her the following week, she sounded hopeful. "I think we're on the right track. The yoga is great for me. I'm sore but it's a good activity to build into my day and

I had zero headaches, just the beginning of one which stopped with the aspirin. I'm finding a daily structure that really works. I start with my two hours of writing, then I answer phone calls and e-mails. I write for a few more hours and I finish the day with yoga. I hope I can stick with this plan."

The final two meetings were spent clearing remaining concerns about letting go of the security of medication and installing positive future images. Jeannie decided she was ready to stop therapy with me and test out all the tools we had developed. As we parted, it was clear that she felt best about relying on the strengths she continued to find inside her family of self.

At six-month follow-up, Jeannie was continuing to feel good about the work we had done. Her writing was going well. She used the audiotapes we had made to start and end most days and reported that her headaches were infrequent. She was continuing to enjoy the benefits of yoga and grateful that she had ended her dependency on the medications.

## Symptom Resolution and Personality Integration

Many clients like Jeannie consult me for help with health problems that appear to be associated with inner fragmentation, which often results from past medical and psychological trauma. I frequently find that helping them achieve more integrative functioning and a sense of greater wholeness through ego-state therapy results in permanent symptom resolution, even when medical and other psychological interventions have not been successful.

This is not a simple task and involves taking the time to work through all four stages of the SARI model in whatever ways and at whatever pace are right for each individual. Some people like Jeannie who have unresolved trauma from past physical traumas or medical events also need a more intensive emphasis on the *relational dimensions* of the ego-state therapy model.

One of the qualities of ego-state therapy that makes it different from other "parts" models like NLP (neurolinguistic programming), psychosynthesis, gestalt therapy, and various types of "inner child work" is that there are four important levels of relationship in ego-state therapy that must be attended to at all times. These are:

1. *The therapist's relationship with the whole of the client's personality.* This is the most essential relationship and must be attended to with the greatest consistent care. In many ways, it is the most important tool in any type of therapy.

2. *The therapist's relationship with the client's individual ego states.* This level requires the therapist to identify and work with key ego states that are contributing to symptoms, as well as with those that can help to resolve them. Although Jeannie's ego states were activated through formal hypnosis, other clients benefit from more indirect, less elaborate work, as you will see in Gretchen's story at the end of this chapter. With some clients, I use even less direct ways, such as metaphor, journaling, drawing, or conversational approaches.

3. *The client's relationships with inner ego states.* It is also important for the client to become aware of his/her self parts in order to form healthier, more cooperative relationships. Often, our way of relating to inner states replicates dysfunctional relationships with parents or siblings and must be confronted and changed. If there is significant dissociation, or splitting-off of parts from awareness, this step will require more effort.

4. *The relationships of ego states with each other.* Finally, the conflicts that exist among ego states that contribute to health problems as well as to other dysfunctional life patterns must be identified, rene-gotiated, and resolved. The end result should be a harmonious family of self that works together as a team.

Focus on these relational dimensions needs to occur simultaneously. This comprehensive approach has the advantage of creating permanent wholeness and integration that may not be otherwise possible. With some individuals like Jeannie, the process can take several years. Others, like Frank, whose story comes next, require less time. Because they experience less inner fragmentation, the road to integration is a smoother one.

### FRANK: IMPROVING SEXUAL PERFORMANCE

Standing well over six feet and sporting a football player's physique, Frank fit perfectly the stereotype of a tall, dark, and handsome man. His life, however, was anything but charmed. Frank was drowning every-where. His business faced bankruptcy, he was being sued by a previous client, and his wife had begun talking about divorce. Frank's psychiatrist had prescribed antidepressant medications, but his depression persisted. He had difficulty concentrating, complained of severe short-term memory loss, and had fleeting thoughts of suicide. He had acute anxiety about his pending court cases and wanted to try hypnosis for stress reduction. He also told me that his sister remembered being sexually and physically abused by their maternal grandmother. Donna believed that Frank and their older brother had also been involved in the abuse but Frank himself had no memories of this.

Fortunately, Frank was a good hypnotic subject and responded well to suggestions for relaxation, mental alertness, and self-confidence. After a year of periodic adjunctive hypnosis sessions designed to stabilize his depression and provide specific coping tools, his depression had subsided and he had weathered successfully the various crises in his personal and professional life.

At this juncture, Frank decided to see his psychiatrist for a few more sessions while he tapered off his antidepressant and antianxiety medications. He wanted to transfer to me as his primary therapist. "I want to find out the deeper reasons why these terrible things keep happening to me," he said. "I don't believe I'm jinxed—there has to be a better explanation than bad luck. And I also want to explore what Donna has told me about what she thinks happened in our childhood. Working with different parts inside was very helpful for her. I want to see if it can help me too."

It seemed important to Frank to experience a technique that connected him with his sister. We decided to begin with ego-state therapy and add in other approaches as well to make sure that his goals were fully addressed. As we clarified our contract, Frank told me that he had some sexual problems that he had not previously revealed because he thought they were linked to the side effects of his antidepressant medication. "If I'm honest with myself, I had problems before I ever got depressed. I've always taken a long time to orgasm, sometimes as much as a half-hour. I know that's not normal for a man. And sometimes when I ejaculate, I giggle like a little kid. I think that's weird too. I want to start with the sexual issues. Maybe they're connected to what my sister's been talking about."

After making sure that Frank had seen a urologist and that his sexual difficulties did not have an organic basis, we began ego-state work. In the ego-strengthening phase (I use the SARI model with ego-state work just as I do with other methods), we used ideomotor exploration to locate three ego states, all of whom were willing to help with therapy goals. These were a 13-year-old, a six-year-old, and a "young" part. When we shifted to the activation phase, the 13-year-old state acknowledged that he knew about Frank's sexual problems because he had "taken charge" of Frank's penis a long time ago. When asked why, he replied, "Well, you already know why. It has to do with what happened with Frank's grandmother. I took over because I didn't want him to get hurt anymore."

After establishing that this ego state had turned off sexual feelings when Frank no longer trusted his wife, Annie, we decided to use a combination of EMDR and ego-state therapy for further exploring. I told Frank that whatever we found was not necessarily what had actually happened in the past, but would give us an idea of how he had stored various experiences inside himself so that we could find and resolve their effects.

We used EMDR alternately with the three ego states where Frank's recent difficulty getting and keeping erections provided us with a target image. Several scenes emerged where grandmother was sexually and physically abusive to Frank. In one of them, the "young part" was describing that his hands felt very heavy. Since this part was unwilling or unable to communicate further in words, I "talked through"[10] to the six-year-old ego state, who agreed to go into that scene and speak for him:

YP/six-year-old: Something very heavy is holding my hands down. . . . Knees are holding them down. . . . I think I'm on a bed. Grandmother is talking to me. She's saying, "How are you going to make love with a girl if you don't get hard?" She wants my penis to get hard. She's hitting me there with a wooden spoon. It really hurts. //

F:   I was thinking of when I went hunting and Frank dragged a big deer out of the woods. I wish we could drag grandmother out of there right now. //

F:   Frank came in and he knocked grandmother down. And he told her never to do that to me again and he dragged her out of there. . . . My hands are starting to feel normal again.[11]

Although Frank's erection problem improved after this session, there was no change in his difficulty with ejaculation. Since he had started to date as his divorce proceedings came toward a close, resolving these symptoms was becoming more urgent.

I wondered if there were other parts inside that might be able to shed more light on Frank's sexual functioning. From an ego-state perspective, if any of the ego states associated with a particular symptom are dissociated from the therapy process, whatever intervention I try, including EMDR, imagery, and hypnosis, is likely to produce incomplete results. This is analogous to trying to make a significant improvement in a family's health when one of its members who is contributing actively to dysfunction is unwilling to participate.

With this principle in mind, we went back to hypnotic ego-state work and discovered two additional ego states who proved essential to resolving Frank's sexual dysfunction. One was an 11-year-old who had learned to masturbate and experienced complete ease in getting erections and reaching orgasm. We also found a 26-year-old who enjoyed great sexual success with the young women he dated in college up until the time of his marriage. These two self-parts appeared to be largely unaffected by whatever childhood trauma might have taken place. Once we began to integrate them into our ego-state work, we constructed a plan that utilized the strengths while taking into account the vulnerabilities of each ego state.

Immediately following the combination ego-state/EMDR session where this plan was put into place, Frank reported normal orgasms for the first time since the beginning of his marriage. We followed with additional sessions to help the younger ego states learn that grandmother was permanently dead (we had them visit her funeral and burial in fantasy since they had dissociated the original experience). They came to believe that she could not come back to terrorize them and that not every woman would betray their trust as grandmother and Frank's ex-wife, Annie, had done.

At this writing, Frank is still learning to cope with dating experiences that trigger dissociation and ego-state division. He continues to use ego-state therapy with EMDR and hypnosis to work toward consistent sexual functioning and to learn about more mature forms of intimacy.

## Somatic Ego States

Sometimes, ego states do not present themselves as readily as they did for Jeannie and Frank. This may be because a self-part is in hiding, protecting the main personality from painful experiences it might be containing. Or the ego state's elusiveness may be due to fears that the therapist will harm or betray it in ways that replicate past hurtful events. Another possibility is that, since an ego state consists of personality energy, it may be encoded at the somatosensory or preverbal level, formed before cognitive functioning was fully developed. This type of ego state is too young to communicate effectively. In these cases, especially when health problems that manifest in the body are involved, it is helpful to focus on possible somatosensory clues to their existence.[12]

### GRETCHEN: RESOLVING BACK PAIN

"I hate to be one more person complaining about her dreary back pain," Gretchen smiled at me self-consciously. "It really is quite mysterious. I never had what you might think of as an injury. The pain started about 15 years ago when I had three young children, and it has been diagnosed variously as lumbar (i.e., lower back) strain, herniated disc, and muscle spasm. One of my children is disabled and I had to carry her everywhere when she was little. I think that's how the problem started. I've been to doctor after doctor. I've had several disc surgeries. And I've done everything that has been suggested to me . . . rested in bed, stayed on the move, given myself plenty of rest, pushed myself to exercise, practiced stretching programs, taken anti-inflammatories. You name it, I've tried it."

It was hard to believe that this stylish, athletic-looking woman in her mid-forties could be suffering from debilitating back pain. Gretchen told me that she knew the pain was stress-related because her discomfort increased just before and immediately after a stressful event. If she was consistent with her hour-long daily exercise and stretching program and managed her life so that there was low stress, her pain was manageable. Yet in the last few months she had begun waking during the night with pain along her spine and in her feet. "I don't understand why the pain has been increasing when I'm so careful with my life. It's discouraging. I hope hypnosis can help me to understand why my condition seems to be suddenly deteriorating, or at least help me to manage the pain more effectively."

Since Gretchen had been referred by several therapist friends she trusted who believed that hypnosis would be the best treatment, we agreed to start with hypnotic suggestion for relaxation and reduction of pain. Gretchen had plans for an extended trip to start in a few weeks, so there was a time restriction that also influenced our plans. I explained that, depending on how she responded, we might want to try several other approaches when she returned. I mentioned that ego-state therapy might help her if there seemed to be an unconscious part of her that could be turning up the pain levels for reasons unknown to her at a conscious level, and EMDR might also be useful to clear any anxieties that might be preventing her from getting better.

We started hypnotic work with general suggestions for relaxation and inner strength (the "S" phase of the SARI model), to which Gretchen responded with ease. Toward the end of the hypnotic experience, I suggested that we do some gentle body focusing with ideomotor signals so that we could begin finding resources to increase her comfort. As we received permission from her yes finger to explore her middle-of-the-night awakenings from pain, Gretchen reported that she felt shrunken in her body on the left side. "I remember now that the shrunken feeling accompanies the pain at night. I had forgotten that," she said.

Since we were running out of time in the session, I suggested that her unconscious mind could help her find the inner resources that would help that part of her body to become full size and reach its full capacity. I also offered her a brief journey into the future[13] to get a glimpse of what it would be like when she had fully resolved the difficulties in her body that were causing discomfort during sleep.

"I had a very interesting reaction to the hypnosis work last week," Gretchen began at our next meeting. "When I left here, my body was shrunken on the left. I felt like a shellfish with no shell on that side while the right half of my body was like a series of wooden planks, very rigid, strong, and straight. I felt very strong as I walked along and I had no anxiety about whether my pain would subside. Later that night I woke with even more pain than usual. I asked myself, 'What is this all about?' And the answer that came is that my back pain has something to do with the difficult relationship I have with my mother. It's like I have no 'back-bone' with her. Fifteen years ago I stood up to her, but that has gotten harder as she's aged. It's like my body is left with the conflict unresolved and so I'm out of balance and in pain about it."

We were beginning to get some clues that Gretchen's problem could be an ego-state conflict. Clues that ego-state work might be helpful include:

1. Use of the "language of parts" to describe a symptom.
2. Awareness of an inner conflict related to the symptom.
3. The symptom is nonresponsive to a wide range of medical and psychological interventions.
4. There are mysterious somatosensory aspects of the symptom that can best be explained in symbolic terms.[14]

After discussing the ego-state model and the benefits it might offer her, we decided to continue our hypnotic work by exploring whether ego states might be linked to the asymmetrical responses of the two sides of her body. Following a brief hypnotic induction, we began with an indirect approach[15] to the two somatic ego states indicated by her somatic awareness:

MP: Just focus your attention alternately, Gretchen, from one side of your body, bridging back and forth, back and forth . . . and tell me what you notice.

G: I feel big and little at the same moment. . . . The upper part of my body is rocking a little now. I don't know why, but it feels very pleasant.

MP: Is there anything that the rocking reminds you of?

G: Yes, I'm seeing a boat rocking back and forth.

MP: Let your whole body be held by the boat and rocking . . . so gently, back and forth, back and forth . . . back and forth, back and

forth . . . soothing you into a deep rest. And, as in any boat, there
may be occasional turbulence, little storms, that arise, but you are
not disturbed because all of you, big and little, can be held and
rest so completely in your own strong boat.

I thought to myself that the young part of her might be the shrunken
left side of her body while the stronger adult with "backbone" was on the
right. Because somatic ego states may be preverbal, I used suggestions
that provided a type of renurturing in the form of the boat image that
could be soothing and facilitate wholeness. I also began with a more indirect, less intrusive approach to the ego states for the purposes of building
trust and "seeding" suggestions for a more integrated bodyself. Later in
this session, we moved to a more direct approach using *ideosensory signals*
to communicate directly with the two states.

**Ideosensory signals** *are a variation of ideomotor signals. Instead of setting
up the signals in the fingers, somatosensory reactions in the body are used as
a focus. Suggestions are given that if the body sensation is connected with an
aspect of the self that can be communicated with, the sensation will increase
as a "yes" signal and decrease as a "no" signal.* Variations include suggestions that images can intensify and become more vivid as "yes" and begin
to fade or dissipate for "no."

I suggested that if the shrunken sensation on the left side of Gretchen's
body were connected to a part of her personality that was important for
us to get to know, that the shrunken feeling would begin to intensify a
little as a "yes" signal to let us know it was there. Gretchen reported an
immediate increase in the shrunken feeling, a confirmation of our intu-
itive hunches.

After also establishing that the strong feeling of "thick planks" on the
right might be linked with an adult ego state, I suggested that they could
help each other stay steady in the boat, perhaps taking turns steering
until they learned to steer together, so that after a while it would feel like
placing two hands on a steering wheel, and knowing both were needed,
both could help, and together they could provide better balance than
either alone.

In response to these suggestions to strengthen connection and cooperation between the two ego states, Gretchen commented that both sides of
her body felt much more similar and in balance with each other. I suggested that she practice using the boat image if her body felt out of align-
ment in any way, including upon awakening during the night. Gretchen
told me she did not know exactly when she would return from her trip,
but that she would phone when she did.

When I finally spoke with her almost six months later, Gretchen told me that she had returned about three months before but had been busy settling back into her life. "I've been unusually busy, but my back has been fine. I've discontinued all medication. I don't even take aspirin. I no longer wake in the middle of the night and I can be as active as I want to be without any pain. I guess I found my whole shell after all!"

# Section III

# IMAGERY:

## OPENING WINDOWS OF THE MIND

# Introducing Imagery

When I was a graduate student in school psychology at Penn State University in the early 1970s, I was first exposed to the art of healing imagery. In the depths of self-doubt, trying to finish what felt like a never-ending master's thesis, I traded visions of the future with a trusted friend on a sparkling spring afternoon at an outdoor cafe. I dreamed about moving to California, which beckoned with its sunny possibilities for practicing the latest methods in psychology. Jerry, my companion, envisioned living in Colorado, working to help athletes extend mental and emotional limits to reach their full potentials.

The futures we painted with such colorful imaginary brushstrokes seemed at the time like impossible flights of fancy that matched our lighthearted decision to play "hooky" from the rigors of graduate school. Yet, two years later, both of us had actualized every one of the important details of those daydreams. Looking back, our whimsical study break was really the beginning of my love affair with the power of images and how they can help make elusive wishes for the future a dynamic reality.

Since then, I've read countless books and taken numerous workshops on the use of images in the healing process. I've read accounts of amazing cures that result from imaging, many of which have been validated by growing evidence published in research studies. I've also had the privilege of observing firsthand the remarkable changes that have occurred for my clients when they have applied different types of imagery to remedy mind-body symptoms.

In my work with imagery, as with other healing methods, I have found that it is usually best to begin with strengths that are already in place. My clients and I identify these strengths as resources, test them just as we do the conflict-free image in EMDR, and modify them so that resources long familiar to the client begin to provide specific kinds of support. Although it may seem sometimes as if the needed strengths are missing, it may really be a matter of knowing where to look. The best place to start is to examine what a person truly enjoys doing every day. These activities often yield buried treasures that can begin to open pathways for healing.

## The Impact of Imagery on Health

Carl Jung wrote: "When we concentrate on a mental picture, it begins to stir, the image becomes enriched by details, it moves . . . and when we are careful not to interrupt the natural flow of events, our unconscious will produce a series of images which makes a complete story."[1] Jung's view of imaginal healing was that our flow of images must be moved or "stirred" to completion. This concept fits perfectly with the principles of energy psychology, which hold that when our flow of qi is blocked, psychological as well as physiological imbalance can occur.

The use of mental imagery has been shown to influence numerous body responses, including blood pressure, heart rate, sexual behavior, and autoimmune performance.[2] For example, there is clear evidence that patients undergoing surgical and chemical treatments for cancer who use imagery increase their likelihood of remission. Although the best results have been found with people who image vividly, the literature has proven that any consistent use of imagery can improve physical health and well-being.

One of the questions asked most frequently by my clients is, "Can I use imagery even if I'm not very visual?" The answer, in my experience, is a resounding *yes*! The only requirements for engaging in imagery are the ability to sustain an inner focus for a period of a few minutes, to *represent* or express our perceptions of an object or experience in somatosensory or symbolic form, and to bring up the image along with its related inner responses for ongoing practice. We form images continuously; the task is simply to discover and use our natural imaging abilities.

Although there are many ways to classify images, for our purposes we will consider two broad categories: *structured imagery,* which is introduced by a professional guide, and *unstructured, spontaneous imagery*.

## Structured Imagery

*Structured imagery involves guiding our thought processes to invoke and use various senses: vision, taste, smell, hearing, touch, movement, and body position and posture.* Imagery provides essential communication links between perception, emotion, and the body.[3] There are four basic steps[4] involved in using structured imagery:

1. First, it is important to develop our abilities to perceive and represent as a sensory image any event or aspect of our experience.
2. The next step is to connect all of the senses with the image so that we make a full connection with it.
3. Then we test the energy of the image to make sure its energy is stronger than the situation we are attempting to correct.
4. The final step is to practice using the image to achieve a desired goal.

Healing imagery is limited only by the scope of our collective imaginations—that is, it is infinite in its possibilities. I've included five kinds of structured imagery that my clients and I have found particularly useful. There are, of course, many, many more to choose from.

### Guided Fantasy
Guided fantasy is useful to stimulate inner journeys, such as an imaginary journey through the body to attack cancer cells. *Guided fantasy imagery* is particularly helpful in stimulating the self-discovery of inner resources and often involves metaphor or storytelling.

### Mastery and Rehearsal
This type of imagery links past experiences of accomplishment (i.e., mastery) and images that project effective responses in future situations (i.e., rehearsal).[5] Mastery imagery is used to retrieve feelings of competence and confidence. When applied to health problems, the imagery of mastery and rehearsal can provide a "back to the future" opportunity to discover inner competencies. People often find strength, for example, in reviewing past illnesses, surgeries, or medical traumas to identify coping resources that helped them weather these crises. These resources can then be used to construct imagery of rehearsing positive ways of responding to future medical interventions and health challenges.

### Imaging Healing Outcomes
A third type of structured imagery involves imagining *specific healing outcomes*. For example, I might suggest that people with chronic pain fantasize taking a tour to the central control room in the brain where they will encounter some type of huge control panel or computer room.[6] They are invited to take a guided tour of the control room to discover where the circuits for physical pain or emotional distress are stored. They then imagine using on/off switches, light-dimmer intensity switches, or circuit breakers to "disconnect" painful reactions to past events or "turn down"

the intensity of discomfort. Dysfunctional or outworn "plugs" can keep someone trapped in habitual or chronic pain can be replaced with new "plugs" that connect to new psychological and physical reactions.

### Imagery to Repair Developmental Conflicts

Still another valuable use of structured imagery is to improve developmental functioning. Structured imagery exercises can be used, for example, to promote experiences of stability with self and others, which helps in learning to hold and integrate healing experiences. People who have difficulty with all/nothing or black/white thinking can also be helped to expand their perspectives through this approach. And difficulties in setting *boundaries*, the limits that allow safe connections, and regulating intense or overwhelming emotions, such as the helplessness and anger that are often linked with health problems, can also be addressed through this method.

### Eidetic Imagery

A final type of structured imagery from this category is *eidetic imagery*. First researched by Ahkter Ahsen,[7] the eidetic image requires an initial focus on a specific image followed by steps to help the image move or emanate. Eidetic images are believed to have three components, called the ISM: the image, which portrays or represents a situation, the somatic state of feelings and affects connected to the image, and the meaning.

Clinical and health difficulties can arise when images of self and others become rigidified or frozen because of past experience. When I work with this approach, the goal is to free the energy that has become frozen in dysfunctional images so that fresh meaning and somatic and emotional responses can evolve.

## Spontaneous Imagery

The second category of imagery involves the impromptu creations of the imagination. They appear nightly when we dream and fill our waking lives in the form of fantasies, daydreams, and visual thoughts. Spontaneous imagery is an important part of the way we symbolize virtually every experience. These images also surface in our responses to EMDR, hypnosis, and other tools of energy therapy.

Experts who have studied the biology of imagery tell us that the right hemisphere of the brain has a primary role in producing the raw imagery that occurs during sleep, muscular relaxation, mind wandering, free association, and dreaming. These raw images are converted and transformed by the left hemisphere into more logical symbols, which we then encode verbally so that we can describe, analyze and work with them.[8]

People who are ill frequently form and operate from negative views of the future that can have a powerful negative destabilizing impact on mind, body, and spirit. Finding imagery that has full resonance with their capacities for hope can often restimulate the flow of life-giving energy again.

# 6

# Structured Imagery:
# Blueprints for Change

ALICE: VIVID IMAGERY WITH HORMONAL HEADACHES

Alice was seven weeks into a very happy pregnancy. She was especially joyful about the pregnancy because, due to her husband's battle with testicular cancer near the beginning of their marriage, she had doubted that she would ever conceive.

Alice was most unhappy, however, with the headaches that had taken over her life during the last few weeks. They started at her temples and sometimes shifted to just above her eyebrows. Rejecting even over-the-counter medication as too risky for her unborn baby, she had tried acupuncture. The treatments were helpful for a few hours, but then the headaches returned with a vengeance. The pain kept her awake nights and made it difficult to concentrate on daily tasks.

She and her doctor believed her symptoms were hormonal, but this diagnosis did not help her cope with them. When I asked her to form an image of her headache pain, Alice gazed toward the floor and remarked that they were "heavy, dark blobs like an eclipse, pushing down." I asked her to consider what kind of image might counteract the headache image. Alice closed her eyes and, after a pause, replied that she was imagining balloons that pushed up and moved her headache toward the top of her head.

As she focused on the effect of the balloons, she noticed remnants of headache stuck to the inside top of her head like cobwebs. I asked again, "What kind of image do you think might help here?" Alice immediately told me that she was watching a large magnet pick up the last shreds of the headache and fling them away from her head. A few moments later, she opened her eyes and smiled. "I feel so relaxed. That was so easy for me to do. But will I be able to do this on my own?" I paused for a moment and said to her, "That's a good question. We don't know the answer yet. Let's see what happens in the next week. If we need to, we can enhance or strengthen the image so that you have just the right one to work with."

When Alice came in the next week, she told me that she had practiced using the balloon and magnet imagery every day at the first signs of headache. Her headaches had consistently dissipated, and she had felt more energized and more confident about being a relaxed new mother. At follow-up after the baby was born, Alice's headaches had not returned.

ALICE WAS ABLE TO FIND HER IMAGES EASILY. She was motivated to practice and use them consistently whenever she thought about or sensed tension building in her head. We can guess that Alice is probably a vivid imager. But what about people who don't have this talent?

Fortunately, there are many ways of learning how to find and use imagery. Sometimes, it's a matter of learning to trust the perceptions we find inside ourselves and to translate whatever symbols appear into usable forms. Other situations might require more of a step-by-step approach, such as learning how to feel comfortable shifting from seeing outer images to constructing inner ones.[1]

An image is a sensory experience. That is, it's possible to have a touch image, a taste image, or even sound and smell images as well as visual ones, or even a general sense image. All that is necessary to create a structured image is to form an *internal* sensory connection that represents or captures any kind of *outside* stimulus, including verbal suggestions given by a therapist or health professional.

### EDDIE: IMAGERY AND STRESS-RELATED COLITIS

Eddie[2] was a rising star. Only 26 years old, he had been transferred recently to a nearby computer company at young executive status. Unfortunately, this career move came at some cost to his health. In reaction to the recent relocation, pressures in his job, and an impending project deadline, Eddie had developed acute ulcerative colitis. His doctor had told him that if his condition persisted much longer, he would need hospitalization and intravenous steroids, a treatment he had experienced in college when he had his first colitis episode. Eddie was seeking hypnotic work with me because he wanted to avoid hospitalization if at all possible.

When I asked him about his previous experiences with hypnosis, Eddie told me that he had participated in a group hypnosis exercise in college, but other than a little reading, he knew nothing else about it. When we discussed our options, Eddie admitted that he was worried that he could not benefit from hypnosis. "I'm really antsy. I'm so uncomfortable, I can't really sit still for very long. Is that a problem?"

I explained to Eddie that that was not a problem for me but that he might feel distracted if he had trouble achieving feelings of relaxation in his body. When we experimented with some general suggestions designed to help him relax, Eddie indeed felt frustrated. "I was afraid this would happen. I just can't relax because my body is too uncomfortable right now. Does this rule out hypnosis for me?"

I suggested instead that we use imagery, one component of hypnosis. Since behavioral medicine research shows that imagery without the use of hypnotic induction has comparable effectiveness to imagery and hypnosis in combination,[3] I told Eddie that we could begin with mental imagery, which did not require a positive response from his body but might end up having a positive impact on his body.

Because his temperature averaged 101 degrees on a daily basis, Eddie visualized a cooling blanket that he could wrap around himself and seal in position with imaginary Velcro. As his temperature lowered, he could begin to unwrap the blanket until his temperature returned to normal. We also concocted a special liquid that he could imagine swallowing to unblock his colon, and I made an audiotape to guide his use of these images during the week.

He practiced daily with the tape and reported improvements at the beginning of our second imagery session: His fever was lower, the frequency of diarrhea and cramping had decreased, and there was less blood in his stool. As we reinforced these images and found new ones, I asked Eddie if he could form an image of a future time when he would be free of symptoms. He told me that he saw a "bright light, like the sun, yellow and green."

A few days later, I received a phone call that Eddie had been checked into the hospital as a precautionary measure to recover from the effects of severe symptoms of several weeks' duration. When I visited him in the hospital, his spirits were good. "I've been using my tape. You were right. My body really is getting the benefits of the imagery we've been using. When the nurse took my blood pressure yesterday, she was really concerned because my blood pressure was so low. I told her that I'd been listening to your imagery tape and she told me it was really working because my pressure had dropped about 20 points from that morning's reading!"

We repeated similar imagery to help him feel general comfort and to encourage his body to release the toxins that had been confined in his digestive system. I again asked if he could imagine a future time when he was free of symptoms and enjoying full health. This time, Eddie saw himself in the park near his new apartment, lying in the sun and feeling tanned, relaxed, and healthy. When I talked to him a few days later Eddie was continuing to improve, and shortly afterward he was released from the hospital.

Three weeks from the time he left the hospital, Eddie was gradually recovering good health. He told me he had started visiting the park on sunny weekends with a blanket and a good book and that it had become one of his favorite places to relax. He had decided to terminate his work with me though he planned to return if he showed further signs of the colitis problem. The last news I had of Eddie was that he was successfully monitoring his diet and stress levels. Since returning to work, he had learned to be mindful of his needs for rest and exercise and was careful to schedule those every day just as he scheduled the myriad of meetings he attended.

## Working with Psychological or Developmental Barriers

Eddie's story illustrates the benefits of looking into the future. As you might have noticed, his image of the future gradually developed more detail until he was able to manifest what he saw in the form of a place he could go for relaxation and replenishment.

Not everyone can produce positive future imagery. Negative future imagery is often a sign that more intensive or different interventions are needed.[4] People with health problems that are not resolving have often lost hope. They may benefit from general strengthening techniques or from medications to relieve secondary or primary depressive symptoms related to health symptoms. Other interventions needed to achieve full stabilization might include supportive psychotherapy, family counseling, and alternative medicine methods such as acupuncture and bodywork.

The psychological barriers that block energy pathways take many different forms. Fears related to the powerlessness and loss of control that often accompany health problems,[5] unresolved emotional wounds,[6] and spiritual crises[7] can all contribute to an individual's failure to heal. If these are at issue, special methods can be added to address and resolve them, leading to a positive future outlook. Such a viewpoint may be one of the most significant predictors of a positive healing outcome.[8]

Some people are unable to make consistent progress toward resolving health imbalance because they have not completed important developmental tasks. For example, they may be unable to sustain positive feelings toward themselves or other people because of early childhood trauma. Another common obstacle to healing can come from boundary problems. We begin in infancy to form psychological parameters that allow us to distinguish between inner and outer experiences and between our own experience and that of someone else. As we establish the boundaries that contain our own experience, we begin to establish a self. Later on in development, boundaries allow us to contain, or hold inside, negative and positive feelings of affect and body sensation so that we can remain comfortable rather than overwhelmed. We also learn to set boundaries or limits with other people, to let them know what we can fully welcome or barely tolerate, as well as what we do not want.[9] When we are unable to set adequate boundaries with others, we mobilize stresses that can propel health problems, as Nancy discovered.

## NANCY, PART I: ADDICTION RELATED TO
## DEVELOPMENTAL NEEDS

"No one would ever believe that I'm addicted to marijuana," said the attractive housewife in her late forties sitting across from me. "I've smoked dope since I was in high school and very few people know about it. I'm not proud of this behavior, and it certainly doesn't fit with my image. At this time in my life, I feel like smoking pot is holding me back somehow. My son, who is my only child, is starting junior high. I'm finding that I have a lot of time on my hands that I don't know how to use. I don't want to wind up sitting alone in my kitchen smoking dope with nothing to show for my life."

Aside from the emotional reasons for wanting to end her marijuana habit, Nancy also mentioned a number of health concerns. "My doctor is worried about my cholesterol levels. My father died about 10 years ago of heart disease. Because I smoke so much pot, I'm always snacking so my diet is lousy. And I don't exercise—I'm just too sluggish most of the time. I don't want to die like my father did but I can't lower my cholesterol without eliminating the pot. And, believe me, I've tried many times to quit. I can't do it by myself; I'm just too hooked."

I agreed to help Nancy with her 30-year addiction, though an inner voice told me it might be a long struggle, since she and her primary therapist had already been unsuccessful with conventional cognitive behavioral methods. First, I referred her to a group for chemically dependent women based on the 12-step model and also to a nutritionist for help with her diet. When we turned our attention to her relationship with marijuana, I asked her to begin by studying carefully the daily situations that triggered urges or cravings. She agreed to keep a diary where she recorded her thoughts and feelings before, during, and after smoking episodes.

After several weeks, some important patterns emerged. First, Nancy discovered that she tended to use the pot to medicate feelings of boredom and restlessness as well as of intense anger or frustration, i.e., times when she felt either overwhelmed or understimulated. She also noticed that she felt pulled away from herself when her live-in partner, Norman, was around. If he were in a dark mood, Nancy soon found herself depressed, though she might have felt happy moments before.

When we discussed her findings in light of her history, Nancy mentioned that she had always felt like she was "out of sync" with the rest of the world. "From the time I was very young, I felt like I was sleepy when I should be wide awake, not hungry when it was time to eat. . . . My mother tried to put me on a rigid feeding schedule that was convenient for her. She also smoked cigarettes and drank alcohol when she was pregnant with me. I've always thought I absorbed her depression and anxiety, probably starting in the womb. And now I'm doing that with Norm too. No wonder I smoke pot—it's all too much for me to handle!"

As it became clear that part of Nancy's recovery from marijuana addiction would involve strengthening her sense of boundaries, we discussed the tools that might help us with this task. Although Nancy might have done well with any of the methods presented in this book, we decided to start with imagery. She had been referred to me by the leader of a week-long workshop on the uses of imagery with mindbody healing. "That was so helpful to me," she explained. "I think I developed real confidence during the workshop. I've always known that I'm very visual, so imagery is a good fit for me." We decided to build on those strengths, bringing in other techniques as needed to treat her dependency on marijuana.

After discussing the concept of boundaries with Nancy, I helped her clarify her strong need to contain and regulate her feeling states, as well as to better define intrapersonal boundaries so that she would not take in the negative feelings of others around her. Nancy expressed her belief that she would have to feel protected from others before she could feel safe enough to handle her own feelings.

I asked her to think about what kind of environment would help even her infant self feel secure and protected from the feelings of others. Nancy closed her eyes. After a short pause, she told me, "I see myself curled inside a beautiful transparent egg. . . . I seem to be floating in warm, blue fluid. . . . It's very relaxing and comfortable." When invited to explore the egg further, Nancy added, "It's good that I can see out but I get the feeling that no one can see in unless I want them to, so that I have complete privacy. . . . And I feel so comfortable. . . . I'm just floating and it's so easy to be here."

Following the four-step model for imagery (p. 107), I asked Nancy to test the image by imagining Norman was in the room with her, to see whether her egg was stronger than the negative energy she was feeling from him. "I see a dark gray cloud coming toward me. . . . I'm starting to feel a little tension because I'm afraid Norman's negativity is going to seep through my shell and reach me."

Our next task was to strengthen the egg image further so it could withstand any challenge that might come from outside. Nancy appeared stuck when asked for ideas so I suggested adding bulletproof glass or some other barrier that would feel stronger than the transparent egg shell. "Yes, that's it," she said, closing her eyes again. "My shell felt too thin. It was almost like one of those big plastic bubbles kids blow through rings. Now it's really thick glass that can repel anything. . . . The gray cloud is bouncing off the glass shell and floating back across the room to Norman. I still feel relaxed and comfortable. . . . This is wonderful."

I suggested that Nancy test the egg image a few more times during our session by recalling recent situations where she felt overpowered by negative feelings coming toward her from someone else. As she used the image in several confrontations involving her mother and a neighbor, Nancy decided to enhance the egg image further by piping in soothing music to drown out intrusive voices coming from outside her space. We discussed how she might practice using the egg in difficult encounters during the next week as well as when she had urges to smoke marijuana. Nancy left, eager to test her "secret weapon."

"I love my egg," Nancy told me at her second imagery session. "I did well with Norman this week, even when he was grouchy. I only smoked pot once or twice during the first part of the week, but then I really lost it on the phone with my mother. It feels like I may have to be inside an army tank or a bunker before I'm safe with her!"

I reassured Nancy that her experiences with the image would help us to see what was still unresolved in learning about her own boundaries. As she recounted the week's events, both of us could see that when Nancy felt suddenly violated by her mother's criticisms, she was unable to activate the egg image. In less challenging circumstances with Norman, however, she had been able to use the protective qualities of the egg environment to help her stay comfortably present within her own positive mood while allowing Norman to express different reactions.

I encouraged Nancy to replay the scene with her mother, imagining that she had activated the egg image *before* starting the phone conversation. This time, Nancy reported more success: "I'm feeling good. . . . Her toxicity feels far away from me. I have this picture of the letters in the words she used to judge me about my weight just rolling down the side of the egg and out of the way."

MP:  Let's test out the strength of the egg now. Can you go back to the phone conversation?

N:  This time, I'm more relaxed. Eventually I tell her I need to get off the phone. This feels really good. Like I'm in control and honoring my own space.

Over time, Nancy learned to use the egg image to better manage her own internal boundaries as well as her interpersonal ones. This greatly enhanced her ability to regulate the negative feelings she had been medicating with marijuana. She also used the egg image for self-calming when she was bored or restless, especially during transitional times. Her marijuana use decreased until she was smoking pot only occasionally. Various life stresses, however, sent her into relapse. Soon she was back to a daily marijuana habit again, struggling to regain the ground she had lost.

You will learn more about Nancy and the body-oriented approaches we used to resolve more of her addictive patterns in chapters 8 and 9.

## Images of Mastery and Rehearsal

Many people with health issues benefit from images that draw on experiences of past mastery in order to prepare for future challenges. This approach can be particularly useful when preparing for medical procedures, including surgery, that are experienced as invasive to the body.

### VALERIE: CONQUERING BLOOD PHOBIA

"I've always hated blood. I even hated the color red as a child. I'm really phobic about seeing blood, like I'm terrified of getting a cut or scrape, not because of the pain but because I'm scared of seeing my own blood. I had a terrible experience a few years ago when I dropped and broke a jar in a grocery store. I cut my hand and there was lots of blood. I almost passed out."

I agreed to work with Valerie for several weeks to help her prepare for the blood tests for her yearly physical. She was adamant that she wanted a practical, change-oriented approach: "I don't want to spend any more time or money probing the past. I want to stay in the present and look to the future now in my life."

Since my agreement with Valerie did not allow us to go into the past for uncovering purposes, we looked into current areas of her life for sources of imagery. The image that seemed most vivid was the one of her running up and down the polo fields in Southern California. She could smell the horses, feel the wind, and sense the heat of the autumn afternoon. She could also experience the strength in her legs and feet when I suggested she focus on how quickly and confidently she could cover the ground with her flying feet. I encouraged her to practice calling up the image using an audiotape that I recorded, especially when anxious thoughts about blood arose.

The next step was to practice using the competencies evoked by the mastery image to prepare for the blood testing that was to occur in a few weeks. An unexpected event also provided us with real-life practice. One morning, Valerie got out of the shower and saw a small vein popping through the skin of her arm. She started to hyperventilate, then rubbed it, and it disappeared. This incident, however, triggered fears that she might find other veins. "It's freaky because veins are connected with blood, of course. And also it brings up fears of getting older. Varicose veins run in my family so I'm going to be in for it. I'd better learn how to deal with this now before it becomes a problem. I think the veins bother me because they seem out of control. They could get tangled, clotted, or collapse. Who knows? It's frightening to think about."

I asked Valerie to bring up the image where she is running on the polo fields as she continued to think about finding the vein in her arm and then to tell me what happened. She noticed almost immediately that her anxiety disappeared as she focused on the strong feelings in her legs and feet along with inner feelings of calm and competence. She was not triggered when a second vein appeared.

We then turned our attention to the blood tests, reducing the event to a series of brief scenes. As Valerie imagined herself sitting in the waiting room of the lab, she brought up the image of the polo fields to reduce the tension she was beginning to feel. When she saw herself sitting down in the chair across from the technician, however, her anxiety escalated. "The running image isn't helping," she said. "I keep losing it. It's hard to concentrate because I'm so nervous."

I reassured Valerie that an increase in her anxiety was to be expected. When that increase occurred, it made sense from a physiological viewpoint that it would be difficult for her to focus, because the chemicals created by her brain during anxiety states interfered with concentration.[10] Therefore, we would need to find a second image and possibly more in order to handle the escalation of fear.

When we searched for other images, Valerie identified a symbol connected with the courage she felt on behalf of the dogs in her care from animal rescue. "I don't know why but I'm seeing a coat of armor. It reminds me that I would and could do anything for my dogs. I've been in some scary situations with them and I'm never afraid because I'm too focused on my concern for them." She also recalled a memory of running up a big sand dune at the beach. "The blood is pumping into my legs as I charge up the hill. I feel energized and strong. I can do anything."

I suggested that Valerie put these two images on a split screen[11] as she imagined sitting with the lab technician, so that she could draw on her strength in both scenes. I thought it was particularly significant that Valerie's second image featured her own blood in a positive context. This time, she was able to go all the way through the procedure, telling me, "I don't have to watch or feel what's happening. I'm strong enough to get through this. I can do it."

VALERIE SEEMED DELIGHTED AT THE BEGINNING OF OUR fifth, and final, session. "The blood tests turned out to be no big deal," she said. "I got so involved interviewing the technician about her dogs and some problems she was having with them that I didn't even notice what she was doing. I'm not sure that the images helped, but it certainly was easy. I plan to use the tapes in a couple of months when I have my mammogram. That's also usually an anxious time for me."

## Eidetic Imagery

Another effective type of structured imagery, called eidetic imagery, emphasizes the mobility of our mental images. The word "eidetic" is used to describe images that are vivid and stable in form over time. Eidetic images can be retrieved again and again with clarity of detail. This type of imagery has been compared to photographic impressions of the outer world. Eidetics appear to provide a kind of living inner mirror of the way we participate in external events.[12]

These unique qualities are believed to distinguish eidetic images from other kinds of imagery such as memory, daydream, guided fantasy images, free association, or nocturnal dreams. One of the most valuable eidetic properties is its propensity to move, or emanate. Because many of our troublesome images have been frozen in time in response to traumatic events, eidetics can be used to help free up the frozen images in our mental pathways that underlie many of our painful emotional responses. From an energy psychology perspective, this is analogous to freeing qi in the meridians of the body.

DARYL: EATING DISORDER FOLLOWING
MOTHER'S SUICIDE

Daryl[13] was a sugar junkie. Referred to me by his group therapist, he struggled with overeating at meals and binge eating on junk food. A recovering alcoholic for 12 years, he participated regularly in both Overeaters Anonymous (OA) and Alcoholics Anonymous (AA). His doctor was apprehensive about his weight because of the hypertension and heart disease in Daryl's family history. He had recommended that his patient lose at least 80 pounds and had proposed various diets, which Daryl had been unable to follow.

Both Daryl and his doctor were also concerned about his depression. Intense episodes of suicidal despair and hopelessness had begun four years earlier, after the death of his mother, who had been terminally ill with cancer. Her death was particularly traumatizing for Daryl, because she had killed herself with a gun while he was visiting in her home and he had found her body while she was still alive. He was besieged with guilt that he should have been able to save her, yet also relieved that her life was over since their relationship had been such a difficult one. Daryl's eating problems had dramatically escalated following her death, and stresses in his marriage had begun around the same time.

It was clear that Daryl's reactions met the criteria for PTSD (posttraumatic stress disorder), with symptoms including frequent and intrusive flashbacks of his mother's death scene, nightmares, emotional numbing through binge eating, and a strong startle response in reaction to loud sounds and violent movies. He was referred for medication evaluation and started on Prozac, which helped to reduce his depressive feelings.

When we discussed possible strategies, we agreed that it was important to resolve his posttraumatic symptoms first before attempting to treat the sugar addiction. Both of us felt this was necessary because the reactions to his mother's death seemed such a clear trigger for overeating. Since Daryl was curious about hypnosis, we began with ideomotor exploration of the time leading up to the death scene. He recalled several attempts he had made to help her get psychiatric help. As we approached his encounter with his mother's barely alive body, Daryl was also able to remember several loving thoughts toward his mother that he remembered having during the moments when he had first found her.

Although the three hypnosis sessions reduced Daryl's anxiety and depression, he still felt haunted by his mother's death. "I just can't shake it," he told me. I commented that it seemed as though his memory of his mother was frozen in those last moments of her life so that he could not complete the grieving he needed to do in order to move on with his life. "That's exactly right," Daryl responded. "What can we do about that?"

I suggested that Daryl close his eyes and make an image of his mother as she appeared in the bedroom when he found her. He began describing the image hesitantly:

D:   The room is dark and I see the gun first in her hand. I panic and then see the blood trickling down the side of her head. I rush over and put my ear on her chest. She's barely breathing. I alternate between terror and anger. I can't believe she's done this when she knew I would be here to find her! I can't think what to do. It's like I'm paralyzed.

MP:  How does she seem to you in this image?

D:   She seems scary, like a monster.

MP:  And what happens inside you when you see this monster?

D:   My body is shaking and I feel scared and angry and very small. I wish I could be anywhere else.

MP:  OK. Now let go of that image, and when you're ready, let another image of your mother appear. . . . Take your time and let me know when mother #2 appears.

D:   My mother looks old and frail as she did right before she died. She felt bad all the time and was bitter but wouldn't do anything to help herself. She was just miserable and I was miserable being around her.

MP:  And what is it like for you to connect with that image right now?

D:   I feel tight and constricted, like I'm tied up in knots . . . angry too. She had choices. She didn't have to approach the end of her life that way.

MP:  When you feel complete with that image, just let go of it. . . . And when you're ready, let mother #3 appear.

D:   This time I'm remembering a fight we had about her getting a doctor to help her with depression. She said she just wanted to be left alone. She looks pathetic and helpless. . . . I feel kind of numb. It's like she's just giving up on life, on me, on everything. . . .

MP:  OK, Daryl, when you're ready, just let go of that image and then let mother #4 appear.

D:   This is interesting. My mother looks the way she did when I was growing up. She is kind of wistful, like she wants to know how to be happy. And she wants me to be happy . . . (*sobbing*) . . . I do remember her being loving and kind with me. I miss getting that from her. And that loss happened a long time ago, long before she died. (*more sobbing*)

MP: Take all the time you need to be with this image, Daryl. You'll find that when you're ready, mother #5 will appear.

D: (*After a long pause*) This one is of my mother after she died. I'm standing at her grave and she's off to one side, like a spirit or ghost. She's telling me that she does not want me to be sad. She says she's free from pain now and has gone to a better place. She also apologizes for killing herself when she knew I would be the one to find her, and for always leaning on me more than she should have, for being a burden. She wants me to be free to enjoy my life now that she's gone, and to forgive her for all the hardships she's caused me.

MP: How is it for you to connect with this fifth image?

D: It's really amazing. I feel different inside, peaceful, like a weight has been lifted. I can give myself permission to move on with my life. I don't have to be held back by worrying about what I did or didn't do for her or being upset at the way she died. Even though it was awful, it was what she chose to do. It didn't have anything to do with me at all. Wow, it feels good to say that!

After this session, Daryl felt much more at peace with his mother's death and ready to tackle the sugar addiction and binge eating. Because he experienced his difficulties as inner conflicts among different parts of himself, we shifted to ego-state therapy. Through this method, we identified an ego state who called himself "the little junkie" and craved sugar to add energy to Daryl's passive, isolated way of life that had started back in childhood when he let his mother dominate him. This ego state agreed to decrease the binge eating as Daryl learned other ways to put energy and vitality into his life. We also worked with "angry coyote," "little boy," and "strong man" ego states, who released unresolved emotional feelings and helped him develop a healthy body image.

I was not using EMDR much at this time (1993) in my practice. If I had been, I might have used it to achieve further integration with the eidetic imagery of his mother as well as to potentiate the ego-state work. By the time of his last session with me, 11 months after his first one, Daryl had lost 31 pounds, changed his exercise and eating habits, and weathered separation from his wife, who had tended to replicate many of his mother's controlling dynamics. He also completed his doctoral dissertation, which he had procrastinated finishing because he wasn't ready to move into a successful future.

At six-months' follow-up, Daryl reported continuation of all positive changes he had made in therapy and believed he had closed completely the chapter of his mother's suicide. He also told me he was in a wonderful new relationship with a woman who seemed very different from his mother. "Maybe that's the biggest change of all," he said. "I'm finally with someone who supports me living my own life instead of taking care of everyone else. That's real excitement. Who needs sugar?"

Eidetic imagery of the self or other people tends to release unfolding images of "personality multiples"[14] that progress from a form that is often negative and trauma-based to a new configuration with the capacity to resolve the past by adding new, often surprising, information.

The eidetic work with Daryl illustrates the special quality of eidetic imagery to generate another image through a process that is similar to the jump of electrical energy across a chasm. Eidetic emanation or movement helps to replace old, frozen states of identity with a freely moving emotional experience that leads to new meaning and form.

Although Ahsen's work with eidetics predated energy psychology, the eidetic method is a good fit. Like any tool presented in this book, however, its effectiveness will depend on many factors, including the client's belief system and readiness for its use.

## Guided Fantasy Images

Many clients respond well to various types of guided fantasy exercises, which help them to produce rich healing imagery. Although there are many excellent scripts available for this method, I usually prefer to co-create the fantasy with my clients.

### MELISSA: IMAGERY WITH NAUSEA AND
### VOMITING RELATED TO RADIATION

Melissa had recently lost more than 40 pounds following a regime of radiation for esophageal cancer. Her clothes hung loosely on her frame and she grimaced as she told me how uncomfortable she felt.

Six months after her ordeal, Melissa's main symptoms were random episodes of nausea and vomiting that occurred frequently during each day. She also experienced intense pain in her chest that dated from before her tumor was identified. In addition, she suffered a gagging reflex when she took her medications three times a day, which sometimes led to more

vomiting. Although her oncologist had prescribed anti-nausea medication, antacids, and anti-anxiety medication, nothing seemed to help. She
had consulted a surgeon who told her that if the nausea, vomiting, and
gagging could not be controlled so that she could eat, radical surgery
might be indicated to eliminate her esophagus and create a new one by
stretching the lining of her stomach up to her throat.

Because Melissa had become quite disconnected from her body in order to escape her prison of discomfort, we began with two sessions of
gentle body relaxation and awareness. She was surprised to find feelings
of comfort and safety in her body that were stable from one week to the
next.

By the time of our fourth meeting, she had begun to shift from having
violent episodes of nausea and projectile vomiting to fleeting moments of
queasiness. Wearing an anti-nausea patch prescribed by her doctor in
combination with learning to focus on a safe place in her body seemed
to make the difference. She had even had a restaurant meal that she enjoyed. Yet she continued to have gagging responses when she took her
medication, which was puzzling to her because she had never had a problem taking pills and capsules before the onset of cancer.

Melissa had learned about imagery in her cancer support group and
had confidence in its efficacy, so I suggested that she imagine swallowing
the pills comfortably with a relaxed throat and passage down to her stomach. Though she easily formed these images, there were no noticeable
results.

At her second imagery session, Melissa reported a discouraging setback. Because she had felt better, she had extended her work hours and
expanded the kinds of foods she ate. Unfortunately, these changes had
resulted in repeated incidents of nausea and vomiting. "What I need at
this point," Melissa commented, "is a miracle."

MP: I tend to agree with you, Melissa. And I think we might need to
engage your imagination in creating the magic we're looking for.
Just close your eyes and let's create together the kind of possibilities that might help you feel more comfortable. Let's start by imagining someone very wise, someone whose guidance you would
trust more than your own. Who would that be? Just tell me what
comes to mind. . . .

M: I see a wise old man who looks like Jack Kornfield [*well-known
Buddhist psychologist and meditation teacher*]. His presence seems
calming.

MP: Does he seem to be someone who could advise you about the
discomfort you're having in taking the pills?

M: Yes, I think so. He thinks it's possible to make some changes that would help. I've been trying to trick my mind by hiding the pill that's the biggest and hardest for me to swallow, but I don't think I'm able to fool myself.

MP: What does he say about how you could take the pills?

M: He says that I'm taking this too seriously, that I should go on with my life more . . . like I could be reading a book or making a list to organize my time for work or thinking about something else that's pleasant.

MP: Does he seem to think the problem is that everything stops while you focus all your attention on the pills and then you can't relax?

M: Yes. I need to distract myself, let taking the pills be less important, along the lines of brushing my teeth or combing my hair. When I do those things automatically, my mind is off somewhere else.

MP: Sounds like interesting advice. Can you imagine following it?

M: I don't know. I'm afraid I'll forget about this. With all the medicine I'm taking, I can get pretty spacey.

MP: Why don't you find out how he can remind you of his instructions?

M: He's waving what looks like a magic wand. I think if I think of him, he will come and wave his wand and that will remind me to let my mind wander. . . . That's interesting, his wand will help me wander. . . .

MP: Yes, why don't you imagine how that would go right now? Just imagine that it's time to take your pills and that you begin to think of him. What happens when you do?

M: I see him and he waves his wand. I wander over to the table and get a book on healing I've been reading. I start reading a paragraph or two . . . and then my hand reaches out for the pills and I just swallow them while I'm reading, you know, like I'm absent-minded. The pills go down easily. I don't even look at which ones I'm taking—I keep looking at the book. That's where my focus needs to be, on learning more about the healing process.

Melissa improved just in time. She told me that when she informed her oncologist that she was taking her pills more easily, his comment was that if her gagging problem had continued much longer, he would have suggested inserting a catheter into her spinal cord to administer the medication.

We met for six more sessions, expanding the guided fantasy imagery and rehearsing how to use it each week. At the time we parted, Melissa had made modest gains. She was eating more regular meals, feeling more confident about her recovery, and expanding her range of activities.

# 7

# Fantasies, Dreams, and Other Spontaneous Gifts of the Creative Imagination

"Don't bother talking to me about the creative resources in my brain. I doubt if I have a creative cell in my body. I'm here because menopause is driving me crazy. My doctor tells me to just accept it. I don't want to take estrogen, because I'm so sensitive that it would probably make everything worse. My marriage is floundering. My teenage daughter tells me I'm turning into a monster. I've tried acupuncture, biofeedback, bodywork, hypnosis, you name it. I'm seeing a nurse practitioner who is also a herbologist. I've tried mountains of herbs and supplements. Nothing makes a difference for very long."

Rarely had I encountered such a tidal wave of negativity. I sat quietly, hoping for inspiration. None came.

Juanita interpreted my silence as rejection. "I don't blame you if you don't want to help me," she said. "If I were a therapist, I wouldn't think I could help me either. I'm so negative. I don't mean to be but that's how I really feel. It's as if because I'm a woman I'm in this prison and I can't get out for who knows how many years because my hormones are changing."

I looked at the neatly dressed woman across from me with what I hoped was a positive countenance. Mentally, I checked off a list of possibilities. Medication for depression? Evaluation by an ob-gyn who specializes in menopausal symptoms? EMDR for the accompanying anxiety and stress? TFT? I had the impression that Juanita and I were wandering through an intricate maze. No matter what path we went down, I sensed we would come to a dead end because of her certainty that nothing would help.

As the minutes of the interview ticked by, I decided to do what I often did in such circumstances. I told Juanita that I honestly was not sure I could help her, that I would not insult the complexity of her difficulties by promising a way out when I did not know yet whether there really was one for her. I offered my services on a temporary consultative basis. That is, I agreed to be available to her during a specified time period while both of us evaluated whether I could be of any significant assistance.

Although I half expected Juanita to decline my offer, she sounded surprisingly positive. "Well, you're refreshing after a whole line of therapists I've seen who have promised the moon and the stars and then could not deliver anything. At least you're being honest with me, so let's give it a try for a couple of months and see how it goes."

When we began to delve into Juanita's history, I could begin to understand why she was so negative. She grew up as the oldest of five children. Both parents were immigrants from Mexico and held perfectionistic standards for their children. Her mother was critical and verbally abusive. Her alcoholic father would rage violently and abuse Juanita and her brothers physically. Juanita also recalled several instances when her father's cruelty became sexualized.

When she was eight, her little sister was killed in freak playground accident. Juanita had been charged with watching the three-year-old as the children played one morning at the neighborhood recreational area. Lucia fell from the top of the jungle gym, landed on her head, and died a short time later at the hospital. The entire family was devastated by this loss. When Juanita's mother openly blamed her for being negligent, Juanita began to have a series of stress symptoms, including a severe outbreak of eczema that left permanent scars on her face and back. The emotional scars of self-loathing and despair persisted into adulthood as well.

"It's as if I've been through a terrible fire fueled by all the rage and toxins in my family. It's still smoldering inside me today and I can't put it out," Juanita said. "I think that when things get chemically out of balance for me, like my hormones, it's like a sudden wind comes up and the fire begins to burn out of control again."

I pointed out to Juanita that she seemed to have a natural way of painting pictures as a way of understanding her difficulties and suggested that we explore and work with these images to see what would happen.

Juanita immediately protested this idea. "I can't imagine that anything I could come up with would be of any value," she insisted. "That's why I'm paying you. The ideas I have don't work or I wouldn't need to come here."

We had a long talk about energy therapies and how they might be beneficial with her menopausal symptoms and the anxiety she felt about them. Unsurprisingly, Juanita expressed objections to each one. TFT sounded "too weird." She was uncomfortable about the idea of making lateral movements with her eyes in using EMDR. Hypnosis hadn't really helped her before when she had tried it. Why would now be any different?

"Regardless of any other changes we may be able to help you make," I explained, "You need to learn to value your own ideas and perspectives and to appreciate the inherent gifts for healing that are lying dormant inside waiting to be discovered. It's as if the fire you talked about earlier has singed you so badly that you can't recognize that there might be any other kind of warmth inside."

Reluctantly, Juanita conceded to the idea that we begin by exploring the images suggested by her daily experiences. Our next few sessions were focused on getting to know more about Juanita's daily rhythms. I asked her to tell me about a typical day and I listened for language that was suggestive of imagery:

MP: What do you do when you're feeling discouraged and really down about everything?

J: I like to ride my bicycle sometimes really fast. I don't even know where I'm going, just anywhere away from home.

MP: Can you take me with you as you ride?

J: What do you mean?

MP: Just tell me what we are seeing as we ride along.

J: Well, at first I'm not noticing anything. I'm too upset. Then gradually, I start to feel a little better and then I look around. Right now, I see the fruit trees in my neighbor's yard and I think about canning peaches with her last summer. That was a lot of fun.

MP: Just focus on that image of canning peaches, Juanita, and tell me what you feel inside of you.

J: I feel kind of peaceful and calm. I see us peeling peaches under the trees in the backyard. We're laughing and talking. The sun is shining. It's a beautiful day.

We repeated this process with activities such as walking her dogs, gardening, and washing dishes. I accepted whatever images appeared along with the feeling responses that were evoked. Juanita's story illustrates the benefit of utilizing as assets the spontaneous mental pictures that surface in descriptions of ordinary activities. Over and over, I sent the message to Juanita that what she thought and saw and felt was valuable and helpful. Although I helped her to develop the images, it was clear that they originated from her experiences.

In the first few months of using this kind of informal approach to imagery, Juanita reported that she felt more in balance with her menopausal symptoms. "I've noticed that my hot flashes don't bother me as much. I still have mood swings but I don't bottom out so far so I can get out of those dark places more easily. And I think the new herbs I'm trying are starting to make a difference along with the sublingual natural progesterone and low doses of plant estrogen I've been taking."

When I asked her how she accounted for these changes, Juanita said, "I really can't explain what's been happening. It's been very gradual, which I can see is better for me. If we got into some sudden dramatic change, I think I'd find some way to sabotage it because it would be too scary."

Several months later, Juanita learned that her mother had moved out of remission and into the terminal stage of pancreatic cancer. Although she had had little contact with her in recent years, Juanita wanted to find a way to support her brothers and make peace with her mother's death. She made the decision not to fly east until after her mother died, when she would support her four brothers in planning the memorial service and funeral. Although we discussed how she might prepare for this event by drawing on the imagery resources we had been collecting, Juanita remained anxious about whether she would be plunged into depression again.

When she received her oldest brother's call that her mother was close to death, Juanita called to let me know she would be gone for a week. At our next meeting, she shared many positive details of her family journey. "The surprising part was that we really helped and supported each other in ways we never had before. It was like her death brought all of us together like the family we had always wanted to be but never could have. Somehow, we were freed from all of that old pain and could heal a little. I mean, we had our moments, but this experience brought out the best in each of us."

Then she leaned closer to me and confided, "But the most amazing thing happened on the airplane ride to New York. My brother called me and said Mom was going down fast and that I should take the next plane. That's when I called you. I knew I probably wouldn't get there before she died so I was thinking a lot about her while I was sitting next to the window there on the plane.

"When I looked out the window, I saw this amazing image. It was like a big white dove. I blinked a few times because at first I thought it was just a cloud, but it was different from a cloud. It had large, graceful wings that moved like a bird would move. And it was flying next to me, almost as big as the plane, keeping me company. And I knew then that Mom had just died. I thought maybe the dove was her spirit, crossing over to the next dimension. I felt very close to her, like I never had while she was alive. It's hard for me to describe but I will never forget that image. It's like God or some higher power sent this dove to me." She paused and then added, "It's the first time in a long time I've felt a deep sense of gratitude that I was alive. And I felt whole and at peace inside. In that moment, I finally found the feelings I'm looking for."

In that moment, Juanita and I shared a profound sense of being moved by an experience that transcended rational explanation. We sat in silence for a while before I let her know how much I appreciated her willingness to share her image with me. I also told her that I believed she would be able to draw on the energy that dove brought to her for a long time to come. I suggested that we could not even begin to perceive the full healing power of her image because its potential would be unfolding gradually while she moved through other challenges and healing opportunities in her life.

Transpersonal and spiritual experiences transform the immediate moment while setting the stage for future transformation. Juanita's negative beliefs about herself could not be the same after she witnessed the dove flying outside the plane window. It's as if the transformative energy of the dove was stronger than all of her doubts and fears.

Six months later, Juanita found out that her father, long since divorced from her mother, was dying of lung cancer. We both thought immediately of the dove. "I think that dove is about more than just my mother dying," Juanita voiced. "I think of it now more as a guardian angel. I've never been a very spiritual person. I've always wanted to be, but I had such a terrible childhood that I couldn't really believe that there was a positive force that was loving enough to heal what was wrong. The dove or angel, whatever it is, is helping me to find that faith."

Although Juanita longed to share some of her newfound spirituality with her father in his final days, there was no shared epiphany, no dramatic bedside scene. Instead, after his death, she shared with me that she was aware of a quiet integration of her feelings about him. "In some ways, my Dad's death is harder for me than my mother's. I had a deep bond of intelligence with him. He was very bright. He abused me terribly when I was a child. No matter how well I did, I never heard any positive feedback from him. Yet I always respected his mind and he has been my model for being a professional in the world.

"Being around his friends and neighbors while he was dying, I was able to see him as a whole person. I only knew the angry part of him when I was little. I'm glad I was able to experience the more warm and loving sides of him. I sensed he wanted me to forgive him for the past, though we never talked about it. I held the image of the dove in my mind while I was with him. It was as if that loving presence followed me to Chicago, to my father's house. I'm going to miss him."

As Juanita moved through her grief process in losing both her parents, as well as attempting to manage hormonal fluctuations, she told me, "I have more of a sense of 'gel' inside me now. It's a feeling of being centered and everything coming together. Sometimes it's a mental feeling, sometimes a physical feeling. I say 'yes' to myself more often and I can tolerate the ups and downs of my moods better. Sometimes I even laugh at my fears."

Can we attribute these changes to the transpersonal imagery Juanita discovered at a time of intense vulnerability? Possibly. But we'll never know for sure, just as we'll never really know how circumstances might have progressed if she had been open to some of the other energy therapies we could have used to help her achieve inner balance, perhaps in a much shorter time period that the three years our therapy spanned.

Toward the end of our work together, Juanita confided in me that since childhood she had had a recurring nightmare. "Before I leave here, I would like to work with that dream. The fact that it keeps coming lets me know that my healing is not finished and I am not whole."

Juanita explained that she wakes in the middle of the night hearing noises and seeing a shadow on the wall. "I can't tell what it is but I know it's something disturbing," she tells me. "My mind starts racing. Is it an intruder? Is it a sign that space aliens are coming to abduct me? I know these are ridiculous thoughts but I can't stop them. When I was little, I had similar fears and nightmares that a wolf or a giant was going to come in and get me."

There are many possible ways of working with this kind of hypnagogic[1] image. The energy therapy approach is different from usual methods, however, because it avoids the interpretation of meaning. The focus is on connecting with the internal energy that the image evokes and releasing that energy so it can flow unblocked, much as acupuncture needles help to release qi. Keeping this principle in mind, I asked Juanita to focus internally as she was telling me about the shadow on the wall. "I feel really tight across my chest. I'm scared and I feel like I can't breathe," she said.

MP: Just stay with that tightness in your chest, your fear, and the feel-
    ing that you can't breathe. Explore that for a few moments.
 J: (*Pause*) It's a little scary to stay with it but now I feel something
    happening around my heart.
MP: Yes, follow what's happening around your heart. What could that be?
 J: Hmmm. I'm not sure. I see some kind of red heart-shaped gelatin.
    It's almost like Claymation, like a friendly cartoon.
MP: And as you focus on that red heart claylike cartoon, what happens?
 J: I feel calmer inside my chest. It's looser and I can breathe . . . (*long
    pause*). Hmmm, my whole body is calmer now.
MP: OK, Juanita. Let's go back to where we started. When you think
    about waking up and seeing the shadow on the wall in the middle
    of the night, what is that like now?
 J: It seems more friendly, kind of like ET from the movie. (*Smiles
    shyly*) That's really interesting. It seems different now.

Juanita had two further encounters with hypnagogic imagery. The first
time, she awoke as before and saw the "alien" shadow on the wall. Juanita
reported that she started to have the old thoughts and fears but then
found herself "talking to" the alien. "I didn't talk out loud because I didn't
want to wake my husband," she said. "But then I found I could just think
my message. I told the alien that I wanted it to go so that I could sleep
well. And you know, it did leave! I just went back to sleep, and in the
morning it seemed more like an interesting dream than something scary."

In her final nocturnal meeting with the image, the shadow appeared
on her wall as a symbol. "I couldn't tell what kind of symbol it was
because I've never seen anything exactly like it, but I think it was spiritual,
like an aboriginal or Native American marking. So I just noticed it and
went back to sleep. In the morning, I didn't even remember it until later
in the day and then I was curious, wondering what form it might take
next or even if I'd see it again."

During the last six months of our work, the hypnagogic images did not
recur. Juanita believed it was "like helping your child to look under the
bed when they're scared of monsters so that they can see that there's really
not one there. You helped me look and now I know there's no monster."

As for her menopausal symptoms, by the time of our final meeting,
Juanita's symptoms were more under her control. A combination of herbs,
acupuncture, low-dose estrogen patches, and low-dose progesterone capsules were managing hot flashes, dizziness, headaches, and mood swings.
Essentially, tools that she had tried before were now consistently working.

What made the difference? As I understand it, the work we did with
spontaneous imagery seemed to help Juanita achieve a steadier state of

inner balance. Juanita's images served early on as nonthreatening teachers for her about her unique and valuable inner resources. Our imagery work also catalyzed shifts of energy that provided wonderful experiences of self-discovery and well-being deeply appreciated by both of us. Such moments of true partnership further solidified our alliance, helping her to trust me while she learned to better manage the limits of her energy and to regulate feelings of anger and despair[2]—less appealing work, yet equally important to her future growth and healing.

Juanita ended her work with me after three years at a pinnacle of health stability and self-confidence. As we celebrated her accomplishments, I left the door open for her to come back in the future, should she want to consult with me.

Nine months later and in crisis, Juanita contacted me again. She explained that a back injury while water skiing had derailed her. She was in constant emotional and physical pain. No intervention seemed to help her and she felt desperate and suicidal.

Her story serves as an excellent reminder of how early childhood trauma can complicate responses to health problems. At this writing, though easily discouraged by her fragile attempts to heal from countless setbacks, Juanita is struggling again in her work with me to reestablish hard-won health stability. On her good days, she can appreciate the creative inner resources that allow her to inch forward again.

### BRAD: SELF-GUIDED IMAGERY FOR HYPERSENSITIVITY

Brad told me in our first interview that he was hypersensitive to sensory overload. As a child, he had been diagnosed with eczema, for which he received shots. He had always been sensitive to loud sounds; leaf blowers, for example, were often excruciatingly painful. In high school he contracted ulcerative colitis and in adult life he had experienced numerous somatic symptoms. "I used to somaticize all my emotional reactions, but eight years of analysis have taught me how to experience my feelings more directly. Still, it's as if I am wired at a higher frequency than everyone else around me."

At the dentist's office, he required more time and anesthesia than other patients. Brad's dentist had told him that he would have to have two crowns replaced. This was very unnerving, because even when Brad had a cavity filled, he felt intense fear and helplessness. "It's a white knuckle experience for me. I feel like I've been assaulted and am usually in a state of shock for a couple of days afterward. I know this is an unusual reaction, but I'm very frightened of having this procedure done and the dentist says I have to have it done in the next couple of months or run the risks of complications. Can you help me?"

Although Brad had contacted me because he believed hypnosis might help him, when we discussed the issues involved in working hypnotically, we both agreed that he might be too concerned with losing control of his sensory experience to feel completely comfortable. We decided to experiment with spontaneous images that might help to prepare him for dental surgery.

At the beginning of our second session, Brad told me that he had scheduled a minor dental procedure, having a cavity filled, for the coming week. We agreed that this would be good practice for him in learning how his mind and body could work together to keep him comfortable and relaxed. Since Brad's dentist was very open to anything that might help him, I proposed that Brad arrange to arrive at the dental office at least a half-hour early and put himself into a relaxed state in the room where the procedure would be done. We also discussed how he could set up three nonverbal signals[3] for "yes," "no," and "stop," so that the dentist could monitor his comfort level throughout.

We began specific preparations for Brad's dental appointment. Since he practiced meditation, I asked him to take a few minutes to guide himself into a relaxed state and signal when he was ready to continue. Brad took about five minutes to reach a level of comfort that was satisfactory. At his signal, I suggested that he focus on the kind of safety he would like to feel in the dental chair and allow an image to come to him that might help him to feel safe there:

B:  (*After a pause*) I can't believe the image I'm seeing!
MP: Just accept whatever comes to mind, Brad. What do you see? Is it OK to tell me?
B:  Well, it's a casket, of all things. Does this mean I'm going to die?
MP: Brad, there are certain conscious meanings that we attach to a casket, but your creative imagination may be working at another level of meaning. Tell me about the casket.
B:  It's snug. I'm lying in it and my whole body fits. . . . It's very dark inside but it's soft and luminous, lined with soft gold satin. It's shaped like one of those mummy cases. There's actually plenty of room for me. I'm surprised at how comfortable I feel.
MP: Can you imagine being inside the case in the dentist's office this week?
B:  Yes, actually I can.
MP: Good. You might want to practice bringing up the image during the week whenever you think about the procedure. Just recall how well it contains your body and how safe and comfortable you feel

inside it. And also, as you practice with the image, if it stays the same, that's fine, but leave room for it to change and develop as our process unfolds here.

Brad was pleased with the results of his dental appointment. "She ended up filling two cavities, not one, and there was a lot of digging but I had no fear of pain. I went 45 minutes ahead of time and I was in a deep meditative state. I found I could come out of it a little bit when she walked in just to show her my signals and then I was relaxed again. I decided to put all of my hypervigilance in my little finger. I told myself that the rest of me could be completely comfortable. The only trouble was that I didn't have enough time to come out at the end and also I was aware of what my dentist was doing more than I wanted to be. I guess I'd say that my body did fine—I was very numb in my hands, arms, and legs—but I need to work on helping my mind relax more."

To prepare for the next dental appointment where two temporary crowns would be installed, we revisited Brad's image of safety. When he found it again, he told me it had changed:

B: It looks like a cello case; it's more rounded. It still has gold satin inside so it's very soft and comfortable and I can open and close it easily.

MP: So it's more rounded and softer this time?

B: Yes, and more flexible. . . . I can look out a little bit or open it all the way, whatever I need.

MP: There's more flexibility there.

B: Yes. But I wish I had something to protect my ears. The sounds of the drill bother me.

MP: See if an image comes that will give your ears just the right amount of protection.

B: Yes, I see little mufflers for my ears.

After Brad imagined using these images successfully in the dental office, he opened his eyes. "I think I know why I saw a casket at first. My parents died in a train accident when I was in my early twenties. It turned out that the engineer had been drinking; he pushed the wrong switch, and nobody noticed. The train derailed and more than 30 people were killed. I think my fantasy is that my dentist will slip somehow, no one will notice, and the drill will go through my mouth into my skull and I'll die."

THE CASKET IMAGE WAS AN INVALUABLE TOOL IN exposing the root of Brad's fears about dental surgery. Once he recognized that he was responding as if his dentist were the train engineer, he could easily distinguish current circumstances from the events that led to his parents' death. "My dentist is really wonderful," he explained. "She is very interested in what we're doing. She's willing to do anything at all that would help. And she watches me closely. She's nothing at all like that train engineer."

At his next visit, Brad told me that his dental appointment went very well and that he felt totally and pleasantly relaxed during the procedure. "It only took me fifteen minutes to get relaxed ahead of time and my face was very relaxed. Even my dentist thought I was deeper this time."

BRAD DISCOVERED AN IMAGE OF A JAGUAR DURING ONE of his daily meditations at home. In exploring this imagery, he believed that the jaguar represented the boundaries of his body, which contained intense energy and had powerful ways to move and release it. He rehearsed using the jaguar as his new image of containment and safety in the dentist's office, and in the process discovered that there were two jaguars: one who could relax yet remain vigilant at the same time, and a second who could stand his ground, ready to strike and release pent-up energy, returning to rest position if aggression were unnecessary.

We discussed how Brad could use the jaguar image during his upcoming dental appointment when the permanent crowns would be installed. He imagined entering the jaguar's body in order to surrender to comfort.

Brad's final and most challenging procedure was his most successful. Brad described his response as a sudden drop into numbness. His entire jaw was relaxed. "Finally, I was receptive to Novocain just like any other patient. They took the old crown off the back tooth and drilled and then sealed and filled the crack. The whole time I had a few moments of discomfort but no pain. I was present but numb the whole time and was able to respond to my dentist's questions, moving out of relaxation a few times and then back into it. I was so numb I didn't even know I had water in my mouth. At the end, I think I fell asleep; I was so safe and comfortable."

He attributed his positive responses to the cumulative effects of our imagery work, especially the jaguar. "I think it's the perfect image to help me. It's strong enough to attack anything that would hurt or invade me and gives me confidence that it can stay alert so that I can relax deeply. It's like he lounges comfortably after marking his boundaries and I can be very comfortable."

The last news I had of Brad was that his dentist had asked him to speak to a local association of dentists about his experiences. "I want to let them know that there are probably a lot of patients like me in their practice. I want them to be sensitive to the fears we have and know that there are ways to resolve them. And," he smiled shyly, "I'm going to tell them that they need to learn that there's more to good dentistry than just filling and crowning teeth."

# Section IV

# SOMATIC ENERGY THERAPIES:

## COMING HOME TO THE BODY

# Introducing Somatic
# Energy Therapies

Vivian's first pregnancy three years before had been a nightmare. Due to several complications, she had spent eight out of nine months in bed. Her delivery was lengthy and painful. Because of similar considerations during her current pregnancy, she had also been placed on bed rest. She was terrified that her second delivery would follow the same pattern as her first and determined to make her experience different from before.

When Vivian came to my office, she was just over eight months pregnant and extremely uncomfortable. She was interested in experiencing formal hypnosis but could not be still in any one position for longer than a few seconds. She had trouble maintaining a focus on much of anything except the discomfort in her body and her fear. My first attempts to help her form images were unsuccessful and she began to feel uncertain that she could have a positive experience with me or find anything that might help her.

Finally, I asked her to tell me what part of her body might feel a little more comfortable than the rest. After a long pause, she answered, "The only place I feel comfortable is my hair. Even the top of my head hurts but my hair is soft. I like the way my hair feels." Relieved to find something positive to work with, I asked her to focus on her hair and just notice what else she might find out about that area of her body. After another long pause, she said, "This is strange. I'm thinking about how my mother used to brush my hair when I was a little girl. It was so soothing. I loved that ritual every morning." We explored further until it was easy for Vivian to recreate that experience and the relaxing feelings that went with it.

Two weeks later, Vivian called to tell me that she had given birth to a baby girl and that she was astonished at how easy the delivery had been. "This time," she said, "the baby practically popped right out. Labor was about an hour and I had relatively little pain. I couldn't believe how smoothly everything went compared to my first baby. . . . I kept feeling my hair and that helped me to relax and think positively. And you know, that scene with my mother kept changing just like you said it might. I saw her in the delivery room with me stroking my hair and soothing me just like she would have if I were a little girl. I needed to feel held by someone older and bigger while I went through the delivery."

THOUGH WE STILL CANNOT DEFINE PRECISELY HOW BODY and mind processes interact, the connection most certainly involves the exchange of subtle energy or energy information.[1] We know, for example, that the diagnostic use of subtle electromagnetic energy technologies found in CAT scans, x-rays, and ultrasounds is accompanied by measurable effects on the physical, hormonal, and behavioral systems of humans and animals. We also know that these types of energies have been channeled to produce positive changes that contribute to health needs such as the regeneration of nerve tissues.

Overwhelming evidence that has emerged in the last 20 years is conclusive in establishing a wholistic mindbody continuum rather than a dualistic model of two separate and independent systems of body and mind. One of the primary ways of studying the effects of the mindbody interaction on health has emerged in study of the relationship between the central nervous system and the immune systems within the field of PNI (psychoneuroimmunology).

Research has indicated a clear impact of stressors on immune system functioning and quality of health. It is conclusive that emotional stress, for example, acts to suppress immune functioning, though it is not yet clear whether chronic, sustained stress is more detrimental than acute, short-term stress. Researchers have also demonstrated that positive mental attitudes and thoughts, such as those that occur through hypnotic suggestion, meditation, and imagery, can enhance the immune system and influence recovery from disease. With such clear proof that psychological processes can have a powerful impact on the strengthening of healthy responses in the body as well as on the resolution of illness, it is surprising that until relatively recently the field of psychology has largely ignored methods that facilitate positive somatic focus.

## Body Awareness

One of the first steps in resolving a health issue is to find a positive way of relating to the body. Many people with health problems have very negative ways of relating to their bodies. It's as if they have decided to blame their bodies for causing the suffering they experience. Others, particularly those who have experienced the long-term effects of abuse and neglect, don't seem to be inside their bodies much at all but stay detached, as if dissociating from the source of their pain.

Although Vivian was easily able to examine her own sense of her body to find the refuge provided by her hair, other people need to be guided through the process. **Body scans** *help people reestablish positive somatic contact by learning how to survey or explore the body.* Body scans[2] also can help to restore severed connections between mental and physical processes and identify areas that may contain somatic resources, as well as ones that may be linked to major problems of concern. I sometimes present these scans as somatic treasure hunts. They are sure to yield invaluable awarenesses that can frequently make the difference between well-being and physical distress.

Chapter 9 presents more information about the use of body scans and other techniques that promote positive body awareness, along with specific ways of connecting to somatic pathways for healing. These kinds of experiences facilitate the restoration of health by working through the body.

## The Body and Energy Psychology

According to Albert Einstein's famous equation ($E = mc^2$), energy resides at the most fundamental level of existence. Essentially, everything in our material reality can be reduced to energy in various forms and can be measured, although it is probably true that there are energies in degrees and types that are so subtle that they cannot be accurately and identified by the current instruments we have developed.[3]

In the health field, the study of energy has moved in several different directions. One is the use of electrostimulators attached to the surface of the skin, such as transcutaneous electrical nerve stimulation devices, called TENS units, which have been found to be useful in controlling pain. Transcranial electrostimulators, conductors attached to areas of the skull, have also been helpful in managing addictions and treating insomnia and depression.[4]

Researchers have found that there is a specific electrical energy current at the site of injury that is instrumental in regeneration of cells, tissues, and bones.[5] Other studies have monitored electrical currents, called L-fields (i.e., life fields), in and around virtually every species of life. Findings have suggested that L-fields seem to control the form into which new molecules and cells are rebuilt, so that they shape themselves into the same pattern as the old ones.[6]

My own experiments with applications of energy theory to psychology have led me to conclude that many clinical problems can be resolved by working with subtle energies in the body. Other professionals, such as Fred Gallo, go even further, claiming that psychological problems may even be a *function of* energy systems or fields. This means that, since psychological disturbances are expressed in our behaviors, thoughts, emotions, neurology, and even biochemistry, there may be an energy component that provides the coding instructions that generate mindbody imbalance. If that is true, in order to fully resolve health problems, it may be necessary to use psychological approaches that operate directly on the energy systems.

## Thought Field Therapy (TFT)

TFT is a recent psychological technology that is thought to manipulate bodymind energies by activating the meridians identified by Chinese medicine. TFT assumes that psychological symptoms originate from disturbances located within subtle energy fields, rather than from disturbances in brain chemistry, thought patterns, emotional moods, or attachment bonds in parental relationships, as traditional psychological theories teach.

Dr. Roger Callahan, the psychologist who developed TFT, practiced traditional methods of therapy before studying kinesiology. One of the applied kinesiology techniques that intrigued him was the use of muscle testing, which demonstrates that negative mental and emotional states tend to disrupt the body's strength while positive states accompany balanced or increased somatic strength. Eventually becoming certified as a kinesiologist, Callahan began testing psychological problems using a variation of the kinesiology diagnostic methods he had learned.

A breakthrough in his work came when he treated Mary,[7] a patient who had a longstanding water phobia that had proven resistant to cognitive, desensitization, and hypnotic therapies. Callahan asked her to think about water while he tested energy "flow" through various meridians. Discovering that only the stomach meridian was out of balance, he had Mary continue to focus on thoughts of water while he tapped with two fingertips on the cavity under her eyes, an area connected with the stomach meridian energy system according to Chinese acupuncture maps. Within a few minutes, Mary reported that the problem was gone and subsequently jumped joyfully into the pool just outside Callahan's home office. Callahan explained Mary's cure, which has held almost 20 years, as resulting from the rebalancing of her body's stomach meridian through tapping on one of the significant meridian points while her thought field contained an awareness of her fear of water.

Although there may have been other explanations for this dramatic change,[8] Callahan has continued to explore links between the meridian energy system and psychological distress. He found that not every patient with phobic symptoms responded to the same treatment as Mary. Eventually, he realized that different configurations of phobias involve the disruption of different energy meridians and require different tapping prescriptions. These discoveries culminated in his theory that it is the *sequence* or order in which various energy meridians are treated, along with their location, that is essential to successful resolution. He has worked out the order of tapping various points along the meridians in his work with hundreds of patients who have exhibited a variety of mind-body symptoms.

Callahan's methods are still evolving, and others[9] are adding to his theories and techniques. The basic TFT approach at this point involves following a program of therapeutic recipes, known as *algorithms*, that prescribe gentle self-tapping with the index and middle fingers of the dominant hand on various acupuncture points in a specific order, depending on the symptom. For example, there are special TFT tapping recipes for specific phobias, addictive urges, depression, anger, guilt, past psychological trauma, physical pain, panic, and different kinds of anxiety symptoms.[10] Specialized diagnostic techniques include the use of therapeutic intuition, muscle testing techniques, neurological balancing, and the more advanced, and expensive, application of voice technology, which analyzes the client's voice as it is presented over the telephone.

If you want to experience TFT before you read about it, find the "v" that is formed on the back of your nondominant hand underneath and between the knuckles of your little and ring fingers (see Figure 2 in Appendix A). Take the index finger and middle fingers of your dominant hand and begin to tap gently with your fingertips on that point, called the "gamut spot." Still tapping with your head held steady, let your eyes focus on the floor beneath you. Then gradually move your eyes slowly from floor to ceiling level, all the while tapping on the gamut spot, keeping your head still, and breathing deeply and easily. This is a brief relaxation technique, usually used to clear symptoms when they have all but disappeared, but can be used whenever you are experiencing slight stress.

Sometimes the benefits of the tapping recipes can be blocked by **psychological reversals** (PRs). *PRs refer to a condition of negative motivation, in which our motivations operate in ways that are opposite to how we hope they will work when we attempt to lose weight, to stop using drugs and alcohol, or to achieve other goals.* There are several possible explanations for reversals, including severe psychological stress, exposure to environmental or ingested toxins, or reversed electromagnetic poles within the energy meridians themselves.

Special tapping techniques can interrupt these reversals, so that energy systems can respond fully to TFT and other techniques.

At this point in its development, TFT appears to be a promising tool of energy psychology, although there is only preliminary research to demonstrate its effectiveness and its scope remains experimental. Part of TFT's growing appeal is its attempt to translate energy theory directly into practice. The use of acupuncture meridians links TFT with the healing legacy of ancient Chinese medicine, and the easy-to-use tapping protocols make its therapy self-therapy. Yet, as Callahan himself notes, the effectiveness of TFT methods rests in the client's willingness to use them consistently and intensively, sometimes over a long period of time. For many people, this level of responsibility can be either overwhelming or impractical.

EMDR, hypnosis, and the other tools presented in this book, as well as many that are not included, work in energetic ways that are complementary to, though very different from, TFT. Since it is highly unlikely that any one method will work equally well for all clients, it is important to consider a variety of tools that involve direct work through the body. One such method is the somatic experiencing model highlighted in chapter 9.

## Somatic Experiencing (SE)

Some years ago, I was teaching a weekend workshop on trauma resolution with my friend and colleague, Peter Levine. Unexpectedly, we heard a loud crash against the window. Peter went to the window to see a small bird lying stunned on the ground. With his biologist's curiosity, he drew all of us into the garden to examine the bird, then rigged up a video camera to study its responses.

Over a four-hour period, we faithfully tracked the bird's recovery, which was documented on film. At first, no signs of life were visible. Then, under Peter's guidance, we detected gradually emerging minuscule responses. Slight color returned around the bird's beak and eyes. Breathing became discernible. Tiny trembling movements occurred in the bird's legs, neck, and wings. Shortly before the end of the workshop day, the bird flew off as if nothing had happened.

Peter commented that this kind of complete recovery from a traumatic event was possible if the body's natural regenerative systems were allowed to operate. Human beings who experience the trauma of injuries and other ordeals are rarely allowed to complete this restorative process, however. In the case of childhood abuse, for example, we cannot risk displaying our responses to trauma for fear of worsening the circumstances. In other traumatic situations, well-intentioned caregivers may rush us through shock responses to speed us toward some fantasy of healing that does not fully consider the biology of the body in its prescription.

Because of his dual interests in psychology and biology, Levine brings a unique perspective to the study of somatic healing. His **somatic experiencing** (SE) model attempts to track and facilitate natural body responses connected to healing so that they can be completed and full equilibrium restored. The therapist's task is to help balance healing and traumatic reactions in the body so that pathways can open to wholeness again and self-regulatory systems are restored.

Levine has proposed SIBAM[11] as a model of internal experience. Normal experience takes place simultaneously across five dimensions: sensation, images (internal impressions of external stimuli that may be visual, auditory, kinesthetic, gustatory, and olfactory), behavior (voluntary and involuntary, including gestural, emotional, postural, autonomic, and archetypal), affects (includes feelings, emotions, and the "felt sense"), and meaning (includes cognition, thought, knowledge, transpersonal, and spiritual elements). When we are exposed to traumatic events, including health crises, dissociation or disconnection from one or more of these dimensions occurs as biological as well as psychological protection. In order to resolve the traumatic experience and related symptoms, we must be helped to reconnect or reassociate the elements of SIBAM.

Some people become overcoupled or flooded by trauma-related experience. Others are uncoupled or dissociated.[12] There can also be a combination of these two basic reactions in the nervous system. In order to resolve these imbalances, it is important to reconnect or link together the aspects of inner experience that have been dissociated, and to separate, contain, and reorganize SIBAM elements that have become overcoupled. Accomplishing these tasks will lead to balanced self-regulation and will facilitate integration somatically as well as psychologically.

In tracking the SIBAM elements of a woman who had chronic symptoms of stiffness in her shoulders and neck, for example, what began to surface was a traumatic miscarriage that she had never grieved. The SE model allowed her to stay with the body sensations, emotions, and movement behaviors that were occurring and then to access a visual memory related to the miscarriage. When she began to connect with her physical and emotional pain related to that event, she could then begin to settle into a state of homeostasis as she surrendered to this loss for the first time.

Although the SE model is too complex to convey within the parameters of a single chapter, its methods are central to the body-focused therapy that I use with clients who have various types of health problems. SE principles follow those of energy psychology, emphasizing methods of achieving and sustaining balance between healing and trauma-related energies and their integration in bodymind systems.

SIBAM provides an effective map to guide reconnection to the essential elements of bodymind processes, from which many people with health problems have disconnected themselves through attempts to manage their distress. Frequently, people who have symptoms related to unresolved health trauma in the past, or who are struggling with the traumatic impact of current health crises, can be helped in a short time to transform symptoms at the core of their traumatic responses using the SE model.

## Integrating Bodywork into Psychotherapy

I am not trained as a bodyworker. For that reason, I do not use "hands on" approaches with my clients. About four years ago, however, I began talking with a friend of mine, Landry Wildwind, about possibilities for incorporating a bodyworker into the clinical setting to work with clients who had significant body issues that were not responding sufficiently to EMDR, hypnosis, and other approaches. Landry had begun working in her practice with Alan van Winkle, a certified massage therapist who is trained in a number of methods, including Rosenwork, the Trager method, and craniosacral stimulation. Alan served as a co-therapist in the room with her and also as an adjunctive provider primarily with women who experienced physical dissociation of bodywork as a result of childhood or adult trauma or in response to various types of health crises.

Since then, we[13] have expanded our integration of bodywork into clinical practice. We now utilize Alan's work with a wide range of clients, including those who are diagnosed with ADD, anxiety disorders, chronic pain, sexual response problems, somatic complaints and injuries, depression, and touch or nurturing deprivation. This collaborative work is also helpful with individuals who exhibit developmental problems such as difficulties with self-soothing, body boundaries, and affect and sensate regulation and tolerance. We have also developed ways of integrating hypnosis and EMDR with Alan's work and have found this method to be highly effective with many individuals who were not achieving significant results using other approaches.

Alan and I have developed several techniques that have been effective in combining somatic and hypnotic approaches. With every client, regardless of the symptoms and problems they present, we begin with *somatic strengthening*. This involves finding a safe place in the body that evokes only positive feelings of safety and security when it is touched. In most individuals, this place is located in the extremities, such as the feet, hands, or arms, away from the trunk or torso, which may have been the site of abuse or inappropriate touching.

We have also been successful in combining somatic approaches with hypnotic ego-state therapy. In chapter 5, I pointed out how some ego states can best be accessed through the body. When this is the case, different types of therapeutic touch can be used to activate somatic ego states in ways that are powerful while providing nurturing attention at the same time.

A third component of our collaboration has been the integration of EMDR and body focused therapy, which is called **rhythmic alternating stimulation** (RAS).[14] In collaboration with Landry Wildwind and Vicky van Winkle as well as in our work together, Alan has developed several effective forms of RAS:

1. Alternating stimulation of the temples conducted as part of craniosacral work
2. Alternating rocking stimulation of the extremities
3. Alternating stimulation of specific meridian points that are significant for a given individual's somatic and health issues

Each form of RAS is used to stimulate lateral eye movements while the eyes are closed and the client is in a state of natural relaxation that occurs in response to Alan's "hands on" bodywork. With some clients, this relaxed state is enhanced through hypnotic suggestion.

We have used RAS to promote somatic strengthening experiences, to deepen positive experiences of sensation and touch, to promote integrated connection with full body experience, to relieve anxiety, pain, and depression, and to calm fear and hyperarousal states. Chapter 9 provides a brief presentation of RAS, and supplementary information is included in Appendix C.

# 8

@

# TFT: Reversing Negative Thought Fields and Their Effects on the Body

MARIA: REDUCING CHRONIC PAIN
FOLLOWING INJURY

Eight months after her car was rear-ended by a large diesel truck during a rush hour slowdown, Maria continued to complain of pain in her right shoulder and arm and left neck area. Her x-rays pointed to soft tissue damage and she had received good care from a chiropractor and a physical therapist. Yet her suffering persisted and she was discouraged.

"My doctor doesn't think there's any more that can be done for me medically. He just says time will heal me further and tells me to keep doing my physical therapy exercises. But I can't accept that. I've got to find a way to deal with the pain in my neck and shoulder. I come home from work at the end of the day and I'm hurting so badly that all I can do is go to bed. My husband has to take care of our daughters and cook. He's supportive, but I'm not sure how much longer he can keep doing all that he is doing. And I have no life at all. What can you recommend?"

We first discussed the benefits of various body strengthening programs, including yoga, Pilates-based rehabilitation, and Feldenkrais movement.[1] Maria decided that participating in one of these several times per week might be preferable to the pain she was feeling. After checking out various approaches, she subsequently enrolled in an exercise studio close to her house that taught the Pilates method.

Our next task was to determine whether any of the energy methods I work with could help Maria to reduce and manage her pain levels. As we examined the options, Maria told me that she had tried acupuncture shortly after her injury and that it had helped the pain temporarily. "The problem was that I had to keep going back to get relief and I had so many other appointments at that time that I just dropped it." When she heard that TFT was based on the same energy theory as acupuncture, and that the techniques could be practiced on her own, Maria wanted to try it.

During her first TFT session, I asked Maria to focus on the area of discomfort in her arm, shoulder, and neck. Since these three areas seemed associated with a similar feeling, we decided to work with them all at once. If this had not been the case, we would have started with the body area that rated the highest SUD level and then moved to the other two later.

As Maria tuned into her arm, shoulder, and neck, she reported a stiff, constricted feeling and a heavy, sharp pressure moving into the back of her head. Her accompanying thoughts were, "I'm not sure I'll ever get rid of this. I may have to live the rest of my life with my body locked up with this pressure." When I directed her to work up as much intensity as she could, the number Maria assigned to her physical and emotional distress was an 8 out of 10 points SUD.

When prescribing medical treatment, identifying the thoughts that might accompany physical symptoms is usually considered unimportant. For example, most oncologists are not interested in what their patients are thinking about while they are receiving chemotherapy for cancer. For TFT practitioners, however, choosing the prescribed tapping treatment sequence is totally dependent on the thoughts and emotional feelings that are linked to the constellation of body symptoms, known collectively as the *thought field*.[2]

*The* **thought field** *is used to understand and prescribe the diagnosis and treatment of a particular problem. When relevant thoughts and feelings related to the energy field that surrounds the body symptom are identified, the important information that is active in a problem comes into focus.*

Alerting Maria that she might find the TFT procedure to be a little odd, I asked her to tap gently with her right index and middle fingertips on the points that comprise the TFT pain protocol. First, she tapped about 30–50 times on a point, called the "*gamut spot*," between and below the knuckles of her little finger and ring finger on the back of her left hand.

Next, she tapped just below her collarbone, all the while focusing on the pain in her arm, shoulder, and neck and the thoughts we identified. As is usual when I'm conducting TFT sessions, I tapped the relevant spots on my own body while Maria was tapping hers. (In order to get a sense of where Maria was tapping, take a look at Diagrams 2 and 3 in Appendix A, which pinpoint many of the energy points used in TFT tapping recipes.)

Next, I asked Maria to measure again her sense of pain. "Nothing much is different," she said. "Maybe the pressure is a little less. I guess it's about a 7." I next led Maria through what is called the mini-psychological reversal sequence, where she tapped the indentation on the side of her hand (i.e., the "karate chop" area) while saying out loud the affirmation, "I accept myself even though I have this pain." This little procedure is designed to clear a reversal, or psychological block, that can intervene during treatment so that significant progress is slowed.

Next, we completed what is called the 9 gamut treatment. First, Maria tapped again on the "triple burner" or gamut point located on the back of her hand in the "v" between and below the knuckles of her little and ring fingers. I directed her to move and swirl her eyes in specific patterns, hum a tune, and count out loud, while she tapped.

When she reassessed her arm/shoulder/neck pain, this time she gave it a 6 SUD rating. "It's a little better, kind of like it's fading." Because the rating was still high, we repeated the mini reversal with the affirmation, "I accept myself even though I still have some of the pain," followed by tapping on the gamut and collarbone spots, then the 9 gamut sequence, and the gamut/collarbone sequence.

This time when Maria reassessed her pain experience, she found that it was a 5. Although we were making gradual progress, it seemed clear that shifts in Maria's problems were being blocked in some way. *I explained to her the concept of* **psychological reversal**, *which suggests a blockage in the energy system so that a person's motivation works in opposition to the ways it should work.* This phenomenon can explain self-destructive behavior from the TFT perspective as well as any reactions that are contrary to what an individual desires or wants to do.[3]

Suspecting that our halting progress might be due to a psychological reversal, I noted that Maria had not responded significantly to the mini-reversal corrections introduced earlier because the pain levels failed to drop at least 2 points. I conducted a brief muscle testing procedure,[4] which involved testing the firmness of her dominant arm muscle while Maria focused on her desire to relieve her pain. Because her muscle weakened in response to the positive statement, "I want to resolve my physical pain," we determined the presence of a specific reversal. To correct this, I asked Maria to repeat the phrase, "I deeply and completely accept myself even though I have this problem," while rubbing in a circular motion the reflex spot on the left side of the chest.[5] Again, we conducted muscle testing, which indicated that the reversal had been cleared. (To avoid encountering a series of mini-reversals as Maria and I did, it is an option to test for and clear any reversals at the very beginning of a TFT session. I chose not to do so with Maria because I wanted to see how well she might move through the protocol. I reasoned that a more direct route, if reversals did not occur, might be confidence-building for her.)

We then repeated the tapping sequences on the gamut spot, the collar-bone point, followed by the 9 gamut treatment. This time when Maria remeasured her pain, she reported that the number had dropped to be-tween a 1 and a 2. "That's amazing; I can hardly feel any of the negative feelings. There's still a little bit of the pressure on the left side of my neck but that's all," she told me.

Since we were approaching zero, I suggested that she tap the gamut spot on the back of her hand, look down toward the floor, and follow my finger as it guided her eyes to rise slowly toward the ceiling. Maria took a deep breath and said, "It's gone completely. I can't find any pain in my arm, neck, or shoulder. All I feel is a slight tingly feeling, like energy is moving again." The eyeroll had done its job of clearing the last traces of the symptom.

We tested our results by having her try to imagine the pain there as it had been in the past by recalling recent incidents after work where her discomfort had been intense. "No. I can't find that feeling right now at all. It just doesn't bother me. I mean, this is great, but will the results last?"

This is a common concern that people have about TFT, especially those who have struggled for a considerable period of time with a chronic prob-lem. We spent some time discussing how and when she could practice the tapping sequences on her own. I suggested that she follow the pre-scriptions on the printed card I provided whenever she thought about or felt discomfort in her neck, shoulder, or arm.

"It seems like I'm going to be doing this every two minutes! Won't people think I'm strange when they see me tapping on myself all the time?" Maria asked as she prepared to leave. "These are worries most people have when they first try TFT," I responded. "You might want to test out your concerns by tapping just the first point and then checking to see if anyone seems to be noticing you. I've had clients who practice TFT on elevators, standing in line at the grocery store, even driving their car. I think you'll find your own way of using it that will be comfortable to you." The session ended as Maria decided that nothing could be worse than the pain she had lived with for so many months. She determined to give TFT a good trial in the next week.

"I DID THE TAPPING PROBABLY 20 OR 30 TIMES A DAY IN THE beginning," Maria said after seating herself for our third meeting. "But you know, I didn't mind like I thought I would because my pain is so much better. It's probably half of what it was when I first came here. My husband can't believe it. I'm having a hard time believing it myself. How could this help me when all the doctors couldn't?"

Skepticism can arise with the use of any technique that is linked to dramatic improvement, yet it seems particularly prevalent with TFT. In Maria's case, we could not prove that her increased comfort was the direct result of TFT because she had started the Pilates program at about the same time. Experts have offered their own explanations of how to demonstrate that the benefits of TFT reach beyond placebo and distraction.[6] In talking with Maria, I simply suggested that we monitor the changes over time to find out whether TFT would be of lasting value to her.

After our discussion, we began our focus on the remaining discomfort she had been aware of during the week in her neck/shoulder/arm area. As Maria tuned into her experience of that place in her body, she reported a different experience from the previous session:

> M: I'm noticing that my arm and shoulder don't really bother me any-more. Right now, it's the left side of my neck that is the problem. It's a sharp, dull ache that feels like it's pressing downward. At the same time, the pressure is also moving up my neck into my head.
> MP: What thoughts go along with these feelings?
> M: I'm thinking about sadness, like I might be about to cry but I don't know why.
> MP: Stay with that and let me know if any more information comes to you about the sadness.
> M: I'm thinking about my little girls and how scared they were after the accident. They weren't with me in the car, thank goodness, but they knew something was wrong with Mommy and they were really worried that I wasn't going to be OK.
> MP: Of course, that was upsetting to you. Do you think you're feeling sad about your daughters and what they went through, or could you be sad about something else for you?
> M: (*Pause*) I'm not sure. . . . I mean, I guess I feel sad about losing all this time out of my life, all this time with them (*sobbing*) . . . that

hurts. I'm missing almost a year of their childhood. I feel so useless at home because I just haven't had the energy to be the mother I'm used to being. I have to keep working to pay the bills, but going to all my doctor appointments is so exhausting. And now there's Pilates twice a week. I just don't have the energy to go to events at school, or make them breakfast, or pack their lunches, or make their costumes for dance class. That's really awful for them and me.

MP: It seems like your sadness is related to a sense of grief and loss. Is there any previous loss that could be related to this? Any accident earlier in your life or in the life of a family member?

M: Well, my father was injured in the factory where he worked when I was about 8 or 9. I don't remember much about it except he sat in his big chair in the living room dressed in his bathrobe. It was a strange time in our family, but eventually he recovered and went back to work.

MP: As you tell me about this experience with your father, Maria, what do you notice about your sadness?

M: Now that you mention it, I can actually feel the sadness now. It's more than just a thought.

MP: OK. I think we need to treat your sadness at this point, so I'd like you to focus on that for a moment and then tell me about the physical sensations, emotional feelings, and thoughts that seem connected.

M: I feel this warm soft feeling behind my eyes. And I have a lump in my throat. I guess my father's injury must have affected me more than I thought.

Maria's feedback as she tuned into her body and its related thought fields led me to shift our direction to treat the sadness and grief that seemed linked to the physical discomfort in her neck. From any perspective, trauma that underlies or is related to a client's presenting symptoms can be complex. In addition to her physical pain, Maria now appeared to experience grief and sadness, for example. In other cases where trauma is a factor, issues of guilt, anger, shame, rage, and related psychological conflicts and emotions can be important aspects of the clinical picture and must be treated to achieve symptom resolution.

This kind of complexity usually requires additional tapping prescriptions to treat all of the important associated issues. As trauma becomes more complex, the TFT tapping also becomes more complex, since several energy meridians may be disrupted.[7] Like other kinds of therapy, including EMDR and hypnosis, TFT appears to work by identifying and treating one layer of the problem at a time, much like the process of peeling an onion.

This time, we began with muscle testing for major reversal, which we found and cleared. As Maria focused on her sadness, which she rated a 7, we worked through the TFT procedure for past trauma and grief. First, she tapped gently on the spot at the outside edge of her eyebrow and then again on her collarbone point while thinking about and feeling her sadness. When she rechecked her SUD measure, the number had gone down to 5. We then completed the 9 gamut sequence followed by tapping once more on the eyebrow and collarbone points. At this point, Maria reported that her sadness was still at 5 on her scale.

Since there was no change in her rating, I asked what she was aware of. "I'm feeling the sadness in my chest now. It's very heavy, kind of a deeper sadness, so I don't think the level decreased." Agreeing with her, I asked her to focus on the sensation in her chest and the thoughts that went with it, which was more of a qualitative change, while she completed the recurring psychological reversal sequence. As she rubbed the reflex point on the left side of her chest, I asked her to repeat out loud three times: "I accept myself deeply and completely even if it's not possible to resolve this sadness completely."[8]

After repeating the tapping sequences for the eyebrow and collarbone points and the 9 gamut treatment, Maria rescaled her sadness. This time, the number dropped to a 2. "I know it's still there but it isn't affecting me very much." We completed the eyeroll from floor to ceiling while Maria continually tapped the gamut spot on the back of her hand, and her SUD dropped to zero. I encouraged Maria to practice the pain and grief protocols during the week, keeping an open mind and a curious attitude about what she might notice related to her body pain.

Maria's pain levels continued to drop during the next few weeks. She told me that it had been very helpful for her to acknowledge and release some of the sadness she had felt about the impact of her recent car accident as well as the long-term effects of her father's injury during childhood.

She decided to end her work with me after five meetings. "I learned that I can control my pain and that is a wonderful gift. I can do the tapping whenever I need to feel relief, even at work. Now I feel confident that I can use the Pilates method to continue strengthening my body, including the areas that still react to the accident." Since Maria promised to contact me if the pain recurred and I have not heard from her, I assume that she is continuing to enjoy a successful recovery.

As Maria's story illustrates, TFT can be effective in relieving pain related to headaches, muscle tension, and other physical problems when symptom relief is appropriate.[9] Often, only a few sessions are needed. Usually, regular practice over time is needed for continued improvement. If there are complex issues involved, such as past trauma or multiple health problems, it is likely that more meetings may be required. It is also common for some people to require several TFT treatments given by a therapist before reaching a level of comfort and confidence that would promote successful self-treatment.

## Advantages of Treating Trauma with TFT

When there are sensitive issues related to past or current traumatic events that may be connected with the physical manifestations of health problems, TFT can be particularly useful. Unlike other approaches, which may trigger painful release of intense physical and emotional reactions related to a traumatic memory, TFT frequently allows the difficulties related to trauma to resolve without overwhelming disturbing emotions and body reactions. And, unlike other methods that require an individual to remember specifics of a traumatic incident, TFT tapping sequences seem effective with only a brief focus on whatever general thoughts, body sensations, or feelings are initially available.

These are distinct advantages with people who have had no previous therapy experience, who have limited resources to fund treatment, or who may be fearful of uncovering or exploring painful issues. Another important benefit is the ego-strengthening aspect of self-treatment. Since TFT is highly portable it can be used as many times as necessary to bring relief in a few minutes of time.

### NANCY, PART II: TREATING ADDICTIVE URGES

Nancy (see chapter 6, pp. 114–117), had several major issues that pulled her toward relapse. These included strong urges to use pot to change her mood, difficulty regulating strong feelings of anger and fear, and heightened awareness of conflicts with Norman, her live-in partner. Without pot, she noticed increased creative and sexual energy, more real connections with other people, better control over her diet and exercise, and increased optimism about the future. She continued to use her egg image to help her manage boundary issues but felt she needed something more to cope with the emotional struggles that threatened her precarious hold on abstinence.

Recalling that Nancy had used acupuncture effectively to help resolve acute physical pain related to a pulled muscle in her back, I discussed with her how TFT might work similarly with the energy systems in the body to resolve emotional pain and related addictive urges. Nancy was intrigued, telling me she had recently joined a class on energy rebalancing taught by a psychic and would like to know more about energy therapies. We decided on a trial with TFT.

Nancy was most bothered by the irritability she experienced without marijuana. "I feel like I'm constantly on edge with a lot of raw feelings that I can't get away from. I don't want to be inside my own skin. I snap at Norman and my son no matter what they do and seem to have no control over my behavior. It's like I'm turning into a monster. It's awful."

I asked Nancy to tune into her irritability at that moment and describe any sensations or emotional feelings that accompanied the thought field she had just described. She immediately responded that she felt like she was vibrating all over her body, could sense a tightness in her throat and stomach, and was aware that her breathing was very shallow, as if she could not catch her breath. As Nancy continued to tune into her irritability, she assessed her distress at a 7 out of 10 points on a SUD scale. We checked for, and cleared, a context or specific reversal before beginning the TFT protocol for anger.

I guided Nancy in tapping gently on the inside of her little finger at the base of its nail and then on the collarbone point while breathing normally and thinking/feeling her irritability. When she stopped and took a deep breath, she rescaled her irritability at a 5 SUD level. "It's still there but not as strong," she commented.

Since the SUD had dropped by two points, we went on to the 9 gamut treatment. Nancy tapped the "triple burner" or gamut point located on the back of her hand, while she moved her eyes, hummed a little tune, and counted aloud from one to five as directed. We then repeated the little finger and collarbone sequences. At that point, Nancy reevaluated her irritability at zero. Just to make sure, we completed the floor to ceiling eyeroll. The zero rating held.

We then tested our results as Nancy attempted to bring back the irritability. "I don't feel anything connected with the irritability," she said. "However, I'm thinking about the stress I feel a lot of the time when I want to smoke pot. Can we work on that?"

When working with TFT, it is common to move fairly quickly from the resolution of one symptom to awareness of another. This is often because disturbances along several different meridians may be contributing to a complex symptom—in this case, Nancy's addictive urges. In working with addictions, it is usually not adequate to treat the addictive cravings themselves, which tend to be anxiety-based. Related factors, such as depression, obsessive-compulsive qualities, social anxiety, and past trauma must also be considered and treated.[10]

Expecting and tracking these kinds of interrelationships with an open, flexible attitude is essential. I questioned Nancy further to determine whether what she was feeling would better fit the protocol for addictive urges, stress, or anxiety. She defined it as stress that sometimes led to an urge but was different than fear. I encouraged Nancy to tune into the stress she had felt in the past to find out how intensely she could activate her experiences of stress at the current moment. She described stress symptoms as shallow breathing, tightness in her chest, a racing pulse, scattered thoughts of confusion, and a "whimpery" feeling. She rated her stress "field" as 8 on the SUD.

She began tapping the points under the eye, under the arm, and on the collarbone. When asked to stop tapping and take a deep breath, Nancy rescaled her stress at 3 on the SUD. After completing the 9 gamut treatment, and repeating the eye, arm, and collarbone sequences, Nancy was amazed to find that her stress was down to a 1. The eyeroll from floor to ceiling while she tapped on her gamut spot brought her stress down to zero.

When I asked her to test the results by attempting to reactivate her feelings of stress, Nancy remarked, "I can't find those feelings anywhere now. I'm feeling very relaxed." We ended the session by discussing how she could practice using the TFT protocols for addictive urges along with those for stress, anxiety, and anger while she was on vacation with her son.

Five weeks later, Nancy delighted in sharing with me her pictures of the wonderful trip to Europe she had enjoyed with her son, Tim. An amateur photographer, she was pleased with how well the film had turned out. "Some of the best ones were taken by Tim," she said proudly. "He's already developing quite an eye. And since I've been back, I've been feeling closer to Norman."

She also had good news about her abstinence from pot. "I stayed pretty level emotionally. I thought about using pot, but my cravings passed quickly. Once or twice I rubbed that sore spot below my left collarbone and it seemed to help. Of course, I noticed the triggers we've already discussed before. I wanted to smoke the most when I was lonely, bored, or uncomfortable in some way but I got through those times without pot and I feel great about that."

SEVERAL MONTHS LATER, NANCY'S SUCCESS WAS SUDDENLY interrupted by a relapse when she smoked marijuana with an old friend at a party. On the positive side, she quickly saw the unhealthy impact of pot. She reported feeling small and emotionally flat, more vague and diffuse, and generally shut down. We agreed to use TFT to treat this setback.

As we explored what might be connected to her decision to smoke pot again, she described deep feelings of angst. "There are these creepy feelings. It's like I'm longing for something I'll never have. I want to numb those with pot because I don't know what else to do. They're almost unbearable." As she continued, she suddenly had an image. "I see myself as a baby all curled up like I can't bear to be alive. Now I also feel nausea and shortness of breath."

Because this description seemed to point to distressing reactions that Nancy recalled having from the time she was very young, the past trauma protocol seemed to be appropriate. And, because this symptom field appeared to be more primitive than others we had worked with, I decided to use the complex version. Nancy scaled her initial distress as a 9 on the SUD scale. Muscle testing did not indicate the presence of a psychological reversal.

When she had completed the complex past trauma prescription, Nancy told me that her emotional distress had dropped to a 3. "I had an image of putting my son Tim on his back when he was a baby so he could drop off to sleep. All I feel is just a small bit of the creepy feeling." Applying a mini-reversal by tapping the "karate chop" spot on the side of her hand and repeating the complex past trauma sequence brought her SUD value to zero. "This time while I was tapping, I had this image of me as a baby," she said. "I was patting her on her back and reassuring her that she was going to be OK. I feel relaxed and comfortable now."

Nancy was free from marijuana for another five months after these two TFT sessions. We occasionally used imagery to help her with boundary issues with family members and to help her continue to regulate successfully the distressing emotional reactions that continued to surface during her abstinence.

## TFT in More Complex Cases

TFT can be used effectively with many kinds of mindbody health issues in a relatively short time, as the stories of Maria and Nancy illustrate. In situations where psychological issues and medical issues interact to create complicated health conditions, however, more advanced TFT diagnostic and treatment skills may be needed, as Lauren's story suggests.

### LAUREN: FIBROMYALGIA, DEPRESSION, AND CHRONIC FATIGUE

"I doubt if you're going to be able to help me. So far, nobody has. But I don't know where else to go, so I'm contacting you. I'm in constant pain, both emotionally and physically. I've been in therapy for more than ten years and I've probably seen 12 different therapists. I was hospitalized for a week and diagnosed with major depression almost 20 years ago following the loss of my second pregnancy. Things got really bad for me after that. I started drinking heavily and abusing prescription medications, and then my marriage fell apart. I've been going to AA and have stayed sober for the past eight years. Antidepressants have helped for a little while but the bottom line is that I'm still depressed. Nothing seems to really take that away.

"For the last two years I haven't been able to work as a social worker because of fibromyalgia and anxiety attacks, which I have even in the middle of the night. I do a little childcare in exchange for room and board and to pay my bills but I won't be able to continue with that unless I can get relief from the fibromyalgia and the depression. Is there anything you can do to help me?"

TO ANSWER THAT QUESTION, IT WAS NECESSARY TO OBTAIN a more complete history. I learned from her most recent referring therapist that she seemed to have a mixed personality disorder and very disturbed experiences of attachment. With each therapist of any duration, Lauren seemed to develop an intense emotional dependency that involved reactions of rage and devastation during any type of separation. With her first therapist, whom she had seen for six years in twice a week psychodynamic therapy, Lauren had experienced painful reactions that appeared unresponsive to all interventions. Her current therapist believed she could no longer help Lauren and hoped that some of the energy therapies I used in my practice might be useful with the fibromyalgia pain and the atypical cycles of depression and anxiety that continued to plague her.

Lauren told me of her beliefs that the origin of her problems dated from infancy. She had been a premature baby and had difficulty taking nourishment. Separated from her mother and family for the first two weeks of life, she was not held by any family member. Her early childhood was affected by her mother's severe depression and a series of losses. Lauren had trouble adjusting to first grade and suffered from daily symptoms of school phobia for the first few years of public school. She also recalled ongoing emotional abuse by her father and sexual abuse by a male neighbor.

In short, Lauren's childhood development was impacted by the trauma of early loss, abuse, and physical frailty. In adolescence, she contracted hepatitis and almost died. Her adult health problems seemed to begin after a string of car accidents in her late twenties and early thirties that resulted in soft tissue damage and chronic pain, which she overmedicated with prescription medications and alcohol. Although the fibromyalgia was relatively recent, the pain seemed to follow the trauma of the loss of her second baby between 18 and 20 weeks of pregnancy. Lauren's tendency to somaticize her reactions to the significant losses that spanned her entire life was complicated by a defensive structure that tended to replicate traumatic bonding experiences and prevented her from forming helpful alliances with therapists.

With this kind of challenging complexity, I am clear with myself as well as with the client that we will explore every possible technique that offers the potential of bringing relief and resolution, *but only* following a time of sufficient assessment and alliance building. Lauren and I spent the first six months trying to forge a healthy relationship different from those with previous therapists.

Because she slipped in and out of despondent, suicidal cycles, we spent considerable time in the "S" stage of therapy, helping her to achieve inner and outer safety in the therapy situation as well as in her everyday life. This was complicated by episodes of destabilization that occurred every time we were separated by the travel demands of my teaching schedule. During this time, we used imagery for ego-strengthening because Lauren was very comfortable with imagery techniques and had regularly used guided imagery tapes in her daily recovery practices related to AA (Alcoholics Anonymous). We also explored her dreams, which were quite vivid and appeared to be rich with symbolic meaning. This approach worked quite well in helping her to feel more stable as well as more connected with me.

As she grew stronger emotionally, Lauren began to want to try new methods and was eager to learn more about the energy therapies that might help her. After discussing all of the approaches described in this book, Lauren decided she would like to explore EMDR to help her with her fibromyalgia pain and its related anxiety. We began using EMDR with positive target imagery to assess and expand her ego strength. After six sessions, she was able to form and sustain a positive connection with conflict-free and other types of resource images during repeated sets of eye movements. We then shifted to a focus on clinical target images linked to emotional and physical pain.

When working with clinical target images connected either to past trauma or current fibromyalgia pain, however, Lauren felt overwhelmed with anxiety and despair. Even though we used safeguards such as very short eye movement sets and appropriate interweaves, she seemed flooded by her emotional and somatic reactions. She reported an increase in depression, fibromyalgia pain, and nocturnal anxiety attacks related to nightmares. After extensive discussion, we decided to stop EMDR treatment and return to imagery for restabilization.

After reestablishing safety and stability in Lauren's functioning, we returned to the question of how to help her find relief for the chronic fibromyalgia pain in her legs, back, and neck. After reviewing various possibilities, we decided on a trial of TFT. Lauren had experienced acupuncture years ago following her car accident injuries. Although she had found it helpful, she did not have the money to continue beyond a few sessions. She was intrigued by another opportunity to work with the same meridian system in her body and also by TFT's self-therapy component.

Fibromyalgia pain from Lauren's right hip down to the knee had been acute for the last few weeks. When I asked her to focus on the pain, she described sharp pains in all the joints in her lower body, including hips, upper legs, and knees. Lauren estimated her pain at a 9 on a 10-point SUD scale.

Initial muscle testing indicated a massive psychological reversal. This was not surprising because her recent and past history indicated abundant evidence of *reversals* (times when her actions were the reverse of her intentions). We treated this by having her rub the reflex point on the left side of her chest and under her collarbone while repeating aloud three times the self-affirmation, "I deeply and completely accept myself with all of my problems and limitations." Subsequent muscle testing indicated that the reversal had been cleared.

We then began with the pain protocol. Lauren tapped the gamut spot on the back of her hand in between and just below the knuckles of her little and ring fingers approximately 50 times and then tapped the point just below her collarbone. When she stopped, took a deep breath and reassessed her pain, she reported that it was at a 6. We then completed the 9 gamut treatment followed by tapping the gamut spot and then the collarbone point. When Lauren again evaluated her pain level, it was a 4. "The pain is different now. It's concentrated in one spot in my right hip. But it's still at a 4," she explained.

Because the SUD rating did not shift further, I guided Lauren through a mini-psychological reversal treatment, asking her to tap on the "karate chop" side of her hand while repeating aloud three times, "I deeply and completely accept myself even though I still have some of this pain." This time Lauren's SUD rating was a 1. Following the floor to ceiling eyeroll, where Lauren tapped on the gamut spot while following my fingers with her eyes, the rating was a zero.

She was pleased that she had responded well but expressed strong skepticism that the results would last. I gave her a printed sheet with the pain protocol and asked her to practice on her own. I also gave her suggestions about TFT treatment related to the positive self-correction we were trying to develop. "I'm not surprised that you are worried that the good feelings you found today might go away. You've suffered a lot of loss in your life and you're afraid that this will bring another one. As you practice, I'd like you to focus on the idea that TFT can help you find feelings of relief by shifting your energy field related to the fibromyalgia again and again. Our energy systems are constantly changing. TFT offers you the same opportunity each time. The opportunity is to make a difference by using a few minutes of your time to follow the formula and find out how much change takes place."

At her second TFT session, Lauren said her pain was slightly better during the week and she felt a bit more hopeful. She wanted to go further so we used part of our next meeting to reinforce the results and increase her comfort and confidence with the technique.

Her pain configuration differed somewhat from the last session. As she attuned to her body, she reported pain in her lower body joints along with tightness and cramping on the left side of her neck. Lauren assigned a SUD level of 8 to her pain. When I conducted muscle testing to check for the presence of psychological reversal, Lauren 's arm muscle weakened when she thought about or imagined herself pain free. We corrected the reversal by having her rub the reflex point in her left chest while repeating three times the affirmation, "I completely and deeply accept myself *whether or not* I still have this pain."

When we refocused on her body to begin the pain protocol, Lauren noticed that her pain level was still at 8 but that she was also aware of emotional pain. "I feel this deep grief," she told me. "The grief often comes with the physical pain. It feels like it comes from a very young place."

Based on her feedback, we shifted to the past trauma complex protocol, which also works for grief. Following the floor to ceiling eyeroll, Lauren's SUD was at zero. "It's amazing that my grief disappeared so quickly. I know it will return but at least I can do the tapping when it does." She agreed to use the past trauma/grief complex protocol when feelings of grief accompanied her fibromyalgia pain.

Several months intervened before our next TFT session. During this interval, Lauren experienced several setbacks in external life circumstances. We agreed on the use of supportive therapy and a return to imagery for restabilization purposes. During this time, she acknowledged that her fibromyalgia pain had fluctuated along with her stress and depression levels. She told me that she used the TFT protocols from time to time and the positive results helped her to feel steadier about the state of her general health. "At least I feel like there's something I can do to help myself," she told me. It was clear to both of us, however, that the fibromyalgia pain persisted and would require continued treatment[11] as soon as other priorities allowed a return to TFT.

We then began a series of four extremely frustrating TFT sessions. Although we continued to identify and clear reversals and to lower her subjective pain levels, Lauren continued to report intrusive feelings of grief, anger and rage, which did not respond to the complex trauma/grief and rage protocols. Even though there was slight improvement, Lauren commented, "I think I could bring all of my symptoms back fairly quickly. The pain in my hips and knees is starting to come back right now and the anger and grief are right behind it."

These four TFT sessions followed a similar pattern, with anger and grief reactions interacting with physical pain to form a formidable maze of unresolving obstacles. Although Lauren generally had a positive response to the prescribed protocols, the constant recurrence of her symptoms left her feeling discouraged. In evaluating our progress, we discussed the possibility of assessment to determine whether what kinesiologists call electromagnetic "polarity switching" might be present.

*From a TFT and kinesiologist perspective, this type of* **neurological disorganization** *or* **switching**[12] *can occur when a client demonstrates symptoms that include physical clumsiness and awkwardness, reversals of letters and words, reversing left and right spatial orientations, and saying the opposite of what is meant.* Lauren believed that she demonstrated all of these difficulties and I had personally observed several of them. Neurological disorganization or switching can interfere with muscle testing, so that problems are not detected or are misidentified, and therefore cannot be treated.

The TFT prescription for neurological disorganization is collarbone breathing exercises. This involves a strange and complex formula of 40 separate exercises. Collarbone breathing involves placing the tips of the left index and middle fingers on the spot under the left collarbone while tapping on the gamut spot on the back of the left hand with the index and middle fingers of the right hand. While tapping, the client follows five different breathing patterns. This sequence is repeated with the left fingers under the right collarbone. Next, the knuckles of the right index and middle fingers are placed under the left collarbone and then under the right collarbone following the same tapping and breathing patterns. Finally, the entire process is repeated using the index and middle finger knuckles of each hand to stimulate the collarbone points.

At the next session, after discussing issues related to Lauren's transfer to a new psychiatrist, we began with a focus on the current symptom that registered in her awareness—a feeling of sadness with a lump in her throat that radiated through the neck and shoulders accompanied by a general feeling of heaviness. This was scaled as 8 SUD. We conducted muscle testing, which indicated a psychological reversal, which we then cleared. We then completed the grief/past trauma protocol. When she stopped to reassess her sadness, the SUD rating was 7.

At this juncture, I led her through the collarbone breathing treatment. When Lauren stopped to reassess, her sadness had dropped to 5 and she reported feeling more well-being. "If this feeling would last, I could live with my symptoms," she said. Because we were out of time for the session, we stopped the TFT and Lauren agreed to add the collarbone breathing sequence on her own to the protocols she was using. As she left, she told me, "A wave of sadness just came back. I'll practice on my own but I think we need to go through the entire sequence next time."

This minor success was followed by the frustrating return of her symptoms. Several times of practicing the collarbone breathing sequence along with prescriptions for reversals and other appropriate protocols provided a lowering of symptoms, followed by an immediate resurgence. At this point, I decided to seek consultation, because I felt I had gone as far as I could with my training in TFT. Through referral, I called Dr. Stephen Daniel, a psychologist and TFT practitioner who specializes in fibromyalgia pain. During our conversation, Daniel explained that some clients are so sensitive that they cannot be adequately diagnosed and treated using basic TFT protocols. In these cases, the most advanced level of diagnosis is provided through voice technology, an approach developed by Roger Callahan, which permits treatment over the telephone through analysis of the client's voice. Only a handful of practitioners are trained in this procedure and Daniel is in this group.

According to Dr. Daniel, people who do not respond to standard TFT treatment often suffer more intensely from reactions to toxins found in ingested foods and environmental chemicals such as pesticides or laundry detergents. The substance causes a toxic effect on the body's energy systems so that they do not respond normally to TFT protocols. Voice technology provides a means of detecting and eliminating the negative agent.

Although voice technology has not been experimentally validated, Daniel and his colleagues who use VT claim high success rates. It is expensive initially, since clients must pay for a block of time in advance. One advantage is, however, that clients are given almost immediate access to the practitioner via a pager number so that help is available while the problem is occurring.

When I explained the details of voice technology and reviewed the printed literature with Lauren, she was hesitant. After much consideration, she decided she did not have the extra money to devote to a trial of VT. Instead, she opted to work with her new psychiatrist, who treated her with a medication regime that brought better pain relief.[13] She continued to use TFT protocols to bring intermittent relief and a sense of symptom relief that she could regulate herself.

After moving to a more supportive living situation and reaching full stabilization on her new medications and supplements, however, Lauren was ready to try VT. Dr. Daniel explained that during our first phone session, arranged in advance, he would analyze Lauren's voice patterns related to her main issues, fibromyalgia pain currently focused in both knees, depression, and grief related to past trauma. The readings he received would determine the prescribed tapping sequences. During four minutes of phone consultation, Lauren responded to his questions and copied down a series of meridian points. She was instructed to call him immediately through his pager if she experienced any return of symptoms. We then terminated the phone call and I led her through the tapping sequences. As we finished, Lauren commented, "I'm feeling different. It's as if I'm trying to find the pain and the grief but I can't right now. I want to have my normal reactions but I'm not having them."

I WISH I COULD REPORT THAT LAUREN'S SYMPTOMS RESOLVED after the first few sessions of voice technology, but this was not the case. She has found Dr. Daniel an able ally in attempting to solve the complex puzzle of her emotional and physical pain. She continues to follow the lengthy tapping sequences he prescribes and is in the process of making other recommended changes. These involve eliminating possible sources of ingested and environmental toxins, removing wheat, soy, and corn from her diet, stopping her 22-year cigarette habit, and changing her laundry detergent. Dr. Daniel believes these are possible toxins that may be contributing to the elaborate reversals that block her progress and prevent her gains from holding over time.

At this writing, Lauren remains cautiously optimistic that TFT will help her consolidate and maximize the progress she has worked hard to make during three years of treatment with me and 10 years of previous therapy. During the time she has employed voice technology, her SUD ratings for fibromyalgia have dropped about 3 points overall, and her depression has improved slightly. Perhaps more importantly, she believes that the extent of the problems she has battled most of her life has been validated and that every attempt is being made to repair them: "Even if we haven't completely resolved my problems, I have a good team working with me. And I know I'm getting a lot healthier. That makes me feel good about myself, which has got to be helping!"

# 9

# Giving the Body its Due:
# Body-Focused Psychotherapy

ERICA: SOMATIC EXPERIENCING AND HYPNOSIS FOR PAIN
FROM RHEUMATOID ARTHRITIS

Erica grimaced in pain as she took her seat. A friend had referred her as a demonstration volunteer for one of my workshops. The hope was that I could help her reduce the excruciating daily pain she lived with as part of her degenerative rheumatoid arthritic condition. Erica was skeptical that any lasting relief was possible. "But I'll try anything," she told me. "I'm very frightened of ending up in a wheelchair. This disease is so unpredictable. Anything could happen."

Two of Erica's family members had struggled with the same disease. Her grandmother lived to be an active 98 years old and only her hands were significantly affected by arthritis. Her aunt, however, began her fight with the condition at 55 and died 33 years later, totally handicapped and dependent on others to care for her basic needs, living out her final days confined to the dreaded chair.

Erica's worst pain was in the joints of her fingers, both wrists, her knees, ankles, and shoulders. She had had surgeries on both wrists, which helped with the pain. Her right ankle had recently undergone a breakdown and was responding to cortisone injections, though the prognosis was uncertain, as the effectiveness of cortisone was likely to taper off.

Erica was most frightened of losing her ability to walk. Surgery was an option to help strengthen the joint but would most likely produce stiffness as well.

Erica coped with her chronic pain by performing an hour or more of daily exercises and using hot compresses on her joints. Bed rest, elevation, and warmth were also helpful in managing discomfort. But her greatest relief was derived from cortisone injections, which brought relief after 6 to 8 hours and full recovery of mobility in a few days. Erica smiled as she described her slow, methodical return to comfort: "I test my ankle on the floor. If I step on it, that ankle has to hold my weight. Otherwise, I might fall. If the ankle feels strong, I feel sheer happiness. It's like being born again. I can carry my own weight, be independent. That's a feeling I'd like to have without the shots."

Because I was to have only one brief meeting with Erica in a workshop setting, I talked with her for a few minutes privately ahead of time to discuss our options. Not wanting to stimulate more internal reactions than we could integrate in a short time, I recommended that we find a way to help her body reveal its resources for healing, which she could then use on her own after the workshop.

Erica was interested in this plan because it made sense within our time frame while fitting her needs. I explained briefly the model and techniques I would be using and elicited her promise to give me feedback about her progress after the workshop.

The first step in the somatic experiencing (SE) model, as with any body-focused approach, is to establish a focus on the body that is experiential. SE focusing is similar to the focusing method of Eugene Gendlin, who developed the term "felt sense"[1] to help clients tune into their body experience. Although difficult to define in words, somatic focusing achieves body awareness through a feeling sense rather than a mental perception or intellectual understanding of the body.

To experience the felt sense, there must be connection with an internal body experience. As I explained to one of my clients who has a dissociative disorder and is massively disconnected from his body, there is a big difference between feeling your foot inside your shoe and having a sense of how your foot is feeling inside your shoe. As I started to work with Erica, my first goal was to help her develop a felt sense of her entire body, including the areas that were impacted by arthritis.

As soon as Erica had settled into her position at the front of the room and we had presented an overview of her arthritis condition to the group, I began to guide her into a felt sense of her body[2] at that moment:

I'd like you to close your eyes and tune into what you can feel in different parts of your body right now. Feel the way your body is supported by the chair . . . feel the way your feet rest on the floor . . . get a sense of what you feel under your skin, below its surface, in your arms . . . your shoulders . . . your hands and fingers . . . your hips . . . your knees . . . your feet. As you feel these places, do you feel more comfortable or less so? Just let your head move yes or no. (*Erica's head nods slightly.*) Good. . . . Now, do you feel energy moving in your body in any particular way? Quickly or slowly, in any particular direction, just feel it happening and notice what it feels like. Is there any kind of rhythm to the movement of energy in your body? Does it feel tingling, tight, loose, heavy, light, warm, cool, electric, or some other way? Take your time and stay with this moving flow. Do the feelings get stronger, weaker, or stay the same? . . . Let me know when you're ready to share some of what you feel in your body with me.

Erica was able to tell me that she felt a familiar constriction in her right ankle and a little wave of fear. That was followed by tingling in her lower body that felt like a pleasant current of energy flowing through her legs. She found that she could make the current stronger by focusing her attention on it. As it increased, the energy flow felt even more pleasant, reminding her of the strength and force of electrical current. Establishing this kind of felt sense of the body accomplishes several things:

- The felt sense establishes a connection to the body that is rich and complex.
- The felt sense helps us shift away from trying to control the body and into an instinctual state of "being."
- The felt sense taps into a flowing stream of life energy. We begin to resonate with this energy stream with curiosity and openness.
- By shifting the body focus as directed, we begin to learn how to regulate troublesome or intense sensations and how to welcome positive ones.

Just by following the felt sense of body experience from moment to moment, we will naturally encounter spontaneous images, intriguing sensations, and surprising remnants of past events that can be used as aids to healing. Most of the time, I simply track or follow the rhythms of the felt sense until one or more of these resources organically appears.

An alternative is to use other methods to tap into the felt sense stream of awareness. Since my demonstration with Erica was part of a workshop on hypnosis, I requested her permission to set up ideomotor finger signals because I felt this method might help us find somatic resources more efficiently.[3]

After setting up the signals, I asked whether Erica's unconscious could connect her with some aspect of her body experience that might help with her arthritis. When her yes finger moved, Erica immediately described a feeling of calm in her upper body followed by an image of her grandmother. "She's walking along the streets looking healthy and strong. She looks like she has a moderate amount of energy—she's not running or walking briskly, but then, she's in her mid-eighties. She looks satisfied and happy with her life."

I asked Erica to continue to focus on the image and to tell me what she noticed. "Grandmother is a wonderful model for me. She managed her own life. She didn't give up or give into the pain (*sobbing*). I'm so glad I knew her."

From the SE viewpoint, the image of grandmother is an archetypal expression of biological energy. Because the energy exists in the way the imagery links it to the nervous system rather than in the content of image itself, it is important to create an environment where the client can resonate fully with somatic resources and the energy links that begin to emerge. SIBAM (see introduction to this section) provides a model for a full cycle of connection, which generally leads to homeostasis in the nervous system.

I asked Erica what she noticed as she focused on and described the image of grandmother. "I'm thinking that grandmother managed her own life by staying in charge of it. I'm the manager of my own life like grandmother. I made a decision shortly after the arthritis started, when my daughter was six months old, that I wasn't going to be a burden to her as I got older. I'm determined to stay in charge and I have, every step of the way."

Here, Erica spontaneously connects with the memory of an important decision she made at the start of her battle with arthritis. I asked her what else she noticed as she explored the fullness of that decision inside of her. "There's a warm sensation in my right ankle. It's a feeling of freedom and vitality. That feeling is somehow going to lead me to more freedom in the future. And that's the ankle I'm worried about right now in my life. Curious, but I don't feel worried, I feel very calm and sure."

In response to my simple invitation to explore her felt sense, Erica has retrieved an image of grandmother, the memory of an empowering deci-

sion and other elements of meaning, along with important emotional feelings and body sensations that are dynamic and flowing. In short, Erica
has moved through a complete cycle of SIBAM to experience sensation,
imagery, behavioral movement, affect, and meaning.

We could have stopped the demonstration there with a full moment
of wholeness. Because she mentioned the future, however, and because I
believe strongly that more complete integration occurs when there is a
positive future orientation related to the presenting problem, I asked Erica
to imagine where her right ankle might lead her in the next few weeks.
She reported being aware of small movements in her ankle that were
very invigorating, like bubbles. When I suggested she imagine what three
months from now might bring, Erica described a little discomfort. "It's
one of those times when I've been active. It doesn't mean anything except
that I probably need a bit more rest than usual."

I then asked her to fantasize even further in the future. "I'm thinking
about one year from now and I feel some tension in the middle of my
ankle. It's like some of my fear is coming back." I directed her to continue
focusing on that future time and consider how her experience of grandmother might be useful. "Grandmother is there walking beside me," she
exclaimed tearfully. "Of course, she will be there with me. I see her and
feel her presence now. I just needed to take her with me, to make her
part of my future. My ankle is fine now."

These subtle, undramatic shifts are the hallmark of the SE model. They
are easily and thoroughly integrated at the physical level as well as at
emotional, spiritual, and cognitive ones. After hundreds of these kinds of
sessions over the years, I have come to take for granted the consistent
discovery of somatic resources that are precisely what is needed to promote permanent healing change.

I received a letter from Erica a year after our meeting. She wrote that
she is still imagining the small bubbles that surfaced in the demonstration
carrying the disease away from her ankle and body. "I continue to give
myself suggestions about my grandmother . . . that she is with me with
her strength and optimism. . . . Thank you for giving me this chance of
working with myself in a different way." Along with hydrotherapy and
other treatment, Erica has used the SE experience to generate more confidence and to support greater muscle strength and mobility.

## Somatic Experiencing and Trauma

Somatic experiencing and focusing can be useful for anyone who could
benefit from a fuller connection with the body felt sense. However, because of its theoretical basis in animal biology,[4] this model is particularly

effective for healing trauma as it is stored in the body. Levine has had extensive experience in working with the entire spectrum of traumatizing events, including prenatal and childbirth stressors, accidents, natural disasters, injuries, surgeries, and invasive medical procedures, as well as childhood trauma, violence, and combat and hostage situations. His work is based on the understanding that much as animals draw on instinctive solutions to improve their chances of survival, we human beings also respond to danger by instinctual, and often unconscious, decisions to make use of the resources inside us as well as those around us.

Although the biological fight or flight response to trauma has been well documented, Levine's work has also focused on the immobility or "shock" response that is our most primitive defense and is generated by the reptilian brain.[5] When fight or flight reactions are blocked or thwarted, which is so often the case in human trauma, the organism instinctively constricts as it approaches the freezing, or immobility, response. If the traumatized individual can somehow shift into flight or counterattack to resolve the danger, traumatic symptoms will be minimal. But if the initial constriction continues, unreleased rage, terror, and helplessness can build until these drives overwhelm the nervous system, triggering massive immobility and inward collapse. This freezing response not only results in extensive constriction of the body's musculature and entire organ systems, but can also trigger emotional numbing and other forms of psychological dissociation.

While animals can move out of shock or immobility states in a matter of minutes or hours, humans sometimes never fully recover. This may be because of the many competing demands in our environments or because our complex neocortex thinking brains override our more primitive instincts, which is not the case for animals.

The good news is that the biological drive to resolve the immobility response is still active, no matter how long the freezing has been in place. Levine has proposed the *renegotiation* of shock/immobility as well as fight/flight responses by tracking and rebalancing these primitive reactions as they manifest through our felt sense of body experience.

The SE model postulates that there are two vortexes of energy that must be navigated. The first is the **trauma vortex**, *which has been created by a breach in what Freud has termed the stimulus barrier, which protects the organism against being overwhelmed by traumatizing stimuli.*[6] Fortunately, a countervortex of healing energy is immediately created. This acts to counterbalance the effects of the trauma.

In order to achieve healing, the therapist must help the traumatized person to *renegotiate the traumatic event and its related reactions by moving slowly back and forth, or* **pendulating**, *between trauma and healing energies,* *gradually integrating them until their energies are released and transformed.*

When renegotiation does not take place in the body, health problems and somatic symptoms may result. Unresolved shock/immobility responses can also explain some of the complications that can arise following surgery and other types of medical procedures that are often traumatizing to the body. It is likely that persistent shock responses also may be related to many psychological difficulties that result from unresolved trauma and can block somatic healing, including severe dissociation.

### JAMIE, PART I: HAND INJURY FROM A CAR ACCIDENT

"I'm living with the nightmare that my body is no longer intact and nothing can change that," Jamie told me quietly as he fumbled with the brace that encased his left hand. "This hand will always look different from my other hand. I want to cover it up. I can hardly bear to look at it because the scars remind me of my defectiveness, of how I couldn't protect myself."

Jamie's injury was the result of a car accident that took place at twilight when he was driving back from dropping off his son at a friend's vacation home after a week of backpacking together in the mountains. No other car was involved in the crash, and Jamie's theory was that he must have dozed off from fatigue at the end of a long drive, though he had no clear memory of what happened.

The car had rolled over off the road and into a ravine. Jamie had been trapped with the full weight of the car on his hand, which had somehow escaped out the driver's window when that side of the car upended as it came to rest. Although Jamie was rescued in a few minutes thanks to a passerby with a cell phone, he was overwhelmed by his ordeal six months later.

After two surgeries on his hand, it remained sore and misshapen. Jamie grieved the losses brought about by his limitations. "I can't type, play my guitar, go rock climbing with my kids, even tie my own shoes. . . . In a million ways, my life will never be the same."

We reviewed multiple options for treatment. I explained the SE model to Jamie and we discussed the benefits in helping him resolve biological and psychological shock responses. Because his healing process would be lengthy, involving multiple surgeries, I also presented EMDR, hypnosis, imagery, and TFT as other energy tools that might be helpful at different junctures. For this session, we decided to use SE to help him resolve some of the shock and immobility reactions I had observed in his body.

I asked him to focus on his hand and tell me what he could feel (i.e., his felt sense). "It's a claw. It's smaller, constricted, squeezed. The fingers are permanently bent. It looks defective, weird. . . . "

I interrupted Jamie at this point, because his responses seemed to indicate hyperactivation in his nervous system and I wanted to prevent traumatic flooding. I also noticed that he appeared stuck in a visual channel and I wanted to redirect him to other elements of SIBAM so that we could expand his constricted processing. "OK, Jamie, let's pause for a moment. As you are aware of the visual appearance of your hand, what do you feel inside emotionally and in your body?"

"It's like all the air has gone out of my lungs. My chest is tight. I feel very sad and exposed. I don't like people seeing this part of me. When I sit in the waiting room before my hand therapy appointment, I look at the other people there. I envy the ones whose hands look normal."

Again, I acted to slow down Jamie's associations by reviewing them as a type of summary. I also noted that when he moved into visual processing of internal representations, he began to detach from, or uncouple, possible resources that might be found in other components of the SIBAM model.

"Jamie, let's stop again. As you began to explore your feelings inside, you began to connect with tightness in your chest, then sadness, shame at being exposed and finally envy. What is it like for you to feel all those feelings?"

"It's overwhelming," he said. "I'm also feeling some guilt because my brother lost his leg 20 years ago in a bus accident. I mean, I'm so lucky compared to him. I feel really awful that I'm making such a big deal of this."

Because Jamie appeared to be moving further into the trauma vortex by activating this memory, I wanted to balance this response by heading toward the countervortex of healing energy. "Jamie, as you describe this, it sounds like it's part of your grief, that you and your brother have both had to go through such terrible ordeals. How do you feel about the way your brother has handled his handicap?"

"He's been a trouper. Really graceful with it. He told me once that he had learned some valuable lessons about himself. In a way, he's more positive than he used to be before the accident. I guess it changed him for the better. . . . I guess that possibility is there for me, too," he finished softly.

After a long silence where I sensed that he was integrating several levels of meaning, past and present, Jamie opened his eyes. "I feel OK," he said. As we tracked some of the shifts that had taken place during the session, I pointed out that color had returned to his face, neck and arms, which had been almost white when we had started. Jamie added that he also felt different, more centered and whole.

At the next session, Jamie shared several healing insights. Yet he still felt burdened by a feeling of shame. "How could I let this happen to me? I've always been so capable, so aware. How could I have spaced out while I was driving? I used to have a sense of being OK in the world. I want that back."

As we continued talking, it became clear that Jamie was not able to extricate himself from feelings of self-blame and guilt. He also had some questions about how the accident had happened because there were gaps in his memory. I suggested that we begin by reconstructing a narrative about that event to help him reconnect to himself more fully.

J: I started off at about 7:00 P.M. I had just dropped off my son and it wasn't dark yet. I still had about four hours to drive to get back home. I brought out a tape I wanted to listen to while I drove along. I had good, healthy food in the cooler. I thought to myself, "This has worked before for me on long drives."

MP: What's happening inside you as you tell me this, Jamie?

J: I'm feeling good, like I'm taking care of myself. I'm thinking that I'm fine but I'm dreading it, too. I'm feeling tired. It's a two-lane straight road and it's stretching out a long way ahead of me.

MP: And as you notice all those reactions what happens next?

J: I feel this tension in my body. I'm thinking that I have a long way to go. I'm holding a container of food and the wheel of the car and I'm feeling tired, more tired than I can ever remember feeling when I'm driving.

MP: OK, just notice the tension and the tiredness.

J: Then I feel this startle. I lose control of the car. I can't believe I can't get out of this . . . it's like the car is doing its own thing. The wheel is turning but it's not doing anything to move the car. . . . *(Jamie's breathing is shallow and fast and his pupils are dilating, signs of shock, and an indication that he is activating trauma energies. My next moves are to steer him to some stabilizing resources.)*

MP: All right, Jamie. Let's slow this down as if we were able to replay it in slow motion. You feel a sudden startle . . . then you begin to lose control of the car . . . you can't believe that you can't get out of this . . . the car is doing its own thing . . . the wheel is turning but it's not turning the car. . . . Just notice how you are working hard to turn that wheel. Notice your hard work.

J: Yes, it's like something took over. Both my arms are braced hard.

MP: That's right, Jamie. Some good instincts inside you took over. Your arms are working hard to hold onto the car. They know what to do even without your thinking about it. How is that for you?

J: It's good for me to see that I'm doing all I can.

MP: That's right, it *is* good for you to see that you're doing all you can.

J: But then, oh my God, something bad is going to happen. I have to hold on for dear life . . . I'm spinning . . . I'm in shock. . . .

MP: And as these thoughts and awarenesses are going through your mind, what else are you aware of right now?

J: I'm feeling like *everything* is wrecked, everything is wrecked. I'm turned upside down now. . . .

MP: And as you feel like everything is wrecked and you're upside down, what is happening in your body right now?

J: (*Pause*) There are these little impulses in my legs like little electric shocks. I'm stiff, I'm frozen, just hanging there. . . .

MP: Jamie, really feel those little impulses in your legs like little shocks of energy. Notice that even while the rest of you feels frozen, there are those important little currents of energy . . .

J: Yes. . . . I'm just holding on, that's all I can do. I remember my hand goes out the window somehow. Then there's a blank. . . .

MP: What's happening now, Jamie?

J: I'm looking at my hand      I can't believe it. I feel horror. I just hope they can fix it. . . . My glasses went flying. . . . I'm thinking about my cell phone. . . .

MP: So many awarenesses go through your mind . . . your hand, your horror, and your hope for it . . . and then what are you aware of?

J: I know people are there now. They're taking care of me. I feel so vulnerable . . . the nurse cut my wedding ring off . . . the paramedics are so warm, like I'm a little kid and they know I need them and it's OK. I remember later in the helicopter, I wanted their names because I wanted to stay connected with them. They stayed with me longer than they needed to.

MP: As you recall how all these people took care of you and stayed with you and it was OK, what happens inside right now?

J: I'm letting go a little more . . . I feel how scared I was. I'm holding onto them because it's all I can do . . . I'm letting the rest of my body hold onto them too. I feel connected now to all of me and to the nurses and the paramedics (*gestures to the left*).

MP: And over on the left near your left hand and arm?

J: Yes, that's where they are. I feel their warmth in the left side of my body. . . . And in the middle, my arm is in the hands of a doctor in San Francisco where they flew me. I'm thinking, "OK, you're it. Whatever you can do for me. I need it all."

MP: And how is that for you there in the middle?

J: OK if I lean toward that place on the left. That feels like where I first started healing.

MP:  Good. And you have discovered a great many things while we've been exploring, Jamie. You've discovered that at the heart of all of this is your commitment to being a good dad. You drove your son to stay with his friend even though it was far out of your way and you were exhausted. You took care of yourself with tapes and food and then, even after that first startle response, something took over and your arms worked hard to turn the wheel and then brace hard when you saw the car was not responding. And when you found yourself suspended in the car, you gathered your awareness to notice what was happening, what help was coming. . . . And then you found so much important healing with the paramedics and the nurses, with some of the doctors. And you learned you could shift within your body to find what was needed, on the inside, on the outside, and bring what was healing on the outside to the inside, and from the inside back outside, and from the left to the right. . . . And now where are you?

J:  (*Long pause*) While you were talking, I was thinking that this whole thing started with my decision to be really present. I was present with my son and we had a wonderful experience in the wilderness. Nothing can change that. And I honored what he needed, to go be with his friend, and I'm glad I did. And I did take pretty good care of myself and I let help from others really make a difference. I feel really good right now. At peace. I'm not so shattered inside. I can look at my hand and I still feel good.

The somatic experiencing sessions helped to stabilize Jamie as well as to promote integration of the injury that had been so fragmenting physically as well as psychologically and spiritually. My work with Jamie also incorporated other energy healing approaches, especially hypnosis. The second part of Jamie's story is told in chapter 11.

Jamie's work demonstrates some of the ways that an SE approach can promote somatic healing. It is particularly effective in helping individuals to integrate aspects of their experience that have been either overwhelming or unavailable due to the coupling dynamics in the nervous system as well as various psychological factors.

In Jamie's first SE experience, we were able to help him both begin to form a different relationship with his hand and body and to work through some of his grief and other trauma-related emotions of guilt, shame, and envy. This was accomplished through gentle reconnection of the SIBAM elements and by tracking and rebalancing the healing and trauma energies related to the aftereffects of the accident. During our second session,

Jamie was able to reconnect with his initial reactions when his car spun out of control and the time period immediately following the collision when he first received medical attention. We were able to retrieve several important external and internal resources that promoted deeper feelings of wholeness and well-being and a more positive sense of self.

Many people with acute or chronic health symptoms that are not related to traumatic events may also benefit from an SE approach, which allows them to achieve a fuller sense of body awareness, a more positive felt physical sense, and the discovery of important inner resources that can help promote healing. Erica, for example, was able to connect with the important life model of her grandmother's style of coping with arthritis, which helped to alleviate her debilitating fears of a helpless future.

Other people with physical symptoms that are not degenerative, as Erica's are, and that have a stronger psychological rather than an organic basis may be able to resolve their symptoms in a session or two of somatic experiencing. I believe this is because many of these individuals have disconnected from their bodies and the innumerable healing possibilities contained within their physical selves.

SE is one of the most powerful, yet subtle, methods I know of for reconnecting with our body selves. As we have noted many times throughout this book, there are many other paths that lead to the same destination. EMDR, TFT, hypnosis, and imagery can also be used to achieve similar benefits. Yet the SE model is unique in offering an understanding of the biology of healing that starts with the body and flows toward the mind, heart, and spirit. It is an invaluable tool for any healing endeavor.

## Collaboration with a Bodyworker

Since I have begun to collaborate with Alan van Winkle, certified bodyworker (see the introduction to this section), I have expanded both the scope and effectiveness of my work with somatic issues. When Alan and I work together, especially if trauma is an issue, we begin by discussing our ground rules so that we can create a secure working situation for all three of us (see Appendix C).

Our next step is to begin gentle body awareness experiences that occur while the client, always fully clothed, is lying on a mat. Alan helps to facilitate these by touching specific areas in the extremities of the body, *always* only after obtaining the client's verbal permission.

During the safety and stability stage, we attempt to stimulate body awareness and a positive felt sense by first establishing a safe place in the body. Usually, we ask the client to lie quietly for a few moments while tuning into the body, letting us know about areas of comfort as well as places where there is tension or discomfort. If clients have difficulty with this step, we guide them through a structured body scan.

We then ask the client to identify a specific area of the body that seems just a little more comfortable than the rest of the body. We ask for a description and then for permission to expand the comfortable location so that it becomes a stable safe place in the body.

## NANCY, PART III: ADDICTION RELAPSE

Nancy (see chapter 6, pp. 114–117, and chapter 8, pp. 155–158) had been using imagery to help her feel a deeper sense of security and safety and TFT to help her manage negative emotional reactions in ways other than using marijuana. Although she had achieved a brief period of abstinence, she pulled several muscles in her lower back while exercising that triggered a return to marijuana.

As we discussed how to work with this setback, I mentioned that I collaborated with a bodyworker and described the different benefits that this type of work had provided some of my other clients. I suggested that adding Alan to our sessions might help her to resolve her injury while also helping us to understand how body issues were related to her addiction. Nancy had enjoyed regular sessions of massage therapy and had recently begun acupuncture. She readily agreed that focus on the body at this point in our work might be a good step.

At Nancy's first somatic therapy session, we discussed the ground rules that applied in our work together and shared a physical health history with Alan that included information about her recent injury. Then we began to establish a safe place in her body. As she lay on the mat, it was fairly easy for Nancy to tune into her body and to describe her felt sense: "I feel sort of a buzzy feeling in my head and some shooting pains in my shoulder and upper back. There's a cramped feeling in my left hip and lower back and a clenched feeling in my stomach. My legs and feet seem OK, but there's a buzzy feeling along the left side of my body."

When we asked her to identify the most comfortable areas in her body, Nancy immediately designated her hands and arms, particularly her right hand. With her permission, Alan began to stimulate the palm and back of her right hand. I asked her to report whatever sensations began to occur. "Alan's hands are really warm so my right hand has this nice relaxed warm feeling." We asked her to expand this positive sensation through diaphragmatic breathing.

Nancy noticed that as she breathed more slowly and deeply from her diaphragm the warm relaxed feelings in her hand began to move up her arm, following Alan's fingers as he began to manipulate her wrist and forearm areas. Gradually, the feelings continued to expand up into her upper right arm. Nancy was able to connect her body feelings with emotional feelings of comfort and safety, sharing with us an image of her son, Tim, snuggling with her under a blanket on the sofa in front of the fire.

Our next step was to determine whether Nancy could hold this body safe place in a constant way while Alan began to work on the areas related to her injury. We began with her left hand and arm, which was most removed from her injury. Directing Nancy to focus her attention on her right hand as Alan manipulated her left hand, she found that she was able to transfer the warm, comfortable feelings from her right to her left hand and then to her left arm.

While Nancy tuned into the positive sensations in both hands and arms, Alan began to work behind her shoulders in the upper thoracic area of her back. With frequent reminders to deepen and slow her breathing and to keep a positive focus on her safe place area, Nancy was able to experience a release of the painful muscle spasms in her neck and shoulders. The buzzy feeling had left her body and she felt relaxed and calm.

Nancy's muscular pain and tension gradually reduced over our next five meetings. She experienced more physical energy and general feelings of well-being. We started each session by reestablishing Nancy's safe place in her body, strengthening her sense of safety as well as her confidence that her body could help her to feel secure in a constant way. Because her marijuana use had not dropped significantly during this time, however, we decided to change our focus to explore the bodymind connection as it might relate to urges to use marijuana.

After reestablishing her body safe place in her right hand and expanding its sensation through most of the rest of her body, I asked Nancy to recall a recent time when she had smoked pot and to notice any changes that took place in her felt sense of her body. Nancy immediately told us that she was thinking of a time when she was angry after a phone conversation with her mother and had used marijuana for comforting. "Something really interesting is happening in my body right now," she said. "I can't feel my upper arms or my legs anymore. It's like the outline of my body has melted in different places."

Because Nancy's sense of the boundaries of her body seemed to be disrupted when she thought about her emotional upset and smoking marijuana, it was clear that our plans needed to emphasize a strengthening of body wholeness or integrity. I asked Nancy to hold her focus on the areas where her body boundaries felt melted while Alan stimulated the strongest area of her body safe place—her right hand—to see if we could restore wholeness. Since this attempt was unsuccessful, we had her return to a more full sense of safety by changing her mental focus to a relaxing scene at the beach while Alan stimulated both her right and left hands.

This time we were successful. We found later that by pairing her egg image as a mental focus with Alan's stimulation of her hands, Nancy was gradually able to maintain full body wholeness or integrity when thinking of emotional events that triggered marijuana use, as long as they did not involve interactions with her mother.

Next, we asked her to focus on more neutral recent experiences involving her mother. Nancy noticed that the left side of her body immediately reacted. She described sensations that reached from her left shoulder and arm all the way to her lower leg as "more vulnerable," containing more "racy" or fragmented energy, and collapsing "like a marionette whose strings are pulled." In comparison, the right side of her body seemed stronger, calmer, and more solid.

With practice, by holding her focus on her body safe place (which she could now intensify without Alan's tactile stimulation), Nancy learned to maintain intact body boundaries while recalling past and present upsetting experiences with her mother. She also reported a stronger sense of wholeness in her relationships with her son, her partner, and friends. "I feel more whole now wherever I am, not just when I'm here. Sometimes when I'm upset and tempted to smoke pot, I focus on my safe place in my right hand. I can make the feelings stronger by stroking it with my left hand, and then I find I don't want to smoke."

During this series of 12 body-focused sessions, Nancy dramatically reduced the frequency of episodes of smoking pot. By the last two sessions, she had stopped smoking altogether and her urges were greatly reduced.

At the time of this writing, Nancy continues to battle relapses of marijuana use that follow increasingly longer periods of abstinence. She told me recently, "It's been a long struggle to shift my dependence from a drug to my own resources. It may even end up being a lifelong struggle for me. I know I might relapse again because that's the nature of addiction, but I believe I have the tools now to get back on track. I feel stronger in myself than I ever have and I'm determined to make this change for my own health and so that I can be a trustworthy model for my son. Without TFT, imagery, and the other tools, I would be tempted to give up."

## Using Somatic Therapy
## to Enhance General Health

Many clients also benefit from body-focused therapy when they have somatic symptoms, unrelated to past trauma, that interfere with their enjoyment of full physical health. A few examples include migraine headaches, constant or chronic pain from injuries, and digestive problems related to stress or anxiety.

We have found that our team approach not only relieves specific symptoms but in many cases has helped our clients to have deeper, more effective responses to psychological and emotional healing efforts as well. When we are addressing any issue related to somatic health, we make sure that the client has received appropriate medical attention and treatment. We are clear that our role is to provide adjunctive healing that can enhance other types of health care provided through traditional as well as nontraditional modalities. Judith, whose story you'll read next, is an example of a client whose general health has been strengthened by this approach.

### JUDITH: THE SUPPORTIVE ROLE OF BODYWORK

Judith is a delightful, intelligent woman who has just celebrated her 85th birthday. I have seen her for supportive psychotherapy for the last six years to help her cope with issues related to her business, interpersonal relationships, and the process of aging. She is fully committed to ongoing personal growth and is a vibrant inspiration to her customers, family, and friends alike.

About two years ago, Judith became concerned about her right knee. She was experiencing pain and weakness in her knee and leg and felt fearful that her mobility might become significantly restricted. Her doctor had diagnosed a bone spur and wanted to send her to an orthopedic surgeon for a consultation. He told her that she might require surgical removal of the spur and that a knee replacement ultimately might be necessary. I encouraged her to follow through with his recommendation and also explained that there were some possibilities that she and I could pursue in the context of our work by consulting with Alan van Winkle. Judith was quite interested in any potential approach that might help her so we invited Alan to our next session. After reviewing her health history, we asked Judith to lie on the mat so that Alan could begin hands-on work.

After establishing a somatic safe place in her feet, Judith gave permission for Alan to begin exploring her right knee. He helped Judith develop a felt sense of the parameters of the bone spur and explained that he might be able to assist her in relaxing the muscles around it that appeared to be inflamed and in spasm. In addition to releasing these areas, Alan pressed some trigger points[7] that were designed to reestablish a more complete flow of energy in her right leg and throughout her entire body.

Judith found the session very relaxing and reported that she had felt less discomfort during the week. After three more sessions, Judith told us that the bone spur seemed less noticeable. "Could it have disappeared?" she asked. When Alan probed her right knee, he found that indeed the spur seemed to have diminished in size and that both legs demonstrated more flexibility.

Eager to hear what her doctors would say, Judith went to the appointment she had scheduled with the orthopedic surgeon. When he examined her right knee, he told her that the bone spur was not a significant problem but recommended future monitoring of the area. Although the specialist she consulted made no specific comments about the bodywork Judith had undergone, he encouraged her to continue with the approach if she felt it had helped her.

"Helped me?" Judith said later to the two of us. "I told him I felt the two of you had saved my knee from surgery. I can't tell you how relieved I am!"

In the next few months, Judith decided that she wanted to continue to include Alan in our sessions because she appreciated the general feelings of well-being she received. "I'm sleeping much better and I notice that my business doesn't seem to cause as much stress as before. When it comes right down to it, I guess I also like getting attention from both of you. I feel really safe and comfortable. It's as if I have two parents to care about me instead of just one." This reaction is one which many of our other mutual clients have shared.

When Judith's business partner, also her close friend, was diagnosed with bone cancer a few months later, Judith immediately took Rachael into her home and became her primary caregiver. Alan and I were concerned about the impact this decision would have on her health and watched carefully for signs of increasing stress.

As Rachael's cancer progressed, Judith began to report difficulty sleeping and her energy levels began to drop as she struggled to cover responsibilities at home and work and remain in balance. In addition to helping Judith obtain supportive care for Rachael in her home, we began to experiment with various techniques to help stabilize Judith's stamina and sleep.

Alan and I found that Judith had a very deep response to the craniosacral stimulation that he applied near the end of every session. During this period of about 10 to 15 minutes, we would pair hypnotic suggestions for relaxation and diaphragmatic breathing with Alan's gentle manipulation of various trigger points, located on the sides and back of the head, that help to release the sacrum. Judith reported an experience of deep relaxation that continued for several hours after her treatment. "It's like I finally begin to let go of all the pressure and worry I feel. My mind stops working overtime. I feel wonderful and deeply cared about. It's a good way to get the nurturing I need."

Because we wanted to provide more lasting results, we decided to add RAS, or rhythmic alternating stimulation (see page 147), to the craniosacral stimulation. To provide this, Alan manipulated the cranial points in Judith's temporal area in a rhythmic fashion to produce the same kind of lateral eye movements that occur in EMDR while her eyes were closed.[8] Not only did this seem to anchor the effects of the craniosacral stimulation so that there was more carryover during the week, but Judith reported some interesting energetic shifts in her body. "I can feel the relaxation moving all the way down into my feet," she said during one of our first RAS sessions. "Now I know what it's like to feel connected to my whole body."

In addition to using RAS to deepen and integrate a more complete relaxation response, Alan and I also used this technique to resolve chronic holding patterns in Judith's shoulders, which resulted from a repetitive lifting motion at work. Because it was difficult for her to let go of the massive tension in this area of her body, Alan stimulated side-to-side eye movements by rocking each shoulder gently back and forth[9] or by stimulating alternate trigger points in her shoulder areas. We have hypothesized that RAS desensitized and reprocessed the anxiety related to her muscular holding so that she could let go of and release the muscles in a much shorter time.

To support this change, Alan helped her with other somatic strategies so that she could lift from a different place in her body with the help of diaphragmatic breathing. I helped her examine and change beliefs that made it difficult for her to ask others for help. We also referred her to an acupuncturist, who helped to further stabilize energy, sleep, and immune functions following Rachael's death and the news of her brother's diagnosis with prostate cancer.

Judith's health remains excellent. She weathered the deaths of Rachael and her brother with grace and resilience. Her knee and shoulders remain flexible and comfortable. When she occasionally overuses those areas of her body, our work helps her to resolve any resulting strain or spasming. We hope that our methods will support her in living an active and productive life for many years to come.

# Section V

# INTEGRATED MODELS:

## ADDRESSING COMPLEX HEALTH NEEDS

# Introducing Integrated Models

When I teach on the topic of energy therapies, two of the most frequently asked questions are, "How do you decide when and which method to use?" and "How do you know when to shift to another modality to get better results?" I usually give my standard answer that this is a matter of knowing and responding to the client's needs and clinical/health situation. And almost always, the questions persist until I address the heartfelt, but unexpressed, need for a specific formula to follow—a recipe that, hopefully, will maximize benefits and minimize any negatives.

Unfortunately (or, fortunately, depending on your point of view), *there is no magic prescription for using the energy therapies.* In the final analysis, the combined best judgments and unfettered creativity of any client-practitioner team will determine the results of healing events, much like pilot and co-pilot navigating a complicated flight plan to stay on course.

However, there are some important guiding principles that may be helpful. The seven guidelines that follow are offered as general markers along the energy therapy trail.

## Guiding Principles for Using Energy Therapies

### 1 Capitalize on the Placebo Effect

Unless there is a very good reason not to do so, I always begin with what my clients believe will work. If a client comes to me seeking hypnosis, TFT, EMDR, or any other specific approach, I will begin with that modality because I want to capitalize on the placebo effect. That is, I want to make maximum use of clients' positive expectations that a certain technique will work for them. Herbert Benson, who has done some noteworthy work in this area, suggests that there are three attitudinal components that contribute to wellness: positive belief and expectancy on the part of the patient, positive belief and expectancy on the part of the caregiver, and positive beliefs and expectancies generated through the relationship.[1]

Because I want to use the placebo effect to potentiate the impact of *any* energy therapy tool, I respect the client's reasoning about its possible benefits for his/her health situation. Sometimes, financial issues may necessitate consideration of a method that I sense might provide more rapid results than the client's choice. And, on occasion, other important standards may override the placebo principle, such as the requirement of sustained attention for formal hypnosis.[2] Aside from these considerations, however, if both my client and I believe an approach will work, our attempts will likely lead to better outcomes.

### 2. Build on Strengths
Throughout *Finding the Energy to Heal*, I have underlined my belief in the importance of beginning the healing process with strengths that are already in place. This principle is the cornerstone of the SARI model and is inherent in most approaches to psychotherapy.

All of the energy methods can be used in different ways to activate and reconfigure the psychobiological energies that move through and organize mindbody systems. Regardless of the particular method being employed, initial interventions should focus on further strengthening. Following this guideline will not only increase the degree of ego strength available for healing endeavors but also provide a safe testing ground to make sure that the selected method is an appropriate choice for the individual's current readiness level.

### 3. Consider Developmental Issues
In my experience, if someone is having a positive response to the techniques being used but targeted symptoms are not improving, it is frequently helpful to consider developmental problems that might be obstructing healing. People who have experienced early loss, abuse, and neglect are obvious candidates for developmental intervention, because it is likely that primitive developmental processes were interrupted or disturbed. Incomplete responses to healing may be indications of significant unfinished developmental business.

The informal developmental ladder I use in my practice[3] begins with the formation and maintenance of internal and interpersonal boundaries. Types of boundaries formed include sensory, cognitive, emotional, verbal, and body parameters. This process begins in infancy and is essential to the development of an intact self that can distinguish between inner and outer, self and others, and real and unreal experiences. Later, the issue of boundary flexibility becomes important, as the growing individual must learn self-regulation by discovering how much external experience to take in and how much internal experience to release so that balance can be maintained.

The developing child also learns to contain, manage, and express strong negative feelings, including rage, fear, and frustration. If this step is relatively successful, the child will begin to develop a sense that attachment to the self, as well as to other people, is positive and permanent. That is, we learn that objects, such as toys or favorite foods, as well as people, still exist even when they are not physically present. We also discover that our connections with self, objects, and other people can remain relatively constant even though circumstances are constantly changing.

We learn ways of soothing our anxieties through these stages with the help of parent figures who can tolerate our feelings and frustrations within reasonable parameters and can help us identify and express in words the reactions that, if left unregulated, may prevent us from moving forward. People who have suffered various types of trauma in early childhood frequently have not had this kind of help. Therefore, they may not have developed an intact, constant sense of self or others, and they may not know how to regulate overwhelming, intrusive internal reactions or how to connect with various types of sensory experience in a way that helps to achieve and maintain psychological equilibrium.

Although there are certainly many other models and theories to consider,[4] using some type of basic map to detect inadequacies and restore sufficient developmental functioning is essential in work with complex health issues. For many clients, it will be impossible to achieve resolution of health problems without resolving developmental problems. It is also important to keep in mind that development lasts a *lifetime*. Since none of us will completely master these issues, some attention to targeted developmental skill areas is likely to be beneficial for everyone.

### 4. Be Flexible Yet Consistent

When making choices about the use of energy therapies, I find it is necessary to strike a balance between flexibility and consistency. Sometimes, I am the first to propose a shift to another technique if the one we are using does not seem to be achieving the desired results. In many cases, my clients' tolerance for the frustrations of failure is much stronger than mine, because experiences of mastery and consistent forward progress are so unfamiliar to them. At other times, the client is more impatient and pushes for new methods, sometimes before I believe we have enough data to properly assess our current intervention.

In either circumstance, the task is a challenging one of responding with flexibility in order to shift with emerging patterns of readiness and needs, yet remaining a consistent anchor to help in evaluating thoroughly all the factors that may be contributing to stalled progress.

The SARI model can be a helpful evaluation tool in avoiding premature decisions about techniques and methods. For example, is there sufficient health stability? Is there enough internal safety to allow for positive responses to the tools being used? Is there enough safety in the therapy relationship and the treatment situation? Is there adequate security in everyday life circumstances? Answers to these questions may point to a need for an additional or a return focus on strengthening in the current situation.

During the second stage involving activation of healing resources, evaluation must center on whether the methods we are using are helping to deliver these results. If they are not, we must consider whether other tools may accomplish tasks related to this second stage of healing more effectively.

During the third "R" stage when health symptoms are resolved, if resolution is not occurring, a thorough review of possible barriers must take place. My list of potential obstacles to healing includes unresolved developmental tasks, unacknowledged relationship issues between me and the client, unidentified external factors such as sudden changes in life circumstances or shifts in prescribed or self-medication use, and unaddressed internal factors, including possible ego-state conflicts. If any of these underlie health problems, progress may remain blocked until they are confronted and resolved. I inform my clients that they may not achieve permanent changes in their health unless they are willing to work through these associated complexities, even though doing so may pose an unexpected detour.

### 5. Promote Integrative Functioning

The fourth step in the SARI model is important enough to require its own separate category. Regardless of the technique being used, or the stage of healing being implemented, the results obtained must be *integrative*. That is, they must promote wholeness instead of fragmentation, a centered sense of self rather than a conflicted one, and a heightened sense of greater competency, not a reduced one.

Individuals are not served at any stage of healing by becoming more dependent on the therapist rather than more dependent on their own resources. Professionals who emphasize the wizardry of their own skills, rather than undertaking the hard work of developing those of the client, risk causing further collapse of health. I tell my clients that if at any time during our work they are not feeling and exhibiting the kinds of strengths that can be used to further their experiences of healing, we will evaluate what we are doing and make adjustments until this *is* the case. My clients soon find out that they can trust what I say.

*6. Find Out What Is Truly Healing for Each Individual*
Although there are some principles, including those stated above, that seem to apply universally, every health situation is different. For some people, humor and playfulness are the best medicine. For others, humor is wounding when it is perceived as a sign that the enormity of their suffering is not being taken seriously. Each individual is the final authority on what is needed to create a healing atmosphere where his/her needs can best be met.

I'll never forget an experience I had some years ago where I reconnected with a distant cousin who suffered from several debilitating health conditions, including adult onset diabetes. Even though we had not seen each other for more than 20 years, she had specifically asked my mother to tell her when I was coming next for a visit because she wanted to speak with me. She drove for three hours, bringing her own food for the meal we shared, not wanting to risk unbalancing her diet. In several other ways, her behavior set her apart from the rest of us who were assembled to see her.

As she gathered up her belongings toward the end of the visit, I remained puzzled as to why she had asked to see me when she had not directed any of her communications specifically to me. Finally, when she turned to say goodbye, I discovered the purpose for her visit. She grasped my hands, looked me in the eye and said, "You're a psychologist, aren't you?" "Yes," I answered, "That's right, I am." "And you work with lots of people who have health problems, don't you?" "Yes," I said, "I do." "I came here today because I wanted to tell you something. Please remember always to listen to your patients," she instructed. "That is what will help them the most." I try to heed her advice every day.

*7. It's the Presence, Not the Technique*
At a recent seminar on mindbody healing, workshop leader Joan Borysenko reminded those of us in attendance that healing is not found in any specific techniques but in the healing presence surrounding whatever curative methods are offered.[5]

Recent studies have demonstrated how the physical presence of doctors impacted recovery from surgery. Doctors who stood in the hallway to talk to patients were correlated with the lowest healing outcomes, while those who sat at bedsides and touched the shoulders of their patients were linked to the most successful results. Other studies have shown that the power of prayer can facilitate faster healing and fewer complications following surgery.

Throughout *Finding the Energy to Heal*, you have read stories about the lives of ordinary people in which spiritual and transpersonal experiences provided pivotal turning points toward health. Full healing may not occur without healing presence that can help us turn from isolation to interpersonal trust and intimacy, and ultimately toward transpersonal connectedness with spirit, with all that is divine. Healing relationships that are open to and encourage spiritual transformation will encourage and maximize energetic shifts.

## Comprehensive Change in Complex Situations

I had a provocative dream as I was nearing the end of the first draft of this book. In my dream, I am the owner of a huge house that covers an entire city block. Various co-dwellers approach me about problems occurring in the basement level. One tenant has identified a disturbing smell she is afraid might be a dead body. I listen to their concerns but rush on to other business. The truth is, I have a lot of responsibilities and don't want to be bothered. Besides, the basement is forbidding. I don't want to investigate.

The next time I venture outside of my own apartment, I am accosted again by other tenants. This time, there is talk about additional problems. Someone mentions incidents of violence, perhaps a stabbing. Another person mentions the stench of garbage that has not been disposed of properly. Finally, at their insistence, I promise to intervene.

Full of dread, I begin my descent to the basement. My first try is terrifying; I only venture partway down the stairs. It is so dark that I can distinguish only the outlines of a long hallway that appears unending. I go back upstairs and try to collect myself. Eventually, I venture back downstairs, this time a little further. After waiting for what seems an eternity in silence, I gather my courage to knock at the first door on the right. There is no answer.

A few minutes later, a woman walks toward me from further down the hall. I am wary of her because of her disheveled appearance but she is warm and friendly, letting me know that she lives there. I tell her about the rumors I have heard. She smiles, "We live differently here. We help each other out. We don't have much by your standards but we like living the way we do. Sometimes things get a little out of hand when people express their feelings but we resolve whatever problems come up." She shakes my hand and thanks me for coming, inviting me to return again.

On my next trip to the basement, I meet a male friend of hers. I am invited into his room with her. His quarters are plain and dark but very clean and neat. We talk for quite a while and I am surprised by how relaxed I feel in their company. At the invitation of these new friends, we go off to a club to hear some music together.

My understanding of the dream is that the huge, above-ground house represents the conscious mind, while the basement represents the unconscious. Often, we do not want to explore the unconscious because its contents seemed too foreboding, dark, and dangerous. Yet when we receive signals we can no longer ignore and are willing to investigate, we discover a way of living that may be more primitive but in many ways more satisfying in its freedom of expression and hidden potentials.

THIS DREAM SPEAKS TO THE NEED TO WORK AT BOTH conscious and unconscious levels, utilizing both take-action male potentials and creative/receptive feminine energies in our healing endeavors, a balance that many methods facilitate. We must heed the fears and concerns of our conscious minds, because they will stir us to necessary action beyond the comfortable limits of what we know. But we also need to examine the more unfamiliar resources of the unconscious that are available for our discovery and use, because they can make us mindful of what may be missing in the ways we are living and what we may need to cultivate in order to find wholeness.

## Three Models for Combining Energy Therapies

One of the most exciting aspects of working with the tools presented in this book lies in discovering the multitude of ways in which they can be combined to provide more comprehensive healing for complex needs that require more than a few sessions. You have already encountered several samples of how the sequential use of multiple energy therapies may result in a more complete resolution of health symptoms. For example, in working with Nancy's marijuana addiction, we first used imagery to address developmental problems, then chose TFT during a relapse period to help her cope with addictive urges and emotional effects of past trauma, and culminated with body-focused therapy to help her heal from a physical injury that triggered renewed use of marijuana. In this last section, I have included three models that I have found effective with a variety of health issues. Undoubtedly, there are many others. Since each person has unique responses, keep in mind that there are countless combinations and permutations of the energy therapies I have presented in this book, as well as other existing methods that were not included. Still to come are the energy technologies at this time still in their infancy, which will continue to evolve.

### 1. The Linking Model
Many health situations can be resolved by helping people bridge from current experiences of limited health to more positive, expansive health realities. Two methods that help provide these vital links to needed mind-body resources from the past, present, and future are EMDR and TFT. Chapter 10 presents the linking model[6] with an extended example to illustrate its benefits.

### 2. The Unconscious Learning Model
A second model, presented in chapter 11, is rooted in the belief that one of the most powerful guides of the healing process is the unconscious mind. This approach draws on extensive experience with hypnosis and imagery as royal roads to the unconscious. The example presented to demonstrate this method of synthesizing energy therapies is the further story of Jamie, first introduced in chapter 9.

### 3. The Braiding Model
A third proposed model involves interweaving energy modalities, much like making a braided rope that has several strands. The specific example that illustrates this approach features the interweaving of body-focused therapy, sensory awareness training, and hypnotic ego-state therapy, although any of the energy therapies could be used in the same manner.

# 10

# The Linking Model: Bridging to New Experiences of Health Through EMDR and TFT

"I know I should have called you sooner, but I've been in a tailspin. The therapist friend who told me about you said that you use techniques that bring fast results. Believe me, I hope that's true." Barely settled in a chair in my office, Angie began to detail a myriad of health complaints that needed to be resolved quickly, since she was scheduled to fly to London in two weeks for a vacation that had been planned to celebrate her 65th birthday.

Angie was most concerned about her energy level, which had plummeted since she had contracted pneumonia three years earlier. "I don't know why I became ill then," she offered. "I had just started retirement, had lost a lot of weight, and was traveling to wonderful places that I adored. Life seemed perfect. I came down with a cold at Christmas and it only got worse. I had never really had respiratory problems before but I certainly made up for it then. I had high fever and was miserable for several weeks. But when I began to feel better, I started binge eating on sugar and gained back all that I had lost—42 pounds!

"Then I got a bad flu two years later, about a year ago," she continued, "and I don't feel like I ever really recovered. My immune function is still depressed. According to my doctor, I now have chronic fatigue as well as fibromyalgia. The pain in my legs is always there from the back of my knee down to my ankle. Then I have pain from the back of my neck down both my shoulders.

"I know we don't have much time before I leave, but I'd really like to improve my energy and pain levels before I leave for my trip. This is a treat for my birthday from a dear friend and I really want to enjoy it. Can you do anything for me?"

Sidestepping her question, I told her that we would need to assess her health needs thoroughly before starting any treatment. She agreed to provide a full health history for the remainder of this appointment and to schedule two additional 75-minute sessions before she left. We would see what was possible.

ANGIE'S CHILDHOOD HEALTH SEEMED NORMAL. SHE RECALLED no allergies, illnesses beyond usual childhood diseases, accidents, or surgeries. Her mother had suffered severe osteoporosis and had died at 52 from a stroke. Her father, still alive in his eighties, had been diagnosed with both adult onset diabetes and kidney cancer. Her older brother, long alcoholic, died two years ago from an accidental heroin overdose. Angie's daughter was also a heroin addict though clean for the last two years and active in the Narcotics Anonymous program. Her younger sister was struggling with both irritable bowel syndrome and respiratory problems.

As an adult, Angie had suffered a major depressive episode at the time of her divorce in 1965 and a second one about 12 years later, when she attempted suicide by overdosing on Valium, alcohol, and antidepressants. She told me she was not depressed currently and felt she had been emotionally stable since her suicide attempt.

In light of her history, Angie was worried about her own addictive tendencies toward sugar and the possibility of contracting diabetes. She was also concerned about her weight, as both her mother and maternal grandmother had died of strokes.

I proposed a plan of intensive focus on improving energy and pain levels before Angie's trip and then reevaluation of goals when she returned, based on how well she had integrated any health gains we were able to make. In discussing possible options, I told Angie that I believed our best immediate strategy was to help her find links to mindbody resources that could strengthen her energy and lower her discomfort.

Although all of the energy methods can help to link to resources that can be used for these purposes, I recommended that, since our time was so limited, we begin with a combination of EMDR and TFT. EMDR is recognized for its rapid identification of links to associational networks.

Since I always begin with positive strengthening targets, I was hopeful that we could maximize EMDR's linking benefits to resources that she could draw on during her trip while minimizing any risk of negative effects.

In suggesting TFT, I explained that this method was based on the energy systems of Chinese medicine. Tapping designated sequential points in her energy meridians was designed to mobilize links to vital qi energy that might help reduce the fibromyalgia pain and increase her energy levels. Because the worst that can happen in my clinical experience with TFT is that there is little or no change but not a worsening of symptoms, I believed that there were few, if any, risks involved in a brief trial with TFT before her departure.

Angie was eager to try both of these approaches. She had tried many alternative techniques, including acupuncture, and was currently finding supplements and herbs helpful to a certain extent for stabilizing her energy. "Acupuncture was wonderful. I would be almost pain free for a day or so, but then it would come back again. If TFT is based on the same principles, and it's something I can do myself when I need to, well, that's inviting!"

When beginning the linking model, or any of the methods for combining the energy therapies, I generally ask people to identify a possible starting place in light of immediate and long-term priorities for comfort and full functioning. If there are multiple health-symptoms, I ask how these difficulties seem to be related to each other, in order to give me additional clues about how to proceed.

Angie told me that when her energy levels were relatively high, her addictive urges for sugar seemed to recede and she could usually find ways of managing fibromyalgia pain. Based on these perceptions, we began with EMDR to identify links from positive target images that represented high-energy experiences to appropriate resources that might be used by Angie to initiate future higher energy experiences. Our second priority, to be addressed following success with this goal, was to use TFT to reduce pain levels.

After discussing the general dimensions of EMDR, I explained to Angie the need to find a conflict-free image based on an experience that she consistently associated with high energy levels in her daily routines. Once we formed a positive target image, we could then link to other related resources during eye movement sets, which could then be utilized for self-regulation of energy states.

Angie first suggested a positive target image of working out in her step class. When she pictured moving to the music in her red leotard, however, she heard an inner voice say, "No, you can't do that now." When asked to describe her inner reactions in greater detail, Angie revealed that this was an activity that she enjoyed when she had lots of energy. She felt frustrated, however, that she could not get to her step class on days when her energy was low.

I explained that this image might be a valuable resource that we could use at a later time but emphasized that we needed to maximize our chances for success by identifying a conflict-free image undiluted by inner conflicts or mixed emotional reactions. Angie thought for a few more moments and then recalled the experience of walking along a special beach that she had visited at various times, feeling exhilarated and excited, drinking in smells of the ocean, and feeling her feet sink into the sand.

Angie's inner thoughts when she focused on the beach image were that she wanted more of this kind of energy in her life. The positive cognition she wanted to attain was "I am capable of creating more experiences for myself that increase positive energy." The beach image was selected as Angie's positive EMDR target image.[1]

During the first few sets of eye movements, Angie connected to wholly positive reactions, which seemed to expand the energy of this conflict-free image:

A: I felt good. I moved faster and faster down the beach. //
A: I want to laugh out loud I feel so good. //
A: I'm just smiling and smiling.

During the fourth set of eye movements, however, Angie began to link to feelings of sadness and loss. Because she seemed to have the ego strength for rapid reprocessing, I supported her in clarifying and moving through them, an intervention that resulted in Angie's finding important links to positive memory material that was integrative and which stimulated additional important resources.[2]

A: I looked in the ocean and saw seals playing. Then I saw a dead seal, and it brought up a lot of loss, a deep sense of loss.
MP: What loss do you mean?
A: My mom's death 27 years ago, my brother's death, the lost innocence of my daughter to drugs. . . . //
A: My feelings are going through me. It's like I'm halfway between the live seals. //
A: I was caught between two forces; I feel released and relaxed, much lighter. It's OK to be sad. The beach still smells good. Life continues in different forms. . . . I feel peaceful. //
A: I saw trees at the end of the beach. There was a wonderful piney smell. I sat down and relaxed. It's like my body is letting go of all

the stuff I've been carrying. I'm smelling the strong smells of the
sea . . . it's very healing, like good medicine. //

A: My mother showed up at the beach. The last place she and I went
together was this beach. She put her hands on my shoulders and
she tells me, "If you stop fighting, it will be OK . . . it's OK to let
go."

MP: How was that for you?

A: It felt so good to feel her hands on my shoulders. I felt her energy
moving inside me. //

A: My grandfather joined her at the beach. I feel so incredibly taken
care of now . . . there is a surge of love without conditions. //

A: They showed me a picture of a tree. My grandfather said, "Just
because you can't see your roots, you need to remember that we're
there holding you and you're safe."

MP: Let's go back and check your positive target now, Angie. Bring up
the image we started with of you walking along the beach. What
happens when you do?

A: The image is peaceful and quiet now. There's such strength and
healing in it . . . it's like I found my family tree (sobbing). I think I
needed to realize that I'm safe, that I come from a long line of
fighters. Since I've been sick, I've been freefalling, not secure, not
connected to my roots. I feel really good now.

The rest of this session was spent discussing how Angie could practice
using the resources she had linked to during this session. She commented
that the strongest image was that of her mother and grandfather with
their hands on her shoulders followed by that of the "family tree." I encouraged her to let the images evolve as she worked with them during
her meditation time early in the morning as well as during other reflective
as well as active moments during the day. "The energy contained in these
images will continue to move inside of you and may take on different
forms," I suggested "Trust that if you move with whatever happens with
them, you will find the resources that you need."

At our next, and final, session before Angie embarked for London, she
reported that she had felt a lot more energy, which she estimated at 6–8
on a 10-point scale, contrasted with 2–4 levels before EMDR. She felt
encouraged, but had identified a new problem common to many pain
patients. Once she began to enjoy greater energy, she began to overdo
her exercise and experienced a setback the next day. "Even though it was
a gentle hike, I realize it was a lot more than I've been used to. The next
day there was a huge price to pay because my pain was much greater,
especially in my right leg," Angie explained.

She revealed that, during her own experimentation, her imagery had transformed to form one image where her mom was on her left side and her grandfather on her right. Each had a hand on her shoulder and their energy came through their hands and down into her legs like grounding. Angie had used this form of the image to help her up the last hill of her hike, as well as at other times.

Since I wanted to shift our focus to the body during this session, I asked Angie to bring up this image at that moment and tell me what she noticed about how the energy of her mother and grandfather moved through her body. "Hmmm . . . I'm noticing that it takes work to move it past the back of my knees. It feels constricted there and then gradually I can feel it keep moving again. It feels like there's a block there." She paused for a moment and then continued, "It reminds me of the emotional block I feel when I drop something. Usually I feel tense and angry. There are negative messages I hear inside like 'You're klutzy.' But this week I pictured how relaxed my grandpa was. I hear him say, 'Gentle, gentle, now,' and then I let go of my irritability. I think these images are really helping."

I suggested that we work on the blocked energy Angie sensed at the back of her knees using TFT. Initial muscle testing indicated no psychological reversals. Angie attuned to the tension in her knees, describing a tightening on her right leg, with the center of the pain below her calf and above the ankle. The beginning SUD was 5 for the pain, and as she tapped through the pain protocol we encountered a mini-reversal that quickly cleared down to a SUD of 1. After completing the floor to ceiling eyeroll, the SUD was down to zero and Angie could not bring back the pain on the backs of her knees.

As Angie scanned her body, however, she identified that her right upper leg now hurt more than her inner knee had. She scaled the pain level at 6 on the SUD and we tapped through the pain formula with focus on this location. The SUD level dropped to 1, yet the physical sensation had shifted location higher in her inner thigh. When this did not respond to either the eyeroll or recurring reversal prescription, I suggested that we shift protocols to the one for past trauma that includes emotional pain or grief.

This time, as Angie attuned to the remaining pain in her inner thigh and tapped through the protocol, the SUD level dropped quickly and easily to zero. "That's amazing," Angie exclaimed. "How did you know we should focus on emotional pain?" I responded that I had remembered the links to loss we had discovered in our EMDR work and thought that loss might be linked to the physical pain and blocked energy in her inner knees as well.

Although TFT links differently than EMDR, I have found that the two methods are often effective energy partners. EMDR is designed to link to important associational and memory networks, while TFT appears to tap into energy networks or meridians in the body. While EMDR tends to reveal links that contain important cognitive and emotional content as well as somatic responses, *in general*, cognitive and emotional content is less prevalent in TFT's highly somatic responses. Often the information obtained through EMDR can be used to guide movement through TFT protocols, as was the case with Angie. And TFT can be used to deepen the somatic dimension of healing that some clients do not experience significantly with EMDR.

After we had resolved the blocked energy in her legs, I was curious about the emotional block Angie had referred to earlier in the session related to "being klutzy." Angie acknowledged a pattern of self-criticism. "When I overdo, like I did on the hike, I tend to get really frustrated. I get in a battle with myself and that further drains my energy. It only makes things worse."

Deciding that this issue would be important to work with because it might come up on her trip if she exceeded her fragile physical limits, we decided to return to EMDR to find links that might help to resolve the inner conflict.

This time, we began with a clinical target image (rather than a positive one for strengthening). Angie targeted the inner turmoil she experienced on the morning after her hike. Because she was not able to identify a past experience related to this inner struggle, we decided to begin with this recent event. The thoughts that reflected her exhaustion after the hike were, "How could I be so stupid as to do too much again? Won't I ever learn?" She commented that the inner voice that delivered these messages sounded like her mother's voice, though she could not recall a specific time when she had heard those criticisms. The turmoil also seemed connected with the negative judgments she felt toward herself for being clumsy and uncoordinated. A tightness in her stomach accompanied these reactions, and Angie's positive cognition was, "I am a competent adult who can learn how to identify and better respect her physical limits." This target resolved in only five sets of eye movements:

A: The tightness in my stomach got stronger. I'm frustrated with limiting myself. //

A: There's a really despairing feeling in my stomach of never being able to get it right . . . a sweeping loneliness. It goes really deep. //

A: I'm so tired. It's a feeling in my whole body like a weight pressing down, I feel so old, so tired. //

    A: I want this all to stop. . . . I don't think I can go through another
       set. I feel a wave of sadness that I keep doing this to myself.
  MP: What might help to remind you that you're a competent adult who
       can better learn how to read and respect her body?
    A: My grandfather . . . I see him now. He tells me, "You're OK." He
       gives me a big hug. My stomach releases . . . I feel a flow of energy.
       There's no block now. //
    A: I saw an image of my grandfather in one of the museums in Lon-
       don with me. He's just taking everything in because everything is
       OK with him. It's so healing and easy to be with him.

When we returned to the target image to check our progress, the SUD
had dropped from 7 to 0. Her confidence in believing that she was competent to learn more about how to honor her physical limits was quite
high. We spent the rest of the session discussing how to use these important links from EMDR and TFT while Angie was visiting London. She
decided to use TFT if she sensed energy blocks in her body and she
would add the image of her grandfather giving her a hug and positive
encouragement if she detected negative self-talk or criticism.

OUR NEXT MEETING TOOK PLACE AFTER ANGIE RETURNED FROM London. She
had enjoyed herself enormously and was delighted by how much her
stamina had increased. "I was able to do pretty much everything I wanted
just by planning ahead and taking good care of myself. There were two
times I overdid it with long walks but TFT took care of the pain. Lots of
times, I would just rub my collarbone spot or gamut spot[3] and that felt
soothing. It's a nice shortcut. I also used the images, and whenever I
was worried about whether my energy would hold out, I would hear my
grandfather's voice reminding me to be easy with myself. Then I'd sit
down and rest or just go back to the hotel. I'm so much more aware of
my needs and my body's limits. My energy just got better and better over
the course of the trip and that hasn't happened in a long time!"

At that point, Angie wanted to focus on her addiction to sugar, which
had resurfaced as a concern in the stress of her return home. We decided
to continue to use our linking model. Since Angie had no known early
trauma, we decided to start reprocessing with the earliest memories related to difficulties with sugar.

What we learned in this EMDR session was that Angie's renewed dependence on sugar seemed to be connected with comforting memories of
her grandmother, with whom Angie stayed after school. Grandmother
made treats, taught her to cook, and talked about many things in the

refuge of her warm, cozy kitchen. Sugar was a way that Angie could recapture that warm, comforting feeling now that her vacation was over.

In the next four linking sessions, we continued to use EMDR to identify links from dysfunctional eating behaviors to old beliefs and memories, reprocess these, and install new behaviors. Several ego states appeared spontaneously during the eye movement sets. They included a little girl of about six who loved to sit in grandmother's kitchen and craved sweets for comfort, an older woman crone who wanted to help Angie rediscover the meaning and purpose in her life, and a young woman of about 26 who was super responsible and had a strong work ethic.

We used EMDR to activate these parts, to find out about the contributions and needs of each, and to help them communicate with and support each other and to begin to work together to achieve goals that would enhance Angie's health: restricting sugar, learning to relax and play more, planning daily meditation and exercise periods. Because the ego states were readily available,[4] EMDR potentiated changes in Angie's inner family very rapidly. Positive behavioral changes were linked to her weekly EMDR discoveries. Angie joined Weight Watchers, lowered her intake of sugar and fat, and enjoyed daily meditation and exercise. She was also motivated to work with her inner parts on a daily basis, which also seemed to support more rapid internal and external changes.

Just as these successes were beginning to solidify, Angie suffered a setback, which brought a recurrence of the fibromyalgia pain along with lower energy and an increase in dysfunctional eating habits. Her resurgence of symptoms followed an incident with her daughter, who was housesitting while Angie was out of town for the weekend. When Angie returned earlier than expected, the house was in disarray and Angie was suspicious that her daughter had used heroin in her absence.

When we explored the meaning of this experience, Angie believed that it may have triggered the memory of an earlier, traumatic, late-night encounter when her daughter had overdosed at her house some years before. We used EMDR to reprocess this earlier event, helping her shift from a state of high anxiety to feelings of compassion for her daughter's struggles and an understanding of her own reactions following both incidents.

At the next appointment, Angie reported that her flu-like symptoms, low energy, and joint pain, which began following the incident with her daughter, had persisted. I suggested that we shift our focus to TFT, which might provide somatic energy links to resources that could resolve her symptoms. We followed the pain and complex past trauma/grief TFT protocols. These allowed her to shift the aches, body tension, and joint pain down to zero. "This is the best I've felt in a long time," Angie sighed as we concluded.

We then used the TFT protocol for addictive urges to focus on the sugar cravings that had begun to plague her again in the evenings. When we moved the SUD down to zero, we shifted over to EMDR to explore any remaining links. During a set of eye movements, an angry, nine-year-old tomboy ego state appeared, who admitted turning on the sugar cravings in order to focus Angie's attention on her needs to be more active physically. The session ended with an image of all Angie's ego states coming together in a circle, agreeing to support and help each other move back on track to health.

AFTER THIS SESSION, ANGIE RETURNED TO A PLACE OF GREATER well-being. "I'm beginning to feel normal and back to myself in ways that I never thought I would feel again. I sense that my masculine and feminine energies are coming together more. I feel more in balance and more sure that I can come to terms with the losses I have experienced as well as my own mortality by discovering the deeper purpose of this time in my life."

We continued to use the linking model to find important health resources and to reprocess links to unresolved trauma and grief, which previously she had discounted as unrelated to her symptoms. When our cues were emotional or behavioral, we tended to use EMDR. When Angie complained of somatic symptoms, which happened only rarely now, we tended to use TFT, though we easily flowed back and forth between the two.

Angie appreciated the sense of mastery TFT protocols gave her when she used them on her own to clear the physical pain and low energy levels that occasionally resurfaced as she learned to regulate the welcome return of stamina and vigor. She also valued the easy access EMDR provided to healing images and to the ego states that facilitated continued emotional, spiritual, behavioral, and physical growth.

At the last of 15 sessions, she felt good about her success. Her fibromyalgia pain was manageable. She had lost 12 pounds in two months, her intake of sugar was under control, and her sleep was better. "I've learned to accept some limitations of my energy and to work within them instead of railing against them. I feel more grounded and more in balance. Even on bad days, I'm confident that I can use the tools I've learned to get back on track within a day or two. When I think now of that image of me in my leotard at step class, I laugh! I don't aspire to be that 'wannabe' stereotype that defies the process of getting older. The awful panic when I first came here is gone. I've learned that this chapter of my life is not all about losses. You've helped me to discover some wonderful additions that I will go on learning about on my own."

TFT and EMDR have helped Angie reclaim vitality in the present and contemplate hope for a promising future. The links these methods provide to valuable resources at every level of mindbody experience can pro-vide similar benefits with constellations of health symptoms that are different from Angie's. When it is a good match, the linking model can activate a more integrated sense of well-being through rapid connection to essential energies that both point to and resolve barriers to good health.

# 11

# The Unconscious Learning Model: Leading with Hypnosis, Somatic Experiencing, and Imagery

"I'm terrified about the surgery I'm going to have next week. So much depends on the outcome. I could find out that I'm going to be permanently handicapped, that there's really nothing more that can be done. Or maybe I'll get a little bit more mobility or a lot. Who knows? No one can predict what might happen.

"The other reason I'm so worried about this next surgery is that I had such a hard time during the last one. I was so scared for so long. There's so much that can go wrong and so little I can do about it. It's such a helpless feeling.

"I want to talk with you today about how hypnosis could help me to prepare for the surgery and help me feel more confident and comfortable. I need to go into this procedure with a more positive attitude. Do you think hypnosis is a good idea for me?"

WHEN JAMIE FIRST CONSULTED ME, HE HAD ALREADY undergone two major surgeries on his hand, which had been badly crushed when his car overturned in an accident five months before (see chapter 9, pp. 172–176, for details of the injury and our work on resolving shock responses). Because the next surgery was quite soon, we had scheduled a two-hour appointment.

I asked for details of his first two surgeries. "I was terrified that I would lose my hand," Jamie told me. "The surgeon spoke to me before the first one and told me that he would do all that he could but that my x-rays looked horrible. What made it worse was that I remembered that when my brother was injured in the bus accident, his doctor told him that he would try to save Ricky's leg, but of course they couldn't. They had to amputate. So I was scared that the same thing would happen to me. It was such a relief when I woke up with all five fingers. But they had to check my circulation every hour so I got no sleep and it was very, very painful.

"I was home for a week," he continued. "But then I had to go back. During the second operation, the doctors took muscle from my leg and grafted it into my hand. I was hooked up to a machine to check the circulation. It felt like my whole life hung on that thing. I was so afraid something would happen, that they'd rush me back to surgery and I'd lose my hand. That whole month I was totally focused on my fear about whether I was going to lose my hand."

When I asked Jamie what the upcoming third surgery would involve, he explained that the doctors had removed all the pins that had been inserted in the first two surgeries. Now that the life of his hand was secure, the question was what could be done with it. Jamie clarified that the surgical plan was to remove some unneeded bones and tendons from other places in his body and graft them into his hand to help with strength and mobility.

We moved on in the interview to discuss his hopes for our work together. "During those two weeks in the hospital when I had surgery, I was really struggling to find meaning and purpose in life. I couldn't work, couldn't drive, couldn't help take care of my kids. It shook my sense of self. Who am I if I'm not someone who can do all these things? I just kept asking myself that question.

"Then I had this nightmare one night. Somehow I had left the hospital when I shouldn't have. I was on top of this barn—I didn't know how I got there—I was worried about my hand and I realized I had to get some help. Somehow I went to my parents' house and they're there but preoccupied, like they were getting ready to go to dinner with some friends. I felt like I was just too much trouble. I was bleeding and messy so I had to go outside. I needed to find my car to go back to the hospital but I had to walk through some low-income housing projects to get there. I thought to myself that it was dangerous but that I could make it. I could do it. Then I was attacked, and that woke me up. In real life, I was attacked one time at gunpoint when I was going to get my car in front of some projects, but I wasn't hurt. It felt really painful that I was such a burden to my parents. I felt like there was nobody else I could turn to. I had to do it myself, even though it was dangerous.

"I guess the dream brought up this conflict I have. I'm afraid of being a burden to others. In my family I was the oldest of four kids, all born within a few years of each other. When we were little, I know my mother was overwhelmed. I had to turn into a caretaker. That was my role and it still is. I need to have a more balanced life, be able to say no to things I don't want to do and have a better sense of what I need help with. Even if my hand doesn't work as well, I need to find that balance because before the accident my life was out of control. I did way too much, was too stressed and had no time for myself. I think the accident was a major wake-up call."

When he paused, I asked Jamie how he felt as he was telling me his dream. I was curious about this because he was, without realizing it, steering our conversation toward clues that his unconscious might be giving him about deeper needs related to the surgeries.

MP: Jamie, what was going on inside of you as you were telling me about your dream just now?

J: I was thinking about my surgeon. He goes over my x-rays with me and tells me all that he can about what he's going to do and what he thinks will happen but there's a point when I have to turn everything over to him. I'm in his hands and I have to trust him. I'm thinking that about you too. I'm not sure what I need. I'm just going to have to trust you to do what you think I need.

MP: It sounds like you're talking about the issue of surrender. Even though it's necessary sometimes, like with your surgeon, it also seems to be your biggest nightmare. I'm thinking how terrified you were after the accident that you might have to surrender your hand. You want to feel like you can do things yourself, like walking into the projects in your dream, yet that leads to danger too. You need to find someplace in the middle, learning what you can let go of and what you can still do yourself to find that balance in life that you're searching for. And we need to find this kind of balance as we begin to work together so that you don't surrender too much to me, but you don't end up feeling that you have to do it all by yourself either.

J: Yes. It's like I need to find a part of me that understands about this kind of balance.

MP: You told me earlier that you had a hard time with your last surgery. Tell me a little more about that.

J: When I was introduced to my surgical nurse, I immediately thought I recognized her. She was the ex-wife of a good friend of mine and an active alcoholic who also abused prescription drugs. I was really in a quandary. Should I check this out? Should I just go through with it? I tried to convince myself that I would be OK but I was terrified. I was afraid that my anxiety about the nurse would have a negative effect on my responses to the surgery. Finally, it was like some part of me came out and said, "No! Look, you have to do something." So I called the head nurse in and asked for another nurse. I ended up with my nurse from the first surgery whom I had really felt comfortable with. It's scary that I could have gone ahead with something that might have been dangerous for me. That's an example of how I don't want to ask for help—I just put myself through things.

MP: It sounds like you need to find that part of you that said, "No! You have to do something!"

J: Yes, that's it.

MP: That's a pretty powerful part of you that can get through your defenses against asking for help *and* all your pain medications to get your attention and say "No!"

J: (*Laughing*) Yes, you're right about that. I need to let that part in more.

Jamie had revealed several important clues that influenced my decision-making process about how to proceed. First, since his was a complex situation, I had known from the first session that we would probably need to combine several methods to prepare him for surgeries. Second, when he shared his dream, I began to focus our conversation more on unconscious as well as conscious levels and found myself using language to elicit information that he could find only through an inner search.[1] Third, I noticed that Jamie framed the problem he wanted help with as a "struggle" or conflict about finding more balance in his life. He also used the language of parts when discussing his goal of finding the part of himself that said "No!" when he was about to go along with the addicted surgical nurse. These are indications that ego-state therapy is an appropriate intervention.

I presented this information to Jamie and told him that I believed that his unconscious mind had already become activated during our conversation. "I think it would be beneficial to start with hypnotic approaches to prepare for surgery because you are drawn to them now. I also think hypnosis can help you find more balance in your life in knowing how much to surrender to the help of others and how much to carry for yourself. And we may also want to use hypnosis to find the part of you that said that strong 'No!' in the hospital."

Jamie agreed with my plan. He indicated that he felt ready to begin and would also be willing to explore other techniques in addition to hypnosis should the need arise. After discussing hypnosis and ego-state therapy, we decided to start our work by finding different self-parts that could respond to the needs that Jamie and I had identified.

Although many clients find their ego states in formal states of hypnosis, others have more positive responses to indirect techniques, including:

- Metaphor and story telling
- Drawing, painting, expressive arts
- Sand tray work or using external objects to represent ego states
- Dreamwork
- Imagery
- Journaling and letter writing assignments
- Indirect activation of ego states through questions and conversational approaches[2]

Since this last approach fit well with Jamie's prior somatic experiencing work with me, I decided to try indirect activation of positive ego-state energies (for strengthening) in the form of a naturalistic age regression:

MP:  Let's try to go back to that moment in the hospital when you heard a part of you say "No! You've got to do something." Can you find that moment?

J:  I'm lying in my hospital bed trying to talk myself into going along with the nurse. I'm getting more and more anxious.

MP:  OK, since that's where you are right now, let's take the opportunity to connect with the anxious part of you that's saying "Just go along with it" first. What's happening inside as you think of that part?

J:  I feel scared.

MP:  Where do you feel the fear in your body?

J:  In my chest, in my arms, my left [*injured*] hand. In my whole body really. . . . . I'm getting more and more anxious and it's scaring me more.

MP:  Then what happens?

J:  Then I hear this voice saying "No" . . . just "No!" (*His voice rises emphatically.*)

MP:  Stay with the no and tell me what, if anything, shifts inside you.

J: The anxiety feels less. I'm still tense but I don't feel scared. My breathing relaxes. The no feels like a protest. "*No!* I don't have to put myself through that!"

MP: OK, just notice those changes and tell me what else you become aware of.

J: My left hand is more relaxed and the right one is more tense. I still feel very activated. . . . Now I'm feeling sad that I had to put myself through all that, that I had to struggle so much, that I couldn't just say no right away.

MP: Jamie, does it seem to you that we're dealing with three different energies here? One connected with fear that says something like, "Maybe you should just go through with it." Another connected with the "No, I don't have to," and a third that feels sad about the struggle? What do you think?

J: Yes, I think that's right.

MP: In the interests of time, let's shift now to find a time of balance . . . a time when your life was in balance just the way you wanted it to be. It may have been a short time or a longer interlude . . . a long time ago or just recently. . . . Just take a few moments and see what comes to you.

J: During college I lived on some land with friends. We grew our own vegetables, lived without electricity like in the pioneer days. We had a wonderful time. I did everything then with my hands. I learned what a pleasure that could be.

MP: It sounds like a wonderful and very important time, Jamie. Stay with that and let's see if we can find a part of you connected with that time on the land. (*Jamie begins to close his eyes.*) Yes, just close your eyes so you can focus fully on that time in your life. You were working hard, yet you had a purpose and a meaning that were in balance. . . . Just let yourself go back there and visit the landscape that you knew so well. . . . When you get all the way there, let me know.

J: I see myself in my overalls in the garden. I have a big smile on my face. . . .

MP: Step into that picture if you can . . . be that person in the overalls back in that time when everything flowed so easily.

J: I feel wonderful. There's plenty of time to do everything I want to do.

MP: Wonderful. Just rest in that part of yourself. With each breath go further into where that energy is inside of you. It's as easy as breathing in . . . and out. . . . Remind yourself of what you felt in your younger body walking around in those overalls . . . connections with the earth . . . the smells . . . the feelings in your body. . . . What are you finding, Jamie?

J: I feel calm, happy. . . . There was so much time to do things that were so deeply satisfying.

MP: May I talk to that part of you?

J: (*Nods*)

MP: So here you are in your overalls with a big smile. You must really enjoy your life.

J: Yeah. I'm doing just what I want to do.

MP: How did you make that happen?

J: Just lucky I guess.

MP: Well, you may have been lucky but I think it must have had something to do with your own strength too. I'm sure there were some obstacles that came up about your lifestyle but somehow you got through them.

J: Yeah, I guess I did.

MP: You went for it and now you're enjoying the benefits, savoring every day. . . . How old are you?

J: I'm not sure. I guess I'm around 19.

MP: You know, Jamie really needs your help. You know what's happened to him, don't you?

J: Yeah, I know.

MP: I'll bet you're not sure you want to leave where you are to come to his aid, are you?

J: Yeah. After all, he was the one who left me.

MP: Jamie did leave you behind, didn't he? Is there any benefit to you to help him now?

J: Yeah, there'd be more connection between us. Jamie was going to come back after graduate school and he didn't.

MP: You've been lonely . . .

J: Yes. It hasn't been the same. . . . He brought the kids back one time (*tearful*). That was really nice.

MP: I can tell you felt really good about being included in Jamie's adult life and that you want more of that kind of connection. So let's find a way to bring you into the present. If you're willing, could you come into his hospital room at the time when he finds out about the alcoholic nurse? Keep your overalls on. . . . Come right in at that moment when he's struggling. (*long pause*) What's happening?

J: I'm just watching. . . . I've got to save his hand. He's really scared and in a lot of pain. I'm going to put some energy into him. I make him sit right up in bed. I give him the strength to call for the nurse. . . . I just step into him and say "*No!*"

MP: Good, do all of that right now.

J: I'm saying, "No! You don't have to put up with that."

MP: Good job! How does that feel?

J: It feels great!

MP: Now, so that you can help in the future, especially during this next surgery, we need to find that part inside who tells Jamie to just put up with it. Do you know why that part of him would give that advice?

The 19-year-old ego state revealed that when Jamie was five or six his mother, with three other small children to care for, felt burdened by his active energy. Jamie's grandmother sent for Jamie and made him feel welcome in her home during the summer and school vacations. Even though he enjoyed his grandmother's special attention, another part of him felt shame about burdening his mother and developed the belief that he should put up with things and not make a fuss. In exploring this experience, we also activated his internal father ego state, who was able to reassure the troubled six-year-old that he was not a burden. Jamie's father ego state also joined the 19-year-old self-part in Jamie's hospital room scene, offering comfort and loving support. Both of these ego states committed themselves to being available as resources before, during, and after the upcoming surgery.

When Jamie came out of hypnosis, he felt very positive about the experience. Because of the surgery and recuperation time afterward, it was likely that I would not see Jamie for some time, but he promised to let me know how the surgery went.

A FEW WEEKS LATER, JAMIE SENT ME A LETTER. He told me that he felt the work we had done had been an important turning point and enclosed a copy of a photograph of himself in overalls during his pioneer days. He shared in the letter that he had felt very fearful before the surgery. While in a meditative state, he brought up images of his pioneer self (i.e., the 19-year-old ego state) and of his father and was able to achieve a level of calm and comfort that helped relieve his fear. His letter related that when he came out of anesthesia, he was in "surprisingly good shape" and "bounced back very fast," leaving the hospital a day early.

We talked by phone after I received his letter. I congratulated him on his successful integration of our previous session in his responses to the surgery. As we discussed briefly the next steps in his healing process,

Jamie told me, "I really need to find a way to help my body heal from these surgeries. I have good resources now to calm my fears. Now, I need to focus on the needs of my body."

When we next met, Jamie told me that his doctors were considering an experimental procedure to lengthen the bone in his hand. Although he was excited about the possibilities, he also acknowledged the risk of infection and the likelihood that the procedure might not bring significant improvement. Sooner or later, Jamie faced accepting that there was nothing more that could be done for his hand. "When that time comes," he said, "I'll be devastated, not just about my hand but also because it means saying goodbye to my surgeon. He's the first person I've been able to trust to really take care of me."

I asked Jamie to tell me about his inner reactions to his expression of those feelings. "I'm getting an image of a little boy who feels so good when he puts himself totally in someone else's hands. I haven't had very much of this and I'm afraid of losing this good feeling."

As we discussed our focus for the rest of the session, I suggested that we explore this little boy image as an avenue for facilitating healing through the SE model.

MP: Jamie, I think it might be helpful to work today with the image of this little boy who is just learning how to trust that it's safe to be taken care of. While you were talking, I noticed that your body was leaning to the right. Were you aware of that?

J: Yes, it was like even my left [*injured*] hand was wanting to lean right.

MP: Stay with the image of the little boy and let your body lean more to the right.

J: I feel this tugging in my chest. That little kid would do anything to please his doctor. He's saying. "I'll be good. I'll thank him so much that he'll want to keep me as a patient."

MP: What's happening in your body now?

J: It's like I'm next to a boundary on my left, like I'm leaning against it and I feel it supporting my body. I notice both kinds of support on my right and my left. I'm looking over the boundary on the left but I can't see the bottom. It's misted over. There are these blue/purple and whitish clouds. . . . It's very pleasant there.

MP: And on the right?

J: I'm having a fantasy of my surgeon going to a specialist with me. We've talked about that and he's willing to go because it would be learning for him. It feels good to have us all together.

MP: And how about back on the left?

J: Well, when I focus on the left, I realize I don't want to give up all that comfort on the right. There are interesting things to explore on the left, though.

MP: Do you feel like you have to choose between the two?

J: I'm realizing that Dr. T and I are building something solid. What we've created won't pass away. . . . Over on the left, the edge of that boundary has dropped down. I don't have to crane my neck to see over it . . . hmmm, now I have an image of holding Dr. T's hand while I'm over on the left. That feels good.

By directing Jamie to focus on both sides of his body and pendulating back and forth, I am helping to promote more somatic integration using two types of resources that are split apart. The resources of a secure, nurturing relationship with his surgeon and a new growthful landscape that is supportive in a different way echo the inner conflict of surrender and autonomy from our earlier ego-state therapy session. I am also using imagery to secure Jamie's body boundaries, which have been compromised by the injury and the medical interventions. By the end of the session, Jamie reports a sense of emotional and physical wholeness.

At the next session, Jamie reported that the last two weeks had gone well in his life, but he looked tired and drawn. He told me that he was beginning to feel stressed out by a job deadline, helping his three kids with their homework, and the approach of the holiday season. "I'm starting to feel like I did before the accident—out of control and exhausted. I need to do some more work on finding balance."

When I asked if he had had a recent experience where he had felt more balanced, Jamie referred to his high school reunion. "It was a wonderful time. A group of us sat around and talked for a long time. I felt relaxed and trusting. There was nothing I had to do to take care of anyone even though we were meeting in my house. Everyone took care of themselves and I felt comfortable when people took care of me when I couldn't use my hand."

We decided to work with this experience to help Jamie generate more ways of replicating it in the future. When I asked him if he thought we could find an inner part of himself that could help, he wasn't sure whether that was the right approach. Since neither of us had a clear idea of how to proceed, I suggested we use hypnosis and ideomotor signals to find out what might be needed.

After we set up the signals, I asked if there were other times when Jamie had had these same feelings of balance and trust. Jamie's "I don't know" finger signaled. When I asked if there were a part of Jamie who knew how to have this experience of balance that he had enjoyed at the reunion, we received a second "I don't know" signal.

At this point, I asked if anything were needed in order to proceed. Jamie's "yes" finger moved and he commented that he did not feel very relaxed. When I asked whether he would like help to go deeper, we received a strong "yes" response. I then gave Jamie some deepening suggestions about finding soft, relaxed energy throughout his body. When I noticed Jamie responding well to these suggestions, I decided to continue taking a more direct approach, deepening his comfort while I continued to suggest ways of finding balance.

Although I checked in with him several times during the session, Jamie appeared to have difficulty talking and signaled that he would like to stay in the experience rather than telling me about it. I continued to interweave different types of suggestions for expanding sensory awareness, deepening relaxation and comfort, and letting go of effort.

After I reoriented him near the end of the session, Jamie told me that he had the experience of looking through light-blue-colored water with little bubbles. He enjoyed the sensation of just floating in the water without trying to make anything happen. "I finally let you be in the driver's seat," he said. "I just enjoyed looking through the water. It was like a rebirth, like I imagine being in the womb would be. And after a while, I didn't know where I was except that I realized I had been very deep when I came out of it."

When Jamie appeared for what would be our third hypnosis session, he had a spring in his step. "I really have different energy after our last session. For a while, I could find the image of looking through that light blue water. Now, the image is faded but I can still reconnect with that feeling of letting go. I've stopped being so hyperresponsible and so wound up. I've been able to stay more fully present with each experience and that's helped me to experience that balance I've been searching for."

Jamie's hand continues to improve slowly. Each surgery is a bit easier, each recovery time shorter. He has come to view the accident as an opportunity for growth and a catalyst for coming to terms with and correcting unhealthy patterns of living and relating. In a recent dream, Jamie was in charge of a baby who fell. The baby was fine and its bruises faded quickly. Toward the end, the baby was talking rapidly and no one could understand him except Jamie. We have viewed this dream, along with other unconscious creations, as a meaningful signpost that keeps us mindful of the transformations he is making toward greater physical, emotional, and spiritual integrity.

# 12

# The Braiding Model:
# Interweaving Modalities for
# Comprehensive Healing

ROBERT: A MYSTERIOUS MUSCULAR CONDITION

Robert slowly dragged his stiff legs and feet into my office. Leaning heavily on a cane, he leveraged himself onto the couch across from me. On the phone he had told me about his symptoms of paralysis, which mimicked those of multiple sclerosis. He had been to more than twenty specialists, including leading neurologists and internists. Numerous MRIs, CAT scans, and blood tests had ruled out various organic causes. His formal diagnosis was idiopathic spastic paraparesis, which, simply put, is a spastic muscular condition of unknown causality.

Aside from his extensive search for an accurate diagnosis, Robert had also consulted a number of treatment specialists offering acupuncture, homeopathy, acupressure, biofeedback, hypnosis, shiatsu, and massage therapy. After a few sessions, most of them dismissed him with "Sorry, I don't think we can help you here."

The only treatment that had helped temporarily was his work with a psychologist at a chronic pain clinic. Here, he participated in approximately 40 hours of different therapies, which included hypnosis, massage therapy, and Feldenkrais. Robert observed some improvement in his balance and mobility, which, unfortunately, diminished over time. He discontinued these approaches shortly after deciding to divorce his wife and make a move across the country to take a new job.

"It's very ironic that I have this problem because pain and ill health have never been problems for me," Robert told me. "I never missed a day of school from elementary through high school because I was never sick. When I went to the dentist, I never needed Novocain because of my unusually high pain threshold. I've never been bothered with extreme temperatures of hot and cold. Of course, I'm aware of dramatic changes but I don't really feel them and become bothered like most people are. Even with my legs, I really don't have pain except when I have a bad fall. Mostly, I have a loss of feeling from just above the knee down to my ankles, with more feeling in my feet. My previous psychologist told me that she thought I had some sort of problem with dissociation but my childhood was pretty typical and I don't think I had any traumas. All of this is a big mystery, but I need to do something because I'm 42 years old. I don't want to end up in a wheelchair. Can you help me?"

SINCE ROBERT'S WAS A HEALTH SITUATION OF LONG-TERM severity and had been largely unresponsive to a wide range of medical and psychological interventions, I negotiated an assessment period for up to 10 sessions. He signed a release form so that I could consult with the psychologist who had treated him with some success and who had facilitated the referral to me.

Dr. Y. told me that Robert had a very poor body sense and that she believed he might have some type of conversion reaction.[1] She had used hypnotic age regression to probe for the possibility of trauma but had found no clear indications. Dr. Y had also used hypnotic ego-state therapy to help Robert connect with a self-part who knew how to walk as well as with other ego states who could support positive changes. These efforts resulted in small gains, as if Robert were beginning to learn to walk again, muscle by muscle. Perhaps her greatest success was to help him begin to examine the impact of his failed marriage on the deterioration of his legs, a process that influenced his resolution to initiate divorce proceedings.

In the first two interviews, I began to obtain a thorough history of Robert's symptoms and of his general life experience. He dated his condition as beginning 18 years earlier, when he noticed in a beginning karate class that he could not respond to the basic movement exercises. Since then, Robert had experienced gradual loss of muscle control in his legs.

His childhood health had been generally good. An intriguing revelation was that Robert had had two injuries playing sports where he had fractured bones. In both instances, Robert did not experience pain but observed that "something wasn't right" and had sought medical attention. A synthesis of other historical information offered additional clues that pointed to the possibility of significant dissociation, or disconnection, from his body. For example, as a very small child, he could not see his toes in the bathtub. "I knew they should be there but they just weren't," he commented.

As I began to fit some of the historical pieces together to form hunches about the origin of his leg symptoms, I suggested to Robert that psychological assessment would be of help to me in formulating a treatment plan. "After all," I said to him, "although you have had every appropriate medical evaluation, you have never had a thorough psychological assessment. And since your medical tests pretty much rule out an organic basis for your problem, I think we need to look for more answers in the psychological realm."

The first step was to refer Robert for thorough psychological testing, a process that required several weeks. During that time, I conducted my own assessment, which included administration of the SCID-D,[2] a structured interview designed to evaluate the presence of a dissociative disorder. Robert scored significantly high on the depersonalization scale, which is characterized by a feeling of detachment or estrangement from one's self, and can include disconnection form one's body or parts of the body.[3]

I also questioned him further to find out more about his relationship history. Robert was initially resistant to this area of inquiry because he did not see any relevance to his leg problems. I explained that we seemed to agree that his difficulties might stem from problems in his relationship to his body. Examining the kinds of relationships he had formed with other people to identify patterns might help us to understand better the ways he related to his own body. Once my rationale was made relevant to Robert's goal of "fixing" his legs, he was immediately cooperative.

I learned that Robert had a brother who was two years younger and that the boys went to two different schools and had very different interests, abilities, and friends. I also learned that his father was raised in foster homes and orphanages. He described his relationships with his parents as pleasant but distant. "They had good intentions," he said, "but they didn't know how to be involved or connected with us." Even when he, his father, and his brother did something together, such as to go on a Boy Scout camping trip, the three of them would move in separate orbits. He does not recall any activities involving all four family members except eating dinner together. He also could not remember seeing any affection between his parents or being touched affectionately by either his mother or father. What was beginning to emerge was a picture of benign neglect and emotional deprivation.

We also talked about his marriage. Robert had married the first girl he dated. His wife Carrie's family was overtly more dysfunctional than his own. Her father was alcoholic and her mother "odd." Robert reported that his marriage was satisfying at first. "Carrie was very attractive and calm and very smart," he related. Yet, soon after the third child was born, Carrie started her own travel business and left childrearing largely up to Robert. Although he tried to support his children's interests, it was clear from his descriptions of their activities that he was woefully uninformed about how to relate to the needs of small children. Carrie, it seemed, was even less equipped than he and rarely participated in family activities. She drifted further and further away, becoming more and more erratic and undependable about keeping family commitments.

We also focused for several sessions on body awareness. I asked Robert to demonstrate and describe the nature of somatic connection, strength, and mobility that was possible at the current time. Robert disclosed that he believed his feet were frequently swollen. "I can only tell when I take my shoes off and look at them. I can feel the floor under them but I don't know where they are unless I look at them or pick them up and put them down."

I learned that when Robert was sitting, he could not move either leg more than an inch off the ground without using his hands to lift the leg up further. He was not able to stand without using both hands to brace. He experienced little trust that his legs would hold him steady without support and had frequent falls, though he taught himself ways of falling that minimized injury. Oddly, or perhaps typically for him, he usually felt nothing on impact. He described the process of falling as "a slow motion movie." "I know I can't recover once the fall begins, so I let it happen rather than hurt myself by bracing on my arms trying to break my fall."

We also invited Alan, the bodyworker with whom I conduct cotherapy, to join us for further assessment. In this meeting, we learned that Robert was unable to hold a felt sense of his legs more than a few seconds, even when Alan directly stimulated a specific area of his lower leg or foot. When Alan began to use Trager rocking motions[4] with both legs, however, Robert reported that the pulses were staying constant and that he felt more relaxed and connected with his legs.

As the session was ending, Robert told us that all of the sensation in both legs had faded. Even when Alan pressed as hard as he could on the tops of Robert's feet or squeezed his toes, the dissociation remained. During our post-session discussion, Alan and I noted that Robert demonstrated several "reversal"[5] phenomena. For example, while deeper breathing usually connects most people more fully with their bodies, it had the opposite effect on Robert, disconnecting him fully from his body. We postulated that rigidity probably helped him to experience his body boundaries, and that if he began to feel too much positive sensation he might become overwhelmed and dissociate as a defense. This type of reaction suggested that Robert might never have formed adequately what Freud termed the "stimulus barrier," meaning that he was not helped to develop boundaries that could screen out or regulate overwhelming or negative sensation or affect. If this were true, then it would make sense that Robert had learned massive dissociation as a way of shutting off intense emotional and body feelings.

It was obvious to me from our discussions that Robert was a very bright man who possessed few social skills. Even though he had an affable manner and was neatly dressed, he demonstrated several oddities that made him significantly different from the norm.

The psychologist who administered the test battery pointed out that Robert's scores were quite high on depression, that he had problems with reality testing, and that there was some evidence that stress might trigger psychotic deterioration. Other results indicated that Robert had a personality disorder, which means that he had certain enduring personal traits that were rigid and somewhat dysfunctional.[6] Supporting data also suggested the presence of conversion disorder and one type of somatoform disorder.[7]

When summarizing the general findings for Robert, I made a rough chart to illustrate the multiple factors that I believed must be addressed in order to achieve permanent resolution of his leg symptoms. These included:

- Dissociation from the body
- Relationship issues (lack of complete attachments to other people as well as to himself)
- Emotional detachment and deprivation
- Spiritual disconnection
- Developmental issues (e.g., confusion in body boundaries, incomplete self/other permanence and constancy)
- Biochemical issues (i.e., medication concerns)
- Sensory awareness limitations

While constructing the list above, I had begun to envision the possibility of interweaving several modalities to provide the type of intensive treatment that Robert's complexity demanded. I struggled with the need to design a treatment plan that would build on skills that Robert already possessed, such as his high motivation to "fix his legs" and his excellent intellectual abilities, while simultaneously addressing some of the immense deficits in his somatic, emotional, and attachment experiences. Unexpectedly, the image of braiding a rope came to mind. I immediately offered the image to Robert as a metaphor for how we could proceed.

"Robert, as we look at this list together, it is obvious that there are a number of important areas here that need our vigorous attention. We must also honor your unique style and the considerable talents you bring to this process to create a structure that will help you integrate the kind of tangible, permanent results we both want to see. One idea would be to choose two of these areas to focus our beginning work and begin to weave them together as if we are braiding a rope so that the two methods we select will fully support and strengthen each other. Once we are building a good strong rope with those two strands, we can add another, interweaving all three strands until we have solid benefits, and then picking up another one, and so on. What do you think?"

Robert was quickly amenable to this idea. When I suggested, however, that one of our first strands needed to be a referral to explore what psychopharmacology might offer, in terms of the high scores on depression, Robert dug in his heels. "Absolutely not," he retorted. "I am not depressed. I've *never* felt depressed. No psychiatrist in his right mind would prescribe medication for me!"

As we explored his objections, I attempted a number of positive ways to present medication to him, all to no avail. Robert remained unmoved. Finally, I told him that if he wanted to work with me, the psychopharmacology referral was non-negotiable, though it would remain his decision, of course, whether to take any medication that was prescribed. He agreed reluctantly, and I went on to explain that the braiding method required a cooperative, team approach, and that the psychopharmacologist I was recommending had served on many successful intervention teams with me. I used the example of how rock-climbing requires strong ropes and team members who communicate well, trust each other's skills, and could perform a number of needed functions.

As we completed the assessment phase, we turned our attention to somatic issues, where Robert's core issues have been expressed. After his first meeting with the psychiatrist, Dr. B, Robert displayed a notable change in attitude. "He really knows what he's talking about," Robert said. "He wants to see me for two or three more sessions to discuss the possible medications that might help me. He seems to believe, like you do, that the problems in my legs are related to some sort of blockage and that certain drugs might help to open things up again."

In the next few weeks, Robert secured the first strand of our treatment braid by agreeing to a trial of Zoloft. We also initiated the second strand by scheduling weekly sessions of body-focused therapy with Alan. After a month of this twice-weekly approach, he reported two significant changes in his somatic functioning. First, his balance had improved so that when standing, he perceived that he did not have to hold onto objects for support as frequently. Second, he experienced an increase in mobility. Robert could now lift his legs without using his hands when he was getting into the bathtub. He could also move his legs more flexibly in a sitting position, a feat he proudly demonstrated by crossing his ankles over either knee, a body position he had not been able to achieve for many years.

During the first few body-focused sessions, we attempted to help Robert form a more constant connection with his legs and feet. After establishing a body safe place in his right foot, we guided him in establishing gradual positive awareness of both feet and the lower leg area below his knees. Alan also activated some trigger points in Robert's feet and ankles designed to stimulate energy flow in his legs. As Robert described the sensations in his legs as vibrations or electrical impulses, he commented, "If my legs were on the verge of moving and I felt these feelings, I would not be able to trust them to hold me up." This comment prompted Alan and me to initiate discussion about the difference between the kind of positive vibrations that are essential for leg movement vs. the kind of leg movement that might signal weakness, instability, or the possibility of collapse.

With individuals like Robert who experience massive dissociation from the body, there are several steps involved in establishing full reconnection. I often find it helpful to explain the steps[8] involved so that people can evaluate their own progress more effectively and feel more confident about extending work from therapy appointments into practice on their own.

- *Body awareness.* This step involves developing a felt sense of various parts of the body, beginning with areas where there is the most awareness and progressing into areas where there is partial or complete disconnection.
- *Sensory discriminations.* Once body awareness is established, the next step is to make more precise discriminations such as identifying which leg is heavier or lighter, which foot is warmer or cooler, whether impulses are electrical or more like undulating waves, etc.
- *Symbolization.* This phase requires clarification of the felt sense of the body by describing verbally various body sensations and other forms of somatic information.
- *Learning.* During this step, heightened awareness of the body is expressed through further explorations and learnings related to specific goals. We emphasize connecting body awareness to relevant cognitive, emotional, spiritual, and other mindbody therapy goals.

- *Integration.* Finally, integration of these learnings is encouraged through the establishment of new, more functional, somatic patterns. In Robert's case, this would involve more flexible movement in his legs as well as in other areas of his life.

During the next few sessions, we began to move through these steps. To focus on step one, for example, we asked Robert to anticipate the feeling of Alan touching his right foot before the touch actually occurred. He was able to experience the kind of warmth he remembered feeling before from Alan's hands. We also asked many questions related to his general awareness of various parts of his lower body followed by inquiries that required him to make more specific sensory discriminations.

After two body awareness sessions with Alan and three individual supportive sessions with me, we noted that Robert's attempts to connect with his body became more rapid and his sensory discriminations more confident. Although he initially struggled for words to describe his somatic experience, Robert became increasingly more adept at finding language to capture the essence of sensations he experienced. As we had hoped, interweaving the biochemical support of Zoloft, successful body-focused sessions with Alan, and sensory awareness/discrimination explorations during individual sessions was beginning to create a strong braided rope that could support Robert's efforts to pull himself toward the summit of full connection with self and others.

During a subsequent body-focused session, we focused on helping Robert walk by holding onto Alan's hands and learning to shift his weight forward to trust Alan's support and find his center of balance. At the next individual session, Robert told me that he had noticed more difficulty in lifting his feet since the last session with Alan. Robert referred to this as a "setback." I wondered aloud if perhaps this step backward was a way that his body could let us know we had attempted too many new accomplishments during a short period of time.

Robert rejoined, "Yes, it's as if part of me is not convinced that all of this is safe for me." When we mused about what could be feeling unsafe for this part of him, I suggested that it was probably too soon for this part to know whether he could trust these new changes, since his hopes had been disappointed so many times in the past. "When you said that just now," Robert added, "I began to feel something inside. It's like that part heard you and thinks you're on the right track."

To utilize this important move of Robert's to share more of his inner world with me, I began to discuss the possibility of adding ego-state therapy to our braiding model.

MP: You know, even though we've had this little setback, I think we've
been making good steady progress during these few weeks. When
you mentioned that a part of you may be feeling unsafe, I began
to wonder about the hypnosis work you did with Dr. Y. and
whether you worked with different parts of yourself then.

R: Yes, we did. I don't remember too much about it now (*long pause*)
. . . but I do remember that we worked with a part of me that
knew how to walk and I think we worked with some parts connected to emotions . . . and then somehow we worked with actual
parts of my body, like pretending that my leg could talk to us.

MP: I want to honor the pace we need to use so that all of you can
hold onto the changes and feel safe. Yet maybe it's the right time
to talk about adding another strand to the rope we're braiding
so that we can address the inner reactions you are beginning
to have about the different moves we're making. What do you
think? We've talked a little about EMDR and imagery and there
are some other approaches we haven't discussed yet that we could
consider.

R: I think we should work with the parts of me first. After all, it
was one of the few things that worked for me before even though
the positive reactions were delayed. I mean, they didn't come
right after the session where we did the work but at least they
came!

MP: That's a good reason to choose ego-state work, Robert. Also, adding this method fits where you are right now in terms of what you
spontaneously shared with me today. And, because there's an issue
of feeling safe, if we add work with inner parts, we're adding a
method that is already familiar to you.

To build further stability, we reviewed previous skills at our next body-
focused session without adding anything new. When we convened for
the individual appointment that followed, Robert reported that he had
experienced no setbacks. Instead, he had experienced only one fall, which
was a significant reduction from his usual frequency. He also told me he
felt he was ready to start the ego-state work we had discussed. At Robert's
invitation, I began to make suggestions for physical relaxation and a deepening of awareness, shifting from external surroundings to a focus on his
inner world where less conscious parts of him could be found. Using
language he remembered from his meetings with Dr. Y, I asked him to
find a special place where he could feel comfortable and relaxed about
being himself. To my surprise, Robert had an immediate response that
featured vivid sensory details:

R: I'm on a raft floating on a big lake. It's a warm day and I can feel the warmth of the boards under my feet. There's just a little bit of a breeze but I can feel this little rocking motion that I remember when I used to be a kid.

MP: Is the part of you around who isn't sure that all we are doing is safe?

R: Yes. He's very small . . . I think he's my age but he's very far away. I can barely see him. It doesn't feel like he's even inside of me.

MP: That's good that you have found him. Can you tell if he knows you are watching him? Do you have his attention?

R: Yes, I think so.

MP: Is it OK with you if I try to talk to him?

R: Sure.

MP: I'm glad you're here, but sorry that you are not sure what we are doing is safe for you. Is there anything we can do that would help you feel comfortable about coming closer so we can try to help you to feel more safe?

R: (Pause) He says, "Make room for me. There are other parts who are stronger than I am and they crowd me out."

MP: Can you let Robert know what you're afraid of, that is, what makes you feel unsafe? If you can tell us, maybe that would let us know how to work with the other parts so we can make room for you.

R: I think he's afraid of getting hurt not just physically but emotionally too.

MP: Hmmm . . . are you scared of getting your hopes up and then when it doesn't always work you feel really bad?

R: Yes, that's it.

MP: Robert, do you think you could invite this part of you to participate in what you are working on outside of our sessions, the exercises in sensory awareness and balancing, when you believe it is relatively safe? That is, could you invite him to be present when you feel the most comfortable about what you are practicing?

R: Yes, that's a good idea. I can do that. Maybe this will help me to feel like I don't have to be constantly testing every move to make sure it's safe. Maybe I can start to relax in my body sometimes.

After this session, we have continued to interweave body and sensory awareness and discriminations with ego-state work. Our three strands served to support and further potentiate each other. The ego state that felt unsafe began to come closer to other parts of Robert and also feel more secure about the variety of somatic learnings that were taking place. Robert began to sustain better balance and mobility between sessions.

We have decided to add TFT as a fourth strand in our work to offer ways of correcting the reversals and neurological switching we have observed in his body experience. Hopefully, TFT will accelerate some of the gains Robert has made in mobility and balance. EMDR will probably serve as the fifth strand in our work so that we can begin to link to and reprocess past experiences of deprivation and loss that may have generated the original barriers to somatic integration.

Robert is continuing to report steady gains from the braiding model. Though this approach might not serve the needs of every client, it is likely that clients who exhibit similar health complexity may benefit from this type of intensive, multimodal intervention.

# Conclusions

Hopefully, you are feeling inspired by what you have read. The stories in this book were carefully chosen to give you a sense of the remarkable possibilities inherent in applying the principles and methods of energy psychology to mindbody symptoms.

There were many more case examples I did not include because they did not "play" as well for a reading audience. Just because they are not as dramatic, however, does not mean that important healing failed to occur. On the contrary, those unpublished stories reflect all the "nuts and bolts" issues of real life—struggles, disappointments, flounderings, and frustrations—as well as the ultimate triumphs.

Of course, like all therapists, I have my share of failures. These usually occur with people for whom my direct style or focused approaches to healing are not a good fit. Energy therapy's action-oriented approach is not for everyone. As one client said to me recently, "I really don't want to change anything. I just want the luxury of being listened to." There are many people for whom the best healing at a given time in their journey may be a supportive and safe place to sort out and clarify their health situations rather than to leap into action. For others, the shift from therapy's usual emphasis on content and meaning to energetic change can feel strange or somehow incomplete. Though the importance of meaning is undisputed, practitioners devoted to energy psychology believe that deeper meaning arises organically when full life energy flow creates wholeness, rather than primarily through cognitive insight.

One of the clearest benefits of the energy methods is that they can resolve health symptoms so quickly. Yet for some of us, rapid change can be frightening. Unless energy therapy is paced properly and respectfully, positive changes can easily unravel. This means that energy methods, particularly the newer, more experimental ones without adequate scientific validation, must be used by well-trained, licensed psychotherapists. It is these professionals, rather than lay people trained only in a technique, who have the expertise to assess thoroughly a person's health circumstance in terms of the appropriateness of energy approaches. Suggestions for how to find a well-trained therapist in each of the featured modalities follow in Appendix D.

Regrettably, there is a small percentage (5–10%) of people with health problems who simply do not heal, regardless of the methods used, just as there are 5–10% of those with severe illnesses who go into spontaneous remissions. Although these cases are well documented, and reflect the ways in which our entire health population is distributed statistically, we do not fully understand the rationale for either end of the continuum, though many theories have been posed. We *cannot* assume that people who don't heal have caused their own problems or that they are not doing enough to help themselves, a condition that has been referred to as "New Age guilt."[1]

Although I am far from claiming a perfect record in resolving health symptoms, I can say with confidence that I have rarely encountered individuals who did not obtain at least partial relief from at least one of the methods presented in this book, provided they were willing to experiment until finding an approach that "clicked." The prospect of experimentation may overwhelm some people's capacities to weather further discouragement and interim defeats. The bottom line is, in order to determine whether any of these methods will work for you, you have to try it to find out exactly how you will respond.

IF YOU WANT TO KNOW WHETHER THE METHODS presented in *Finding the Energy to Heal* would be useful for you or for someone you know or work with as a client, there are a few factors to consider. It is difficult to draw specific conclusions about the viability of each method from the results shared in the stories you have just read. This is because, in most cases, multiple methods were used. As a clinician, my interest was in obtaining the best results for each person who consulted with me, rather than proving or disproving the effectiveness of any particular approach. I hope that professionals more oriented toward research will do the hard work that will help us to make more scientific comparisons.

In addition to the guidelines presented in "Introducing Integrated Models," however, I can offer the following points to factor into the decision process for selecting energy therapy methods:

*EMDR*

I always consider a trial of EMDR when the health symptom is stress or anxiety based, especially if trauma is part of the picture. Since EMDR works rapidly with single incident trauma, it is highly effective with medical trauma that results from surgery, injuries, accidents, and catastrophic events. EMDR is also valuable in helping people achieve any type of multifaceted health change—at cognitive, sensory, emotional, physical, and spiritual levels—in a relatively short time.

Advantages of EMDR include the ability to help someone reprocess, or transform, distressing events that may be contributing to health imbalance so that they are no longer stressful. I also find that when I use the EMDR model with positive target images, the strengthening and stabilization phase of treatment can be completed more quickly. Finding out how mindbody pathways to healing may be blocked by dysfunctional beliefs or thought patterns can also be determined and corrected relatively quickly using this approach.

I have heard a few complaints about the mechanics of EMDR (for example, that the eyes tire or that eye movements stimulate unpleasant sensations like light-headedness). Some clients also feel unduly pressured to produce useful associations during or after each set. These difficulties are rare, however, and can usually be overcome with supportive discussion and further experience.

*Hypnosis*

People who have conversion symptoms or dramatic physical symptoms such as paralysis or pain in the absence of organic causes usually respond well to clinical hypnosis, as do those who have dissociative disorders and symptoms that result from trauma.[2] This is because these are trancelike conditions that suggest high hypnotic ability. I also choose formal hypnosis with people who are curious about hypnosis and feel some affinity for the method. Even if a person is not an excellent hypnotic subject, it is possible to obtain excellent results with practice and training.

Ericksonian suggestion is a fundamental aspect of my communication style. I find the principles invaluable in establishing a "mutual yes set," that is, a context where my client and I are in complete agreement about what we are attempting to accomplish. To increase motivation, defuse resistances, and introduce indirect routes to change in almost any health situation, Ericksonian hypnosis is a natural choice.

Direct or indirect ego-state therapy is, for me, an essential tool when dealing with inner conflict related to health issues. When past trauma has created fragmentation or division in the personality, I combine ego-state work with clinical or Ericksonian hypnosis in order to detect and solve the problems among self-parts that may be contributing to the formation of mindbody symptoms and to ineffective efforts toward resolving them.

Because these interactions usually occur at an unconscious level, some form of hypnosis may be useful. EMDR is also highly effective in work with ego states, potentiating or speeding up hypnotic efforts to resolve barriers to inner cooperation and sometimes achieving good results without hypnosis.

One of the disadvantages of hypnosis involves the complexity of formal trance states. Sometimes when people have personality structures that are very fragile, they can become overwhelmed quickly by anxiety-producing imagery, sensations, and emotional feelings. Although hypnosis helps us relax by lowering our defenses, for some individuals relaxation removes important barriers that have protected them from painful awarenesses. Without sufficient preparation, hypnosis may be inappropriate for people with severe, multiple psychological traumas in their histories or who have longstanding clinical problems such as psychosis, major depression, or personality disorders. Careful screening by a well-trained professional is *always* recommended.

*Imagery*

Although imagery is not thought of as an energy therapy approach, it is a basic staple of human experience, and therefore of any treatment. Though not a trendy element of the emerging energy frontier, the healing effects of imagery with mindbody health symptoms are perhaps more widely documented than any other healing method. Some experts believe that the bioenergy that flows between images and neurotransmitters, the informational messengers of the brain that turn on healing responses throughout the organism, is where mind and body meet.[3]

I use imagery with people who are drawn to hypnosis but need more control over the process of exploring the unconscious. I also use imagery as a convenient way of tapping into the abilities of the creative imagination, which is an essential ingredient of every healing path. Since imagery occurs spontaneously as a rich element of our fantasy lives, it is rare *not* to encounter imagery in responses to all of the other methods of energy psychology.

*Thought Field Therapy (TFT)*

TFT is the most experimental of the energy therapies presented. I tell people that I do not know whether TFT will help them and that there is no solid research validating over time any positive results we might get. TFT's advantages include the fact that it is easily taught and can obtain fast results without overwhelming the client with information related to the symptom, a distinct benefit for people who are not cognitively oriented. TFT seems to work directly to stimulate the energy centers of the body by tapping on specific meridian points that are high conductors of electrical energy, and many people who use it report feeling pleasant energy shifts along with cessation of symptoms.

I usually include a trial of TFT for health problems with a pain component that has not responded to more conventional methods. I have had clients who do not obtain significant results with TFT, but I have never encountered a situation where someone's symptoms were made worse. Usually, the worst that occurs is nothing at all. The only real downside, aside from its odd appearance, is that with more complex problems shifting back and forth to various protocols and lengthy tapping sequences can seem tedious.

### Emotional Freedom Techniques (EFT)

This is a model developed by businessman Gary Craig, who based his approach closely on Callahan's TFT approach. EFT differs in the fact that one basic tapping "recipe" is used on every problem, whether emotional or physical, and in its folksy style. Craig's rationale is that by including all of the major meridians in the recipe, most problems can be helped because the affected meridian will be addressed. This is a shortcut intended to streamline diagnosis and treatment procedures, which can be cumbersome and time-consuming. The downside is that EFT does not offer the precision of Gallo's energy diagnosis and treatment method and Callahan's TFT methodology.

### Somatic Experiencing (SE)

The body has a central position in the practice of energy psychology. When there is clear trauma to the body, SE is a gentle, highly effective method for exploring and resolving physiological roots of traumatic events as well as for helping people with health problems learn to regulate somatosensory states of pain and hyperarousal. SE can also help most people to integrate their awareness of their bodies into a more complete range of experience.

Occasionally, I encounter people who have difficulty finding, or following, the SIBAM elements once they collide with powerful, trauma-related energies. In these cases, introducing relaxation, imagery, hypnotic techniques, or EMDR can help provide more rapid stabilization and the needed resources to achieve self-regulation.

THESE ARE EXCITING TIMES. THE FIELD OF PSYCHOLOGY IS joining behavioral and Chinese medicine to deliver accelerated, yet integrative, healing opportunities for the whole person—mind/body/spirit—that were never before possible. If I have tempted you to open the door of curiosity even a fraction more, then *Finding the Energy to Heal* has fulfilled its mission.

# Glossary

## EMDR

**Clinical target image:** An image that represents the symptom, or past disturbing experiences related to the symptom, selected for EMDR processing.

**Conflict-free image:** An image that represents a time of wholeness and completely positive feelings. Inner conflict, anxiety, stress, discomfort, and health symptoms are absent. Ideally, this is a time of activity built into one's regular routine. Examples include playing a musical instrument, gardening, hiking, meditation, playing with grandchildren. This type of image can be used with any of the energy methods.

**Interweave:** New information added to speed up blocked processing. Ideally, the interweave contains needed information that would have been available except for blockage of inner pathways by trauma responses. Types of interweaves include:

*Cognitive interweave:* New cognitive, adult perspective added by the therapist in the form of questions or statements designed to help the client find missing information.

*Counterbalancing interweave:* Added when someone is looping or overwhelmed by traumatic feelings. Designed to facilitate complete processing by adding new information that is "counter" or opposite to the activated state or feelings.

*Developmental learning interweave:* Important information designed to help people learn to better manage inner or interpersonal boundaries, regulate powerful emotions, and hold positive attachments to self and others.

*Resource interweave:* Important information revealed by associations during EMDR or in life experiences. The therapist identifies and utilizes this resource to facilitate ego strengthening and more complete reprocessing of the target.

*Renurturing interweave:* Resource interweave offered to repair past experiences of parenting that were abusive, incomplete, or damaging to facilitate reprocessing.

*Safety interweave:* New information that adds to the safe place image and introduced as a positive target image or used during processing of clinical targets to increase sense of safety and stability.

*Temporal resource interweave:* New information that helps us realize that instinctual reactions at the time of a stressful event are useful and that important learning has taken place as a result of the traumatic experience.

**Looping:** When EMDR processing seems stuck. The client may be repeating similar associations, feelings, thoughts, or images and is not progressing.

**Positive target image:** A sensory image used to represent an experience that evokes only positive feelings when symptoms are not present (e.g., pain-free interlude).

**Protocol:** A recipe or step-by-step formula for dealing with specific types of symptoms. For example, there are special EMDR protocols for depression, dissociative disorders, illness and somatic disorders, and phobias.

**Reprocessing (also processing):** Rapid free association of information between trauma memory networks and informational networks during eye movement sets which results in the reduction of distress, as measured by SUD, and a "metabolizing" of the trauma.

**SUD (Subjective units of disturbance scale):** This is a personal scaling of distress (from zero to 10) activated by a clinical target image chosen for reprocessing. Used in EMDR (and TFT) to measure baseline emotional or physical pain and also to assess progress being made.

**Target:** A goal for reprocessing related to past trauma or distressing events believed to contribute to current symptoms. Can be a full or partial memory, dream image, sensory fragment (feeling in the body, image, sound or voice, etc.), or current awareness.

# Hypnosis

**Age progression:** Direct or indirect suggestions used to imagine future possibilities and positive consequences of current changes. A positive progression suggests integration and good use of the healing method applied; negative progression can indicate a need for more strengthening or different approaches.

**Age regression:** Direct or indirect suggestions to travel back in time for reviewing or recalling a past experience or memory.

**Direct suggestion:** Directives given in straightforward language to appeal to conscious logic. Examples are: "Close your eyes now," and "Begin to feel comfortable."

**Ideomotor signals:** Used in hypnosis to link the body's motoric responses in hands or fingers to suggestions or questions. Basic responses are "yes," "no," and "I don't know or I'm not ready to say."

**Ideosensory signals:** Involuntary sensory responses linked to suggestions or questions. Examples are body sensations, images, auditory thoughts, kinesthetic or affective feelings which can increase as a "yes" response and decrease as a "no" response.

**Indirect suggestion:** In hypnosis, subtle, covert directives given in vague, permissive language designed to appeal to unconscious, creative process. Example: "Many people believe it is helpful to *close your eyes* in hypnosis because *you can feel more comfortable.*"

**Induction:** A series of suggestions designed to bridge from the normal waking state to a less conscious one by dissociating the conscious attention while activating and amplifying unconscious. Some inductions are structured and formal (e.g., fixating the eyes on a stimulus, visualizing a relaxing scene, or relaxing progressive muscle groups). Others are indirect, such as conversational and naturalistic techniques that utilize moments of inner attention and relaxation occurring naturally in a given situation.

**Posthypnotic suggestion:**   Direct or indirect suggestions given while in hypnosis related to desirable future behaviors, feelings and experiences.

**Utilization:**   A basic principle of Ericksonian hypnosis, which holds that *every* symptom, attitude, behavior, and experience, whether negative or positive, can be useful as assets or resources in the healing process.

## Imagery

**Eidetic imagery:**   A type of image known for its vivid, stable qualities and its ability to emanate or move, generally progressing from negative to positive meanings.

**Guided imagery:**   Complementary to hypnosis though independent. Imagery approaches can be suggested to enhance healing, promote positive physiological, emotional, and behavioral changes, and expand insights and awareness.

**Hypnagogic imagery:**   Thought of as a sleep disorder. Infrequent hallucinations (usually visual) that occur with a subjective sense of being awake. Accompanied by anxiety or panic.

## TFT

**Neurological disorganization (aka "switching"):**   A condition where the central nervous system misinterprets nerve impulses. Signs include reversal of letters and numbers, directions, spatial sense, etc. Can block muscle testing and responses to TFT and other energy methods.

**Neurolymphatic reflex point:**   A lymphatic point in the left and right chest, approximately one inch below the collarbone notch and three inches toward the right or left. Connected to the lymphatic system and used to clear reversals.

**Nine (9) gamut treatment:**   A rather bizarre series of tapping sequences where the client taps the back of the hand in the gamut spot "v" or apex underneath and between the little and ring fingers. So called because nine different actions are performed while tapping the gamut spot continually. These include moving and rolling the eyes in prescribed directions, humming a tune, and counting aloud.

**Protocol:**   A formula or recipe for treating presenting symptoms consisting of directions to tap specific energy points along the meridians in a particular sequence or order.

**Psychological reversal:**   This is a complex interference phenomenon, which includes psychological and bioenergetic blocks to TFT methods, including ambivalent motivations and fears, reactions to toxins, and neurostructural impairment. Correcting a reversal typically involves repeating affirmations related to self-acceptance while rubbing the neurolymphatic reflex point in the left chest. Types can be general, context or criterion specific, recurrent (symptoms recur after a decrease), or intervening (progress comes to a plateau).

**Thought field:**   The cluster of cognitive, sensory, emotional, neurochemical aspects of a symptom and its surrounding energy field, which is thought to be electromagnetic.

# Body-Focused Psychotherapy

**Body scan:** A basic technique used to survey or scan the body from head to feet in order to identify a wide range of positive, neutral, and uncomfortable body responses, and to enhance connection to the body.

**Counter vortex:** A configuration of healing energy that develops in response to the trauma vortex. Expansive and transformative, it is used to counterbalance and renegotiate traumatic experiences in SE.

**Felt sense:** A term originally used by Eugene Gendlin to describe a sensory or body awareness rather than an intellectual understanding of a person, situation, or event.

**Pendulation:** Bridging between trauma and counter vortexes of energy, following the oscillation of these opposing forces to create a new response, that of renegotiation.

**Rhythmic alternating stimulation (RAS):** A method developed for bodyworkers to incorporate into body-focused therapy. Stimulates lateral eye movements of EMDR through alternating stimulation of craniosacral points, alternating rocking movements of the extremities, and alternating stimulation of specific meridian points. Used to provide safe and strengthening somatic experience, to relieve pain, somatic symptoms, anxiety, and depression, to enhance general health, to provide somatic nurturing experiences, and to calm fear and hyperarousal states.

**SIBAM:** A therapeutic model proposed by Peter Levine to describe the flow of integrated inner experience. The five components include sensation, sensory imagery (internal impressions of external stimuli), behaviors as voluntary and involuntary movements, affects, and meaning. During trauma, one or more of these elements are split off from our awareness due to the mechanisms of dissociation. When we are fully connected to the first four dimensions, the fifth component naturally follows.

**Somatic experiencing (SE):** A method developed by Peter Levine, which involves tracking and rebalancing biopsychological responses related to trauma including shock/immobility/freezing responses, dissociative or uncoupled reactions, overwhelming/flooding/hyperarousal responses, and constrictions, or holding in the body.

**Trauma vortex:** In SE, a metaphorical concept of the organization of trauma-related energies in the body that contribute to physical, emotional, cognitive, and spiritual symptoms.

# Notes

INTRODUCTION

1. An excellent discussion of qi can be found in *The Web That Has No Weaver: Understanding Chinese Medicine* by Ted J. Kaptchuk, O.M.D., especially pp. 35–41.
2. See Kaptchuk's discussion of the *Nei Jing*, a resource from Chinese medicine which presents the impact of emotions on illness, pp. 129–131.
3. For a fascinating discussion of this possibility, see Fred Gallo, 1999, *Energy Psychology: Explorations at the Interface of Energy, Cognition, Behavior, and Health*, especially pp. 14–15.
4. Defining "energy" and "energy systems" is a complex process. The reader is referred to Gallo's (1999) varied and comprehensive discussion of the body's bioenergy systems in chapter 3, "The Energy Paradigm," pp. 33–49.
5. See Gallo's presentation of evidence for the positive results of energy stimulation on pain and other correlates of illness, pp. 36–43, in the same text.
6. The reader might want to consult such references as: Alman & Lambrou, 1992; Erickson, Hershman, & Secter, 1961; Hammond, 1990; and Weil, 1995, for more information on applications of hypnosis with health symptoms.
7. Some authors who document the use of imagery in healing are: Achterberg, 1985; Pelletier, 1977; Weil, 1995.
8. See Francine Shapiro, 1995.
9. Professionals who have documented these clinical applications of EMDR include (in order of topics mentioned): van der Kolk, 1997; Fine & Berkowitz, 1998; Phillips & Frederick, 1995; Phillips, 1997; Parnell, 1998; Manfield,1997; Manfield, 1998b; Wildwind, 1993; Frederick & McNeal, 1999; Lovett, 1998.
10. An exception is the chapter in Shapiro & Forrest (1997) on "The Final Doorway: Facing Disease, Disability, and Death," pp. 201–221.
11. Perhaps the most readable presentation of thought field therapy is *Thought Field Therapy and Trauma: Treatment and Theory*, written by Callahan in 1996.
12. See the article written by Wylie in the *Family Therapy Networker* (1996) describing the study by Charles Figley that compared the effects of EMDR, TFT, V/KD (visual/kinesthetic dissociation), and TIR (traumatic incident reduction). A more scholarly review of this study is given by Gallo, 1999, chapter 2, "Highly Efficient Therapies," pp. 17–49.
13. This four-stage model of treatment was developed by Claire Frederick and me in *Healing the Divided Self*. See pp. 36–43.
14. Thich Nhat Hahn (1999). "Buddhism and psychotherapy: Planting good seeds."

## INTRODUCING EMDR

1. Claire Frederick, M.D., and I wrote *Healing the Divided Self: Clinical and Ericksonian Hypnotherapy for Post-traumatic and Dissociative Conditions* in 1993 and finished it in 1994. It was published in early 1995 by W.W. Norton. This is a book for professionals about the uses of hypnosis with the whole spectrum of trauma-related conditions, including PTSD, dissociative symptoms and disorders, and dissociative identity disorder (DID).
2. Joseph Wolpe is a distinguished psychologist who contributed to the development of the cognitive behavioral approach to psychotherapy.
3. I stimulate eye movements primarily with hand passes using my index and middle fingers as a guide. Many other therapists use special light panels to provide alternating visual stimuli, offer alternate tapping on hands and knees (alternating kinesthetic stimuli), and use alternating auditory stimuli (earphones with musical or sound tones). Although these are viable alternatives, and in some cases necessary to provide effective reprocessing, I usually prefer my hands and fingers.
4. Shapiro presents a discussion of this theory in both her 1995 and 1997 books.
5. For a comprehensive treatment of the cognitive, emotional, physical, social/developmental effects of trauma, see van der Kolk et al. (1996).
6. Shapiro clarifies that memory networks can be thought of as metaphorical in nature. She theorizes that they are a series of channels where related memories, images, thoughts, emotions, and physical sensations are stored and linked. See Shapiro, 1995, pp. 32–33. A related concept is that of state-dependent memory which helps to explain why a traumatic event is likely to evoke aspects of previous traumatic experiences. For a discussion of this, see Ernest Rossi, 1993, pp. 47–68.
7. See Peter Levine's presentation of these mechanisms in his book, *Waking the Tiger*.
8. Laurel Parnell presents this view in *EMDR in the Treatment of Adults Abused as Children*, pp. 7–8.

## CHAPTER 1

1. For a thorough description of how to select appropriate clinical targets for EMDR, see Francine Shapiro, 1995, pp. 74–76.
2. I first developed the concept of positive EMDR targeting in my work with conflict-free imagery presented in a 1997 workshop on ego-strengthening at the EMDRIA conference in San Francisco.
3–4. For a succinct description of the relationship of cognitive interweaves and looping, see Philip Manfield's chapter on EMDR terms and procedures, 1998a, p. 25.
5. My term "resource interweave" is similar to Andrew Leeds' term "resource installation" (see Leeds, 1998, pp. 272–278). The main difference is that while I utilize resources that occur spontaneously for the client, Leeds usually suggests or constructs them with the client.
6. I could certainly have shifted to the use of the standard EMDR protocol at this point. However, I believed that a second session with positive targeting would prove to anchor and integrate the positive changes she had made and might

even resolve the symptom since she had made such a dramatic behavioral change following the first session.

7. For a complete discussion of transference and countertransference issues in the therapeutic relationship, see Robert Langs, *Interactions: The Realm of Transference and Countertransference.*

8. From an ego-strengthening perspective, the principle of mastery is used to enhance self-efficacy, the confidence that one can accomplish a particular task, such as reinstating the sleep cycle following an episode of insomnia. The term "mastery" is used to describe a state of accomplishment, command, or proficiency.

9. In ego-state therapy, it is possible, and sometimes advisable, to acknowledge the current needs of a particular state without probing experiences of past trauma so that stability can be maintained.

10. To learn about the ego-state model therapy, see Jack and Helen Watkins' book, *Ego States.*

11. The renurturing interweave is derived from the hypnotic tradition of renurturing which produces profound affective responses. See Hammond, 1990, pp. 326–328, and Frederick and McNeal, 1999, pp. 185–189.

12. The inner state Richard is describing here is a precursor to personality integration or wholeness. From an ego-state therapy perspective, integration occurs when the ego states of the internal family are working together cooperatively. See *Healing the Divided Self*, pp. 167–169, for the stages that lead to integration in ego-state therapy.

13. For detailed information about cognitive interweaves, see Shapiro's 1995 discussion, pp. 244–271.

14. Shirley McNeal's application of Heinz Hartmann's concept resulted in the development of several important ego-strengthening tools, including the "Inner Strength" technique. A script for Inner Strength can be found in *Healing the Divided Self*, p. 88, or on p. 141 in Frederick and McNeal's *Inner Strengths.* McNeal's and Frederick's contributions in this area have had primary influence on my development of conflict-free imagery.

15. When using the standard EMDR protocol, it might be unusual to encounter such frequent negative looping early on. However, I have found that any negative looping that occurs during positive targeting for ego-strengthening brings two important benefits. First, negative looping at this point can identify specific barriers that are blocking healing and that will continue to block progress if left unaddressed. Second, this occurs in an early context of safety where there is usually less resistance from the client toward the process of identifying and resolving longstanding obstacles.

16. Although I studied developmental concepts as part of my training as a psychologist, it wasn't until I met Elgan Baker in the early 1990s that I began to grasp the significant impact of unfinished developmental issues on current adult problems, including mindbody symptoms.

## CHAPTER 2

1. See Shapiro & Forrest, chapter 11, "The Final Doorway: Facing Disease, Disability, and Death," pp. 201–221. The protocol for illness and somatic problems is in Shapiro, 1995, pp. 229–243.

2. There is a growing body of literature on PTSD (posttraumatic stress disorder) resulting from medical procedures and from health crises. For a recent review, see Shalev et al., 1993.

3. There are no data regarding the occurrence of headaches with eye movements during EMDR. Practitioners are instructed to test the speed and direction of eye movements, and if headache occurs, to modify eye movements accordingly.

4. In order to help the client create a safe place image, the steps of the safe place exercise in the standard EMDR protocol are highly recommended (see Shapiro, 1995, pp. 122–124).

5. These techniques can also be used, as Laurel Parnell (1999, pp. 45–54), has mentioned, to help the client stay connected to traumatic memories, to chronicle progress, or for additional exploration of meaningful imagery that surfaces during EMDR.

6. The best available interview scale for suspected dissociative disorders is the SCID-D (Structured Clinical Interview for DSM-IV Dissociative Disorders-Revised), developed by Marlene Steinberg (1994).The Dissociative Experience Scale (DES) developed by Bernstein & Putnam (1986) and the PTSD module of the SCID (Structured Clinical Interview for DSM-III-R) developed by Spitzer et al. (1990) may also be useful.

7. The SARI model is a spiral, not a linear progression. As clients' needs for restabilization change, we recycle through earlier stages of work.

## INTRODUCING HYPNOSIS

1. For a comprehensive review of this issue, see Brown, Scheflin, & Hammond, 1998.

2. See Rossi, 1993, and Rossi & Cheek, 1988, for a complete presentation of ideodynamic healing.

3. T.A. Wadden & C.H. Anderton draw this conclusion in their 1982 review of the hypnotic literature.

4. See Norris, 1989, pp. 275–277.

5. My approach with Ted resembles one of Milton Erickson's cases, which can be found in Haley, *Advanced Techniques of Hypnosis and Therapy*, pp. 34–35.

6. Highly recommended for the study of Milton Erickson's work is the four-volume set of his collected papers (Rossi, 1980).

7. An interesting discussion of techniques that can interrupt habitual patterns can be found in Steve Gilligan's *Therapeutic Trances*, pp. 240–261.

8. See Carole Kershaw's book, *The Couple's Hypnotic Dance*, for an extended discussion.

9. See Lankton & Lankton, *The Answer Within*, for presentations on internal resources and how to retrieve them.

10. For a comprehensive guide to this approach, see Watkins & Watkins, 1997.

11. An example of a more indirect approach to activate ego states for healing can be found in my 1995 article on using ego-state therapy with an AIDS patient where I used ideosensory signals.

## CHAPTER 3

1. Although this is true, there are also good outcome data for cognitive behavioral approaches to addiction, which emphasize personal responsibility and choice,

in contrast to 12-step programs, which are based on the medical model and teach that addicts are victims of forces beyond their control. In general, I believe that most people in recovery are best served by a combination of individual therapy and group experiences that provide social modeling support.

2. Some people in early recovery have difficulties with disrupted attention that can make sustained inner focus difficult. Uncovering approaches with hypnosis are problematic because they may stir up inner memories and feelings that the newly recovering person is not equipped to handle and may trigger relapse. Other contraindications include people who tend to use hypnosis, or any other therapy technique, to avoid confronting and dealing with addiction as a central issue. However, hypnosis, especially self-hypnosis, can be helpful in teaching recovering addicts the values of positive self-attention and the use of relaxation to help regulate overwhelming negative emotional reactions. This is the approach I used with Mason.

3. The Inner Strength technique and script can be found on pages 140–146 of *Inner Strengths* by Frederick and McNeal.

4. See Phillips and Frederick, 1995, pp. 45–50, for information about informal assessment using different types of hypnotic suggestion.

5. Many people find self-hypnosis challenging at first and report difficulty in achieving satisfactory depth on their own. I find it helpful to introduce the client to hypnosis for several sessions first so that there is comfort and familiarity with a range of hypnotic experiences before introducing self-hypnosis. It can also be useful to have clients practice leading themselves into trance during the session so that they can get help and encouragement before they practice at home.

6. I have found Stephanie Brown's developmental model of addiction very helpful. See her book *Treating Alcoholism*.

7. I wrote my doctoral dissertation on self-efficacy and alcohol/drug treatment. One of the main findings was that high scores on self-efficacy predicted completion of a four-week program, whereas low scores predicted premature dropout.

8. This approach is useful when a client requests any specific technique, but is especially true of hypnosis. Because of sensational portrayals by the media, which has sparked controversy over many years, there has been a high incidence of public misconception. It is important to discuss and clarify the context for clinical uses of hypnosis, which is quite different from stage or media hypnosis, for example.

9. For discussions about the importance of achieving mastery over symptoms that activate traumatizing reactions such as helplessness and anxiety, see Phillips & Frederick, 1995, pp. 82–100, and Frederick & McNeal, 1999, pp. 42–47.

10. Ideomotor signaling requires the client to identify several communication signals (usually *yes, no*, and *I don't know*, a privacy signal). Although some practitioners assign signals to the client, I use a permissive approach, allowing clients to find their own signals. Most identify finger signals, some their hands, or some combination of fingers and hands.

11. For a recent review of the uses of hypnosis with acute and chronic pain, see Donald Lynch's article, "Empowering the patient: Hypnosis in the management of cancer, surgical disease and chronic pain."

12. There are many good books on mindfulness. My favorite is Jon Kabat-Zinn's *Full Catastrophe Living*.

## CHAPTER 4

1. Indirect suggestions are designed to relate indirectly, rather than directly, to a person's conscious experience. Use of indirect suggestion can require the receiver to search his/her inner experience in order to find meaning; therefore, it stimulates unconscious involvement in the change process.
2. See my 1993 article, "Turning symptoms into allies."
3. Individuals react to medical and health trauma in similar ways to the PTSD that can occur as a response to other stressors. Intrusive symptoms such as nightmares, anxiety, uncontrolled thoughts, and sensory flashbacks and other reenactments are common, as well as avoidance symptoms such as physical and emotional numbing/detachment, avoidance of thoughts that are painful, and restricted range of emotional reactions. Gwen appeared to have mostly avoidance responses to her surgeries and health problems. She also reenacted the traumas by repeating the sense of specialness, safety, and comfort that accompanied them.

## CHAPTER 5

1. One of the indications for ego state therapy is that the client reports an inner struggle or conflict related to symptoms.
2. The technique of calibration was developed by Richard Bandler and John Grinder, co-creators of Neurolinguistic Programming (NLP), a model based on their study of Milton Erickson's work in hypnosis.
3. These include: hypnotic imagery, ideomotor signaling, interspersal, metaphor, suggestion to create anesthesia, time distortion, amnesia, and displacement of pain. For examples, see Hammond, 1990, pp. 45–84.
4. For an understanding of how ego states are positioned on a dissociative continuum, see Watkins and Watkins, 1997, pp. 31–33.
5. For a presentation of internal self-helpers, see Christine Comstock, 1991.
6. See Phillips and Frederick, 1995, pp. 66–73, for direct and indirect techniques used to activate ego states.
7. This statement suggests that Jeannie's ego state has converted her terror to shame, a defense mechanism used by many children who have been traumatized. Here is an example of how ego states have their own distinct feelings, beliefs, needs, and means of protection that may differ from other parts of the personality.
8. Therapists should always be alert to the possibility of emotional and/or physiological dependency on pain medication. When there is no other reason for lack of progress, it is a good idea to check for overuse or abuse of medicine.
9. When using EMDR to activate an ego state, often all that is necessary is to ask for an ego state to come forward, answer a question, or offer information. I used this technique at this point because I wanted to strengthen internal cooperation among Jeannie's ego states rather than to supply some other type of help.
10. "Talking through" is an indirect approach used to activate an ego state. The therapist directs communications to an inner ego state and asks the client to report any reactions that occur. This method is used when an ego state is unwill-

ing or unavailable for direct communication. In this instance, it was simply more convenient to ask the six-year-old to take over, rather than taking the time to access him more directly and risk disrupting an emotionally charged experience.

11. This is an indication that the young part's cataleptic response of heaviness is a state-dependent memory. That is, when he begins to resolve the memory, the body response shifts.

12. For further information, see Phillips and Frederick, 1995, pp. 78–81, and the Frederick and Phillips article, "Decoding mystifying symptoms."

13. This is a reference to the hypnotic technique called age progression. In contrast to age regression, which suggests that the client explore past experiences, progression suggests that the client explore future possibilities.

14. For more information about the indications for ego-state therapy, see Phillips and Frederick, 1995, p. 18, and Watkins and Watkins, 1997.

15. Indirect techniques are usually best used when the ego state is thought to be a somatic state. This is because the state was likely formed at a preverbal age or might be otherwise incapable of verbal communication.

## INTRODUCING IMAGERY

1. See Carl Jung, 1976/1926.
2. See Sheikh et al., 1989, pp. 493–503.
3. See Jeanne Achterberg, "Introduction," *Imagery and Healing*, p. 3.
4. These steps are based on the work of Elgan Baker, who developed his structured techniques when working with people who had psychotic difficulties. See Baker, 1983.
5. For a good discussion of mastery and rehearsal, see Frederick and McNeal, *Inner Strength*, pp. 44–46.
6. This is based on a technique by Don Price, which can be found in Hammond, 1990, pp. 343–346.
7. See Ahsen, *Psycheye*.
8. See Rossi, 1993, pp. 35–36.

## CHAPTER 6

1. For a more complete description of how I teach imagery, see Phillips & Frederick, 1995, pp. 48–50.
2. This case was first published in my 1992 article with Claire Frederick on the use of age progression with acute psychosomatic symptoms.
3. Sheikh et al. make this point in their chapter, pp. 496–497.
4. Implications of negative age progression are discussed in Phillips & Frederick, 1995, and Frederick & Phillips, 1992.
5. Joan Borysenko, *Minding the Body, Mending the Mind*.
6. Carolyn Myss, *Why People Don't Heal and How They Can*.
7. Jean Shinoda Bolen, *Close to the Bone*, and Herbert Benson, *Timeless Healing*.
8. This is one of the significant findings in my current research project on factors that contribute to successful recovery from childhood trauma. Claire Frederick and I also drew this conclusion based on our case studies presented in the 1992 progressions article.

9. For a readable discussion of boundary formation and maintenance, see Kroll, 1993, pp. 108–109; 114–120.

10. For a detailed presentation of mindbody interactions related to anxiety, see Reid Wilson, *Don't Panic*.

11. The split screen technique was developed by Spiegel and Spiegel, 1978/1987, pp. 230–233.

12. For an expanded definition of eidetic imagery, see Ahsen, *Psycheye*, p. 47.

13. This case was first published in my article "Our Bodies, Our Selves," pp. 114–116.

14. This term was used by Ahkter Ahsen in *Psycheye*, page 89, and relates to the multiple self-images constructed out of many past experiences.

## CHAPTER 7

1. Hypnagogic hallucinations are included in the *DSM-IV* under parasomnias. They may be experienced sporadically by people who are otherwise asymptomatic. Hypnagogic episodes usually trigger anxiety and are characterized by vivid imagery and a subjective sense of being awake. In my experience, there is a correlation between childhood trauma and hypnagogic hallucinations during childhood and also in adulthood.

2. Specifically, I modified several of Marsha Linehan's exercises related to affect modulation. These can be found in M. Linehan, 1993, *Skills Training Manual for Treating Borderline Personality Disorder*. The exercises can be used successfully with any clients who have developmental issues, not just those with a borderline personality disorder diagnosis.

3. This is a variation of ideomotor signals. Brad decided ahead of time what the signals would be and discussed the method with his dentist.

## INTRODUCING SOMATIC TOOLS OF ENERGY PSYCHOLOGY

1. See the model of mindbody interaction proposed by Kenneth Pelletier and Denise Herzing in their chapter "Psychoneuroimmunology: toward a mind-body model."

2. For a thorough understanding of the body scan technique, see Jon Kabat-Zinn's *Full Catastrophe Living*, pp. 75–93.

3. Gallo presents a thorough review of the energy paradigm in his 1999 book, *Energy Psychology*. See pp. 10–15.

4. Gallo cites several experts. Two references are: Rubik, 1995, and Schmitt, Capo, & Boyd, 1986.

5. See Becker, 1990.

6. See Burr, 1972.

7. This case was first presented in R. Callahan, 1981, A rapid treatment for phobias. *Collected Papers of the International College of Applied Kinesiology*.

8. Gallo presents an annotated description of the case of Mary, which suggests that her cure, and the positive effects of TFT, might also be attributed to various chemical changes stimulated by tapping on energy meridians, such as elevations of neurotransmitters or endorphins. See Gallo, 1999, pp. 94–96.

9. Gallo (1999) has extended Callahan's Thought Field Therapy model and contributed extensively to greater understanding of TFT theory, principles, and techniques. In his latest book (2000), he has added his own methodology, en-

ergy diagnostic and treatment methods (EDxTM), developing more precise manual muscle testing, identifying additional treatment points, suggesting further corrections for neurological disorganization, and proposing general recipes for rapid change that can be used for a wide range of symptoms. Gary Craig (1995) has created emotional freedom techniques (EFT), which are also closely based on the TFT model but offer a more streamlined approach for clearing reversals and a "one recipe fits all" approach, which taps into all of the major meridians in one protocol as a general intervention for all symptoms.

10. For specific algorithms and TFT procedures, therapists may consult Gallo, 1999, chapters 7 and 8, pp. 123–235. Of course, the most thorough training is provided by attendance at one of the Level I or Level II workshops taught by Callahan and other approved TFT experts.

11. This model is analogous to the BASK model of dissociation developed by Bennett Braun. I prefer Levine's model because there is more emphasis on the body.

12. Levine discusses these general dynamics in his book *Waking the Tiger*. For a more detailed presentation, also see his 1991 article, "The body as healer: A revisioning of trauma and anxiety."

13. This group includes Landry Wildwind, LCSW, Vicky van Winkle, MFCC, and me, although Alan is now branching out to work with other therapists. We eventually hope to offer training to clinicians and bodyworkers interested in this kind of collaborative approach.

14. The term RAS was first developed by Landry Wildwind, Vicky van Winkle, and Alan van Winkle. Their approach was introduced in a workshop presented in Richmond, California, on May 8, 1998. The workshop was titled *In the Body: Rapid Alternating Stimulation using EMDR in a Bodywork Context.*

## CHAPTER 8

1. Yoga is a form of moving meditation from the Buddhist and Hindu traditions. Feldenkrais is a type of movement therapy created by Moshe Feldenkrais. Pilates is a rehabilitative exercise program developed by Joseph Pilates, a physical therapist who worked with dancers, including Martha Graham's dance troupe.

2. See Roger Callahan's definition of thought field in *Thought Field Therapy (TFT) and Trauma: Treatment and Theory*, p. 126.

3. See the extensive information on psychological reversals in Gallo, 1999, pp. 153–161, and 2000, especially pp. 83–86, 90–99, and 182–189. Also see Callahan's definition in Callahan and Perry, 1991, *Why Do I Eat When I'm Not Hungry?*, pp. 40–41.

4. Manual muscle testing originated in the field of physical therapy as a way of testing muscle function. Goodheart brought the technique to applied kinesiology to assess problems of central nervous system imbalance. Callahan, Gallo, and others have extended muscle testing to psychological problems. See Gallo, 2000, pp. 35–58, for an excellent discussion of this technique.

5. This is the neurolymphatic reflex point which is often tender and sometimes called the "sore spot."

6. Callahan refers to this as the "apex problem." He suggests that when people experience rapid results with a technique such as TFT, they will experience cognitive dissonance or disbelief. They will then use defensive maneuvers to resolve the dissonance, such as insisting that the TFT was just a confusion technique or a distraction.

7. See Gallo's (1999) discussion of the use of TFT with PTSD and traumatic complexity, pp. 198–200.
8. This verbal affirmation is based on criteria-related reversals proposed by Diamond, Durlacher, Gallo, and others who have researched the TFT model. See Gallo's (1999) discussion of criteria reversals, pp. 158–161, and Gallo, 2000, pp. 91–99.
9. When working with pain problems, it is always important to make sure that relieving the pain will not interfere with the body's natural way of alerting the person to imbalance or danger of decompensation. For this reason, it is essential to make sure the client has had a thorough medical evaluation and that pain control techniques are an appropriate intervention.
10. Gallo, 1999, pp. 182–187.
11. Callahan has acknowledged that complex trauma can require up to 40 treatments.
12. See Gallo, 1999, pp. 111–114, and Gallo, 2000, pp. 59–79.
13. In addition to Wellbutrin for depression, and Desyrel for sleep, Lauren is prescribed Neurontin for fibromyalgia pain.

## CHAPTER 9

1. See Gendlin's book *Focusing* for definitions and ways of activating the felt sense.
2. This exercise is based on one by Peter Levine in *Waking the Tiger: Healing Trauma*, pp. 74–77.
3. There are other techniques I might have used, but since I had only one session with Erica, I believed that ideomotor signals would give her more of a feeling of control, since this technique literally places the control for pacing in the hands of the client.
4. Levine has an extensive background in biology. His book *Waking the Tiger* draws heavily on animal reactions to trauma to help the reader understand the human response.
5. See Levine's chapter "How Biology Becomes Pathology" in *Waking the Tiger: Healing Trauma*, pp. 99–107.
6. Freud believed that traumatic "neuroses" were the result of a rupturing of the stimulus barrier. This is another way of saying that when our boundaries are violated, we can no longer trust them for self-regulation. Therefore, we cannot make healthy decisions about which sensory experiences to take in and which to shut out.
7. This is an acupuncture term which refers to points which trigger desirable responses in corresponding parts of the body.
8. I have also had some good results with other ways of stimulating lateral eye movements while the client's eyes are closed. This method has been studied and developed by Harriet Hollander, Ph.D., who calls the approach ECEM (Eyes Closed Eye Movements).
9. This is an application of the Trager method developed by Milton Trager, M.D.

## INTRODUCING INTEGRATED MODELS

1. See Herbert Benson's book, *Timeless Healing: The Power and Biology of Belief*, pp. 28–38, for discussion and research studies related to the placebo effect.

2. There are a few requirements for the use of formal hypnosis. One of them is the ability to sustain attention to verbal suggestions. People who are in states of sustained physical pain or extreme emotional arousal, may not be able to make good use of formal hypnosis. For other considerations for the use of hypnosis, see Brown & Fromm, 1986.

3. I learned this developmental model from Elgan Baker in a series of workshops that I organized in Berkeley, California, in 1993–1996.

4. Examples of other important developmental theories include those advanced by Erik Erikson, Jean Piaget, and Margaret Mahler.

5. This view was presented by Joan Borysenko at an Omega Mind/Body workshop and in her 1994 book.

6. Joan Lovett presents a related technique of interest called bridging in her chapter "'Am I Real?' Mobilizing Inner Strength to Develop a Mature Identity," 1998, especially pp. 197–199.

## CHAPTER 10

1. Ideally, the positive target image is an example of the therapy goal that has already been actualized to some extent and is already well integrated into everyday life. However, because the beach image seemed to contain the greatest degree of unconflicted ego strength available at that time, it was selected as Angie's initial positive EMDR target image.

2. It is best to find out first whether the client has sufficient ego strength to confront and reprocess trauma-related feelings. I was watching carefully here. If Angie had started looping negatively when she moved into the grief feelings, I would have had the option of introducing appropriate interweaves to add more information so that reprocessing could continue. Although I felt concern about too much loss surfacing in the timeframe we had because of her previous depressive and suicidal episodes, another consideration, as Shapiro (personal communication, 1999) has pointed out, is that premature introduction of interweaves can interrupt and fragment accelerated reprocessing.

3. Angie is referring to the neurolymphatic reflex point an inch below the collarbone and about three inches to the left as the "collarbone spot." It is also called the "sore spot" because in many people, it is tender when rubbed. The other spot is the point between and below the knuckles of her little and ring fingers which are part of standard TFT protocols. I have had several clients find those "shortcuts" helpful.

4. The accessibility of ego states is related to the degree of dissociation that exists in the personality. When there is greater dissociation between the main personality and various ego states, or among the ego states themselves, hypnosis can be employed to find and work with self-parts in similar ways. Once there is a substantial amount of co-consciousness, EMDR can then be used, as it was with Angie, to facilitate integrative movement toward desirable changes.

## CHAPTER 11

1. See Phillips & Frederick, 1995, pp. 23–24, for information about interviewing styles that utilize an informal, conversational approach derived from the hypnotic tradition.

2. For more information on indirect approaches to ego-state therapy, see Phillips & Frederick, 1995, pp. 66–74.

## CHAPTER 12

1. A conversion disorder, as defined by the *DSM-IV*, is a condition with symptoms affecting voluntary sensorimotor functioning, which suggests a neurological or other medical condition. Psychological factors are believed to be associated with the symptoms—in fact, they are thought to be converted into sensorimotor symptoms. See *DSM-IV*, pp. 452–457.
2. The *Structured Clinical Interview for DSM-IV Dissociative Disorders-Revised* was developed by Marlene Steinberg, M.D.
3. See *DSM-IV*, pp. 488–490, for more information about depersonalization disorder.
4. Trager Psychophysical Integration was created by Milton Trager, M.D. Hands-on work, conveyed through rocking, cradling, vibrating, and stretching the body, is designed to set off waves in the body that lead to deep relaxation and greater joint and muscle mobility.
5. I'm borrowing this term from thought field therapy. Although Robert's reactions don't fit the exact definition of TFT reversal, he does demonstrate in this case that his behavior is the opposite of his intentions.
6. Robert's diagnosis was schizotypal personality disorder, means that he held odd beliefs, had extreme discomfort with close relationships, and reported unusual body and perceptual experiences. See the *DSM-IV*, pp. 641–645.
7. I had considered both of these diagnoses before the psych testing so the data simply confirmed my hunches. For an understanding of conversion disorder, see note 1. Somatoform disorder is a larger diagnostic category of which conversion disorder is one subtype. Robert's symptoms clearly met the criteria for the conversion type of somatoform disorder.
8. Although my steps are different, the interested reader might find helpful the excellent work by Susan Simonds in *Bridging the Silence*, which presents various nonverbal modalities appropriate for resolving a wide range of body issues.

## CONCLUSIONS

1. The important issue of New Age guilt is addressed by Ken Wilber in *Grace and Grit*. Wilbur's basic premise is that we prefer guilt to helplessness in our reactions to death because we feel more in control.
2. These points, along with fascinating case examples, are discussed in Deirdre Barrett's *The Pregnant Man*.
3. Karen Olness makes this point in her interview with Bill Moyer in *Healing and the Mind*.

# APPENDICES

# APPENDIX A

## Diagrams for EMDR and TFT

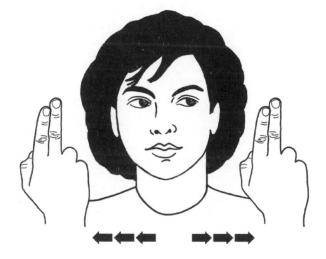

*Diagram 1. EMDR Lateral Eye Movements*

Lateral eye movements in EMDR are usually stimulated by passing the index and middle fingers of the dominant hand about 10–12 inches in front of the face while the person is holding in mind an image, cognition, or somatic response for reprocessing. With some people, the movements are more effective if shifted to a diagonal direction. Others appear more responsive to eye movements activated by hand taps, alternating lights, or sound cues. Although there is no conclusive proof, the effects of eye movements in EMDR appear to be similar to those of the rapid eye movement (REM) stage of sleep in reprocessing disturbing experiences.

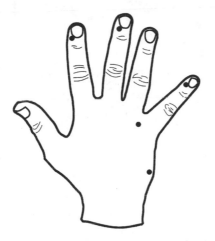

*Diagram 2. TFT Hand Points*

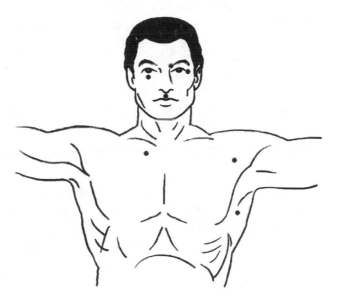

*Diagram 3. Other TFT Tapping Points*

The TFT points shown in Diagrams 2 and 3 feature those used with individuals described in this book. Additional tapping points located in other meridian sites have been suggested by Fred Gallo (2000). See his book for information on additions and alternatives. Gary Craig (1995), originator of EFT (emotional freedom therapy), has proposed a universal tapping protocol for all mind/body symptoms. Some of his tapping points are not included on the diagrams here. The current EFT training manual provides relevant guides and diagrams.

# APPENDIX B

## Protocol for Ego-Strengthening in EMDR

1. *Use the safe place at the beginning and end of every EMDR session.* Introduce the safe place image as indicated in the standard EMDR protocol before beginning processing. In addition to reminders that the safe place can be evoked at any time during EMDR sessions or at home and offering occasional reinforcement of safe place imagery through eye movement sets, safe place imagery can be used as a way to begin and end every EMDR processing session. This practice can promote further stabilization and integration of important changes that occur through processing. In individuals where self or object constancy is an issue, this approach can also facilitate a stronger sense of constancy.

2. *Expand the safe place concept.* People who demonstrate more complexity may benefit from working with the transitional properties of safe place imagery. With this expanded approach, safe place images are explored over time rather than identifying and using a single safe place image that meets established criteria. Much can be learned about the client's ego functioning and ability to use internal boundaries for containment and about the nature of internal conflicts that may block processing and lead to negative looping.

It is important to note that only safe place imagery that consistently evokes a sense of inner calm and safety should be installed with eye movement sets and used during processing. Other imagery that emerges during expanded safe place exploration and evokes more varied inner responses, especially negative affects, should be reserved for other kinds of therapeutic processing.

3. *Begin with a conflict-free target image for stabilization.* Follow the standard EMDR protocol first using positive target experiences. During this step, a conflict-free image is identified (Phillips, 1997). This is a current

area of functioning free of presenting symptoms and anxiety. Different from the safe place image, the conflict-free image is action-oriented. It focuses on a positive sense of self that has already been actualized rather than positive affect associated with a location or setting.

To find the image, instructions are: "Think of a time in your life currently when you are just the way you want to be. You do not have any of the difficulties or symptoms you came here to change. All of you is engaged in a positive manner and you experience only positive feelings about yourself." Once identified, a positive target image related to the conflict-free experience of self is then installed using eye movement sets. The client must be able to hold this image in a consistently positive manner and actually strengthen the image through the sets. If this does not happen, the therapist must help the client look further for a true conflict-free experience.

Results can increase the ability to observe and experience the self in a positive way, thus strengthening observing and experiencing ego functions. This step also provides an important opportunity to observe whether the client has sufficient ego strength to continue on to more challenging target images for reprocessing.

4. *Utilize the positive thoughts and beliefs that accompany conflict-free imagery as positive cognitions.* When the client has been helped to identify, install, and expand the conflict-free image in step 3, positive cognitions will often emerge spontaneously. For example, someone might remark while installing the conflict-free image: "It's really important to remind myself that I have times of feeling strong and confident just the way I want to feel. This makes me think I can make the changes I want to make here." Such a positive statement may then be used to develop a positive cognition during subsequent sessions when the clinical target image is reprocessed.

If there is difficulty forming an appropriate positive cognition during reprocessing, the therapist can link back to positive cognitions spontaneously expressed during step 3 by asking, "Is there anything from the previous session that might be relevant here in terms of what you want to be able to believe about this?" If there is no response, previous statements can be offered as possibilities more directly. It is usually more empowering to clients to use their own statements rather than to accept ones constructed by the therapist.

5. *Link conflict-free imagery with cognitive interweaves.* During the processing of more distressing material related to the clinical target, if resistance or negative looping occurs, the conflict-free image introduced in step 3 can be used as an interweave of more positive experiences of self. Install-

ing the conflict-free image and its related positive cognitions and affects can serve to bring in needed new perspective and information from the client's own resources, rather than from the therapist's questions and suggestions. This method can be further strengthening, helping people to tolerate negative affect, and to elicit and incorporate positive and new information using their own experiences. Usually when the conflict-free image is installed as an interweave, the client reports spontaneous shifts in awareness that lead to new associations and progression through the reprocessing procedure.

6. *Install other positive imagery as needed for additional resource interweaves.* Hypnotic approaches offer numerous types of imagery that might be used to stimulate resources for interweaves, much like the client's conflict-free imagery is used in step 5. This type of imagery can often be potentiated when introduced and reinforced in hypnotically deepened states of highly focused awareness and relaxation. Such images might include, but are not limited to:

- The Inner Advisor: An aspect of self that represents wisdom, balanced perspective
- Inner Strength: An aspect of self that is fearless and oriented toward survival
- Ideal Mother: An aspect of adult ego that can renurture the child self
- Ego states that are inner helpers
- Nurturing figures from the past outside of the family of origin (e.g., neighbors, relatives, teachers)
- Inner Love: An aspect of self that has the capacity for selfless, compassionate agape love

Several EMDR therapists have reported the use of resource installations (Leeds, 1998; Parnell, 1999) to serve as interweaves. These interweaves are based on the identification of special resources needed to complete reprocessing. Images, thoughts, feelings, or positive memories related to the target resource are installed during subsequent bilateral stimulation sets. The use of shorter sets is recommended because some clients tend to polarize during the installation.

I have used various types of hypnotic imagery, including those listed above, to develop a variety of resource interweaves to meet the specific needs of clients who demonstrate trauma-related difficulties during EMDR reprocessing. These include safety, renurturing, and affect regulation interweaves (see Glossary).

It is important to note that the overuse of interweaves can interrupt reprocessing (F. Shapiro, personal communication, 1999). Therapists should check carefully to determine whether negative looping occurs after the installation of conflict-free imagery and other resources installed as interweaves. This phenomenon may be an indication of the incomplete processing of underlying traumatic material.

7. *Expand the positive template.* Some people, even after successful EMDR desensitization and reprocessing, may be unable to imagine appropriate future behaviors so that they can use the positive template to help integrate shifts made during processing. This may be because other clinical material related to that already reprocessed may be generating anxiety that is blocking a positive future orientation, or it may be that there is underlying depression or trauma that requires treatment prior to approaching this step.

When someone appears ready to initiate a focus on the future, it may be best to use a series of structured experiences to help enhance the client's ability to engage in future-oriented activity. This could include a future self visualization, a hypnotic age progression (Frederick & Phillips, 1995; Phillips & Frederick, 1992), or a hypnotic exercise designed to explore the ideal self (Brown & Fromm, 1986). These are all activities designed for strengthening so that expansion of future orientation is possible. Images produced during the exercises can then be used as the basis for future rehearsal with the positive template.

# APPENDIX C

## Bodyworker and Psychotherapist Collaboration

### Factors to Consider

Preparation Phase:
    Locating a bodyworker
    Negotiating working agreements
    Arrangements (cost, place, time, conditions, and ethics)
    Discussion of issues specific to each client
    Screening the client:
        Informed consent
        Assessment of indications and contraindications
        Creating specific framework needed for each client (when, how, for how long, for what)
        Discussion of goals
        Using preparation as screening
        Providing client with appropriate written materials about bodywork and outcome
Adding Bodywork:
    Indications for working jointly:
        Monitor development of possible sexual transference
        Severe mistrust of touch, especially male touch
        Strong possibility of splitting (i.e., good bodyworker, bad therapist, or vice versa)
        Provide opportunity for two-parent nurturing
        Reality testing difficulties
    Indications for working separately:
        Shame and privacy issues
        Maximizing financial resources
        Convenient scheduling
        Maximizing continuity of verbal work with psychotherapist
        Maximizing nonverbal benefits of bodywork

Ground Rules for Joint Collaboration:

    Client is always fully clothed except for shoes.

    Bodyworker must dress professionally (especially if opposite sex of client).

    Bodyworker only addresses somatic (not psychological) issues with client.

    Bodyworker understands and respects all policies and ground rules of the psychotherapist in interactions with the client.

    Therapist shares with bodyworker all relevant information related to transference and countertransference and anticipates how collaboration may impact these issues for each client.

    Therapist explains model of treatment (e.g., SARI model) and ensures that bodyworker can work within this framework.

    Therapist determines that bodyworker can track subtle changes in body related to relevant healing goals, particularly those related to trauma, and can recognize and respond appropriately to signs of flooding, dissociation, and immobility.

    Goals for each session are mutually agreed upon by client, therapist, and bodyworker and progress is evaluated regularly.

    Bodyworker begins work by helping client find and explore safe place in the body; understands how and when to return to safe place focus to prevent destabilization.

    Bodyworker always asks for and awaits verbal permission from client before entering a new area of the body.

    Therapist and bodyworker develop nonverbal as well as verbal signals to communicate during body-focused therapy.

# Appendix D

## Resources

### How to Find Qualified Therapists and Training in the Energy Modalities

EMDR

(EMDRIA) Eye Movement Desensitization and Reprocessing International
    Association
P.O. Box 141925
Austin, TX 78714–1925
TEL: (512) 451–5200
FAX: (512) 451–5256
E-mail: emdria@aol.com
Web site: www.emdria.org

This organization provides referrals to therapists who have completed approved training in EMDR in specific geographical areas, offers information on Level I and II training for therapists, and sets criteria for certification and approved consultant status. The Web site provides general information about EMDR and answers questions and answers about its uses and effectiveness.

HYPNOSIS

American Society of Clinical Hypnosis (ASCH)
2200 East Devon Avenue, Suite 291
Des Plaines, IL 60018–4534
TEL: (847) 297–3317
FAX:
Web site: www.asch.net

The Milton H. Erickson Foundation
3606 N. 24th Street
Phoenix, AZ 85016
TEL: (602) 956–6196
FAX: (602) 956–0519
Web site: www.erickson-foundation.org

The Society for Clinical and Experimental Hypnosis (SCEH)
2201 Haeder Road, Suite 1
Pullman, WA 99163
TEL: (509) 332–7555
FAX: (509) 332–5907
Web site: www.sunsite.utk.edu/IJCEH

International Society of Hypnosis (ISH)
Level 1, South Wing
Repatriation Campus
Austin Medical Centre
Heidelberg West 3081
Australia
TEL: 61–3-9496–4105
FAX: 61–3-9496–4107

These four groups are the main professional hypnosis groups inside the
U.S. and abroad. They can help you locate a therapist referral in a specific
geographical area, provide information about training and workshops,
and answer general questions about hypnosis on their Web sites. The
Erickson Foundation is devoted to the study of Ericksonian hypnosis and
psychotherapy; the other three groups are more oriented to clinical applications of formal hypnosis and scientific research efforts. ASCH is the
best source of information about training in ego-state therapy and therapists who use this approach.

IMAGERY

The Academy for Guided Imagery
P.O. Box 2070
Mill Valley, CA 94942
TEL: (800) 726–2070
FAX: (415) 389–9342
Web site: www.interactiveimagery.com

This group offers intensive and home study courses in imagery to professionals. It also offers a certification program accredited by the American Psychological Association. Books and tapes on imagery for self-healing can be purchased through the Imagery Store at (800) 726–2070.

TFT

Roger Callahan, Ph.D.
Callahan Techniques
TFT (Thought Field Therapy)
45350 Vista Santa Rosa
Indian Wells, CA 92210
TEL: (619) 345–9216
FAX: (619) 360–5258
Web site: www.tftrx.com

Callahan Techniques provides referrals to therapists trained in TFT, updated information about approved training workshops nationwide, and access to a printed newsletter. The Web site gives extensive information about the uses of TFT and access to numerous case reports of its effectiveness.

Fred Gallo, Ph.D.
Psychological Services
40 Snyder Road
Hermitage, PA 16148
TEL: (724) 346–3838
FAX: (724) 346–4339
Web site: www.energypsych.com

Gallo developed the Level I and Level II workshops in TFT. He has been a pioneer in energy psychology methods and has developed his own model, energy diagnostic and treatment methods. His Web site offers excellent information about energy psychology. The site also describes EDxTM, which is based on TFT, and gives access to Gallo's training schedule.

EFT (Emotional Freedom Techniques)
Gary Craig
P.O. Box 398
The Sea Ranch, CA 95497
TEL: (800) 231–6132
FAX: (707) 940–4333

Web site: www.emofree.com

EFT is a popular cousin to TFT. Gary Craig, the originator, has streamlined Callahan's TFT protocols into one general tapping protocol that can
be used for most symptoms. The general training program, consisting of
manuals, audio and video cassettes, can be ordered through the Web site
or by phone or fax through the office. The Web site offers extensive anec-
dotal information, clinical cases, and an almost daily e-mail newsletter
from Gary Craig.

## SOMATIC EXPERIENCING (SE)

Peter Levine, Ph.D.
The Foundation for Human Enrichment
P.O. Box 1872
Lyons, CO 80540
TEL: (303) 823–9524
FAX: (303) 823–9520
Web site: www.traumahealing.com

This organization offers books, pamphlets, and articles on somatic experiencing. The Web site and office provide referrals to SE practitioners,
schedules of training worldwide, and helpful information about the SE
model.

# References

Achterberg, J. (1985). *Imagery and healing: Shamanism and modern medicine.* Boston: New Science Library.

Ahsen, A. (1977). *Psycheye: Self-analytic consciousness.* New York: Brandon House.

Alman, B.M., & Lambrou, P. (1992). *Self-hypnosis: The complete manual for health and self-change* (2nd ed.). New York: Brunner/Mazel.

American Psychiatric Association (1994). *Diagnostic and statistical manual, fourth edition.* Washington, DC: American Psychiatric Press.

Baker, E. (1983). The use of hypnotic techniques with psychotics. *American Journal of Clinical Hypnosis, 25,* 283–288.

Barber, T.X. (1984). Changing "unchangeable" bodily processes by (hypnotic) suggestions: A new look at hypnosis, cognitions, imaging, and the mind-body problem. In A.A. Sheikh (Ed.), *Imagination and healing.* Farmingdale, NY: Baywood.

Barrett, D. (1998). *The pregnant man and other cases from a hypnotherapist's couch.* New York: Times Books.

Becker, R.O. (1990). *Cross currents.* New York: Putnam.

Benson, H. (1996). *Timeless healing: The power and biology of belief.* New York: Fireside.

Bernstein, E.M., & Putnam, F.W. (1986). Development, reliability, and validity of a dissociation scale. *Journal of Nervous and Mental Disease, 174,* 727–735.

Bertrand, L., & Spanos, N. (1989). Hypnosis: Historical and social psychological aspects. In A. Sheikh & K. Sheikh (Eds.), *Healing east and west: Ancient wisdom and modern psychology* (pp. 243–253). New York: John Wiley.

Bolen, J. S. (1996). *Close to the bone: Life-threatening illness and the search for meaning.* New York: Scribner.

Borysenko, J. (1988). *Minding the body, mending the mind.* New York: Bantam.

Borysenko, J., & Borysenko, M. (1994). *The power of the mind to heal: Renewing body, mind, and spirit.* Carson, CA: Hay House.

Borysenko, J. (2000, March 3–5). *Omega mind/body healing workshop.* Mt. Madonna, CA.

Brown, D., & Fromm, E. (1986). *Hypnotherapy and hypnoanalysis.* Hillsdale, NJ: Erlbaum.

Brown, D., Scheflin, A., & Hammond, D.C. (1998). *Memory, trauma treatment, and the law.* New York: Norton.

Brown, S. (1999). *Treating alcoholism.* New York: Jossey-Bass.

Burr, H.S. (1972). *Blueprint for immortality: The electrical patterns of life.* Essex, England: Saffron Salden.

Callahan, R. (1981). A rapid treatment of phobias. *Collected papers of the International college of Applied Kinesiology*. Shawnee Mission, KS: International College of Applied Kinesiology.

Callahan, R. J. (1996). *Thought field therapy (TFT) and trauma: Treatment and theory*. Indian Wells, CA: Author.

Callahan, R., & Perry, P. (1991). *Why do I eat when I'm not hungry?* New York: Doubleday.

Comstock, C. (1991). Countertransference and the suicidal multiple personality disorder patient. *Dissociation, 4*(1), 25–35.

Craig, G. (1999). *Emotional freedom techniques: The manual*. Sea Ranch, CA: Author.

Eden, D. (1998). *Energy medicine*. New York: Tarcher.

Erickson, M. H., Hershman, S., & Secter, I. I. (1981). *The practical application of medical and dental hypnosis*. Chicago: Seminars on Hypnosis Publishing Co.

Fine, C., & Berkowitz, S.A. (1998, March 18). The use of hypnosis and EMDR in the treatment of DID. Paper presented at the 40th annual scientific meeting of the American Society of Clinical Hypnosis, Fort Worth, Texas.

Frederick, C., & McNeal, S. (1999). *Inner strengths: Contemporary psychotherapy and hypnosis for ego strengthening*. Mahwah, NJ: Erlbaum.

Frederick, C., & Phillips, M. (1992). The use of hypnotic age progressions as interventions with acute psychosomatic conditions. *American Journal of Clinical Hypnosis, 35*, 89–98.

Frederick, C., & Phillips, M. (1995). Decoding mystifying signals: Translating symbolic symbolic communications of elusive ego states. *American Journal of Clinical Hypnosis, 38*(2), 87–96.

Gallo, F. (1999). *Energy psychology: Explorations at the interface of energy, cognition, behavior, and health*. Boca Raton, FL: CRC Press.

Gallo, F. (2000). *Energy diagnostic and treatment methods*. New York: Norton.

Gendlin, E. (1982). *Focusing*. New York: Bantam.

Gilligan, S. (1987). *Therapeutic trances: The cooperation principle in Ericksonian hypnotherapy*. New York: Norton.

Hahn, Thich Nhat. (1999). Buddhism and psychotherapy: Planting good seeds. *Journal of Contemplative Psychotherapy*, VI, 97–107.

Haley, J. (1967). Further techniques of hypnosis—Utilization techniques. In J. Haley (Ed.), *Advanced techniques of hypnosis and therapy: Selected papers of Milton H. Erickson, M.D.* (pp. 32–50). New York: Grune & Stratton.

Hammond, D.C. (1990). *Handbook of hypnotic suggestions and metaphors*. New York: Norton.

Hartmann, H. (1961). *Ego psychology and the problems of adaptation*. New York: International Universities Press.

Jung, C. (1976/1926). The symbolic life. In R.F.C. Hull (Trans.), *Collected works*, vol. 18. Princeton: Princeton University Press.

Kabat-Zinn, J. (1990). *Full catastrophe living: Using the wisdom of your body and mind to face stress, pain, and illness*. New York: Delta.

Kaptchuk, T. J. (1983). *The web that has no weaver: Understanding Chinese medicine*. Chicago: Congdon & Weed.

Kershaw, C. J. (1992). *The couple's hypnotic dance: Creating Ericksonian strategies in marital therapy*. New York: Brunner/Mazel.

Knaster, M. (1996). *Discovering the body's wisdom*. New York: Bantam.

Kroll, J. (1993). *PTSD/Borderlines in therapy: Finding the balance*. New York: Norton.

Langs, R. (1980). *Interactions: The realm of transference and countertransference*. New York: Jason Aronson.

Lankton, S., & Lankton, C. (1983). *The answer within: A clinical framework of Ericksonian hypnotherapy*. New York: Brunner/Mazel.

Leeds, A. (1998). Lifting the burden of shame: Using EMDR resource installation to resolve a therapeutic impasse. In P. Manfield (Ed.), *Extending EMDR: A casebook of innovative applications* (pp. 256–282). New York: Norton.

Levine, P. (1997). *Waking the tiger: Healing trauma*. Berkeley, CA: North Atlantic Books.

Levine, P. (1991). The body as healer: A revisioning of trauma and anxiety. In M Sheets-Johnstone (Ed.), *Giving the body its due* (pp. 85–108). Stony Brook, NY: State University of New York Press.

Linehan, M. (1993). *Skills training manual for treating borderline personality disorder*. New York: Guilford.

Lovett, J. (1998). "Am I real?": Mobilizing inner strength to develop a mature identity. In P. Manfield (Ed.), *Extending EMDR: A casebook of innovative applications* (pp. 191–216). New York: Norton.

Lynch, D. (1999). Empowering the patient: Hypnosis in the management of cancer, surgical disease and chronic pain. *American Journal of Clinical Hypnosis, 42*(2), 122–130.

Manfield, P. (1997, December 9). *EMDR with personality disorders*. EMDR Level II training workshop, Sunnyvale, CA.

Manfield, P. (1998a). EMDR terms and procedures: Resolution of uncomplicated depression. In P. Manfield (Ed.), *Extending EMDR: A casebook of innovative applications* (pp. 15–36). New York: Norton.

Manfield, P. (1998b). Filling the void: Resolution of a major depression. In P. Manfield (Ed.), *Extending EMDR: A casebook of innovative applications* (pp. 113–137). New York: Norton.

Myss, C. (1997). *Why people don't heal and how they can*. New York: Harmony.

Norris, P. (1989). Current conceptual trends in biofeedback and self-regulation. In A. Sheikh & K. Sheikh (Eds.), *Healing east and west: Ancient wisdom and modern psychology* (pp. 243–253). New York: John Wiley.

Olness, K. (1993). Self-regulation and conditioning. In B. Moyers, *Healing and the mind* (pp. 71–85). New York: Doubleday.

Parnell, L. (1998). Helping a new mother to bond. In P. Manfield (Ed.), *Extending EMDR: A casebook of innovative applications* (pp. 37–64). New York: Norton.

Parnell, L. (1999). *EMDR in the treatment of adults abused as children*. New York: Norton.

Pelletier, K. (1977). *Mind as healer, mind as slayer: A holistic approach to preventing stress disorders*. New York: Dell.

Pelletier, K., & Herzing, D. (1996). Psychoneuroimmunology: Toward a mind-body model. In A. Sheikh & K. Sheikh (Eds.), *Healing east and west: Ancient wisdom and modern psychology* (pp. 374–375). New York: John Wiley.

Phillips, M. (1995a). Ego-state therapy in the treatment of aids patients. In G.D. Burrows & R.O. Stanley (Eds.), *Contemporary international hypnosis* (pp. 127–139). West Sussex, England: John Wiley & Sons, Ltd.

Phillips, M. (1995b). Our bodies, our selves: Treating the somatic expressions of trauma with ego-state therapy. *American Journal of Clinical Hypnosis, 38*(2), 109–121.

Phillips, M. (1997). *The importance of ego-strengthening with EMDR.* EMDRIA Conference, San Francisco, CA.

Phillips, M. (2000). *Exceptional healers from childhood trauma: Variables that predict success.* Unpublished manuscript.

Phillips, M., & Frederick, C. (1995). *Healing the divided self: Clinical and Ericksonian hypnotherapy for post-traumatic and dissociative conditions.* New York: Norton.

Price, D. (1990). Corporate headquarters of the mind. In D. C. Hammond (Ed.), *Handbook of hypnotic suggestion and metaphors* (pp. 343–346). New York: Norton.

Rossi, E. L. (Ed.). (1980). *The collected papers of Milton H. Erickson, M.D.* (Vol. 1–4). New York: Irvington.

Rossi, E. (1993). *The psychobiology of mind-body healing: New concepts of therapeutic hypnosis* (2nd ed.). New York: Norton.

Rossi, E., & Cheek, D. (1988). *Mind-body therapy: Ideodynamic healing in hypnosis.* New York: Norton.

Rossi, E., & Ryan, M.O. (Eds.). (1985). *Life reframing in hypnosis.* New York: Irvington.

Rossman, M.L. (1993). Imagery: Learning to use the mind's eye. In D. Goleman & J. Gurin (Eds.), *Mind body medicine: How to use your mind for better health* (pp. 291–300). New York: Consumer Reports Books.

Rubik, R. (1995). Energy medicine and the unifying concept of information. *Alternative Therapies, 1*(1), 34–39.

Schmitt, R., Capo, T., & Boyd, E. (1986). Cranial electrotherapy stimulation as a treatment for anxiety in chemically dependent persons. *Alcoholism Clinical and Experimental Research, 10,* 158–160.

Shalev, A., Schreiber, S., & Galai, T. (1993). Post-traumatic stress disorder following medical events. *British Journal of Clinical Psychology, 32,* 247–253.

Shapiro, F. (1995). *Eye movement desensitization and reprocessing: Basic principles, protocols, and procedures.* New York: Guilford.

Shapiro, F., & Forrest, M. S. (1997). *EMDR: The breakthrough therapy for overcoming anxiety, stress, and trauma.* New York: Basic Books.

Sheikh, A., Kunzendorf, R., & Sheikh, K. (1989). Healing images: From ancient wisdom to modern science. In A. Sheikh & K. Sheikh (Eds.), *Healing east and west: Ancient wisdom and modern psychology* (pp. 469–515). New York: John Wiley.

Simonds, S. (1994). *Bridging the silence: Nonverbal modalities in the treatment of adult survivors of childhood sexual abuse.* New York: Norton.

Spiegel, H., & Spiegel, D. (1978/1987). *Trance and treatment: Clinical uses of hypnosis* (pp. 230–233). Washington, DC: American Psychiatric Press.

Spitzer, R. L., Williams, J. B. W., & Gibbon, M. (1990). *Structured Clinical Interview for DSM-III-R (SCID).* Washington, DC: American Psychiatric Press.

Steinberg, M. (1994). *Structured clinical interview for DSM-IV dissociative disorders revised.* Washington, DC: American Psychiatric Press.

van der Kolk, B. (1997, July 12). *Current understanding of the psychobiology of trauma.* EMDRIA Conference, San Francisco, CA.

van der Kolk, B., McFarlane, A., & Weisaeth, L. (Eds.). (1996). *Traumatic stress: The effects of overwhelming experience on mind, body, and society.* New York: Guilford.

Wadden, T.A., & Anderton, C.H. (1982). The clinical uses of hypnosis. *Psychological Bulletin, 91*(2), pp. 215–243.

Watkins, J., & Watkins, H. (1997). *Ego states: Theory and therapy*. New York: Norton.

Weil, A. (1995). *Spontaneous healing: How to discover and enhance your body's natural ability to maintain and heal itself*. New York: Fawcett Columbine.

Wilber, K. (1993). *Grace and grit: Spirituality and healing in the life and death of Treya Killam Wilber*. New York: Shambhala.

Wilson, R. (1996). *Don't panic: Taking control of anxiety attacks*. New York: HarperCollins.

Wildwind, L. (1993). *Chronic depression*. Workshop presentation. EMDR Conference, Sunnyvale, CA.

Wylie, M.S. (July/August, 1996). Going for the cure. *Family Therapy Networker, 20*(4).

# INDEX